Marx's ethics
of freedom

Marx's ethics
of freedom

George G. Brenkert

Routledge & Kegan Paul
London, Boston, Melbourne and Henley

First published in 1983
by Routledge & Kegan Paul plc
39 Store Street, London WC1E 7DD,
9 Park Street, Boston, Mass. 02108, USA,
296 Beaconsfield Parade, Middle Park,
Melbourne, 3206, Australia, and
Broadway House, Newtown Road,
Henley-on-Thames, Oxon RG9 1EN
Set IBM in 10/11 pt Press Roman by
Columns, Reading, Berks, Great Britain
Printed in Great Britain
by St Edmundsbury Press
Copyright © George G. Brenkert 1983

SB 24619 £14.95 · S·84

Library of Congress Cataloging in Publication Data

Brenkert, George G.

Marx's ethics of freedom.
Bibliography: p.
Includes index.
1. Marx, Karl, 1818-1883 – Ethics. 2. Ethics – History –
19th century. I. Title.
B3305.M74B718 1983   171'.7   82-24999

ISBN 0-7100-9461-2

To my Parents,
To Antoinette, Jurgen, and Hannah

Contents

Preface

In the last quarter century, interest in Marxism has risen to a level comparable only to that which existed in the first third of this century. There are important differences, however. The claims of some one country to particular insights into Marx's thought are no longer credible – as they apparently were to many in the early part of this century. Further, a wealth of previously unknown or unpublished manuscripts of Marx is now available. Thus, a major current of recent interest has been the return to Marx himself.

The discussion of Marx's ethics has played a significant, though not uncontested, part in this return to Marx. It has frequently been held that Marx had no ethics, though he is readily admitted to have had an economics, a theory of history, a political science, and a sociology. I think this view is mistaken and shall attempt to show this in the following study.

A number of methodological presuppositions should be noted at the outset. To begin with, I have looked only at Marx's own writings and those co-authored with Engels in which he is thought to have played a significant, if not dominant, part. I have not drawn in any substantial way on the writings of Engels. My reason is that there is noteworthy disagreement concerning the extent to which Marx and Engels shared the same views on various topics. Since my concern is not to write an account of what Marxists in general have said about ethics – which would be as difficult as writing an account of what liberals or Christians have in general said about ethics – I have omitted consideration of Engels, as well as Lenin, Mao, etc.

I have also assumed that there is a continuity to Marx's thought. Though this has been doubted or denied by many, I believe that the notorious 'problem' of 'the Young Marx versus the Mature Marx' is one which has been resolved. Commentators such as S. Avineri, R. Bernstein, and D. McClellan, among others, have shown that Marx's thought is of a piece. This is not to say that it did not change and develop during Marx's lifetime; but through the oftentimes bewildering maze of his thought there are continuous threads that one may follow in the reconstruction of his ethics. Thus in the discussion of Marx's views on morality and ethics I have drawn on all of Marx's writings, though particularly those after 1842. From these we can formulate a reasonably coherent account of Marx's ethics. To this extent, but only to this extent, can the present work be seen as entering into this now past dispute.

In reconstructing Marx's views on ethics, I have not attempted to psychoanalyze Marx. It may or may not be, for example, that some of Marx's views were occasioned by latent psychological conflicts against various family members or various social groups. Whether or not Marx's thought was influenced by such conflicts is a matter of indifference here. Furthermore, to proceed in this manner is in accord with the spirit of Marx's own views. He did not approach other philosophers or economists such as Kant, Hegel, and Adam Smith by seeking their inner psychological motivations or by simply writing off their views because of their class origin or class bias.

Finally, I do not maintain that Marx was completely consistent. Marx wrote for over forty years; he wrote for many different audiences and under many different conditions. It would be asking a great deal to believe that he was never inconsistent. Still, since Marx himself placed important emphasis on the systematic nature of his thought, one can hope to reconstruct a consistent interpretation of his ethical views. The task, perhaps, is not unlike that of an archaeologist who finds various bones that he tries to reconstruct into the skeletal form of the ancient animal. Some bones may be missing and others may be mixed in so as to allow for the reconstruction of animals of slightly different appearances. His task would be successfully accomplished so long as he reconstructed an animal that fitted most consistently and organically with our most complete knowledge of ancient animals. Similarly, I have tried to reconstruct the most consistent ethics to which Marx can be said to have subscribed and I have done this from the widest possible consideration of Marx's theoretical and practical work.

I begin in Part one with a consideration of Marx's critical remarks on morality and ethics, as well as his views on historical materialism, determinism, and ideology. This amounts to a consideration of Marx's metaethics, i.e. his methodological views concerning the nature of morality and moral justification. This discussion allows me to respond to various objections traditionally raised against the view that Marx had an ethics at all, as well as to establish certain parameters for the reconstruction of Marx's normative moral views.

In Part two I discuss Marx's normative moral theory, central to which is the notion of freedom. Accordingly, I see Marx's moral philosophy as a continuation of long-standing German and European traditions in ethics. I maintain that it is upon the basis of freedom, not distributive justice, that Marx condemns capitalism and bourgeois society. Marx's views on violence, revolution, punishment, and communist society must be understood in light of his views on freedom.

In Part three I draw some conclusions about the insights and the value of Marx's ethics. Marx approaches the problems of ethics from a unique and instructive perspective. Not all his conclusions and suggestions are plausible or acceptable today. But of what philosopher or social scientist of any century could we say otherwise? Since Marx has been such a significant and influential figure, higher evaluative standards are often applied to him than to others. As a consequence, when he is not viewed simply as a misguided scientist, he is frequently taken for an immoralist or anti-Christ of sorts. The evidence is the evils perpetrated in his name throughout the world. But who, among the great thinkers and leaders of the past, would be spared if their views were appraised in light of consequences effected by their supposed followers? Jesus's followers have helped establish inquisitions, have gone on crusades, and fought holy wars both ancient and modern. Admirers of Nietzsche have goose-stepped their way into history. These facts should not be forgotten in our appraisal and understanding of Marx. To do otherwise is to skew the conclusions of many away from an important intellectual and practical thinker.

In writing this book I have used as far as possible the standard and widely available English translations. In this past decade a complete English translation of Marx's works has begun to appear which, it seems certain, will become the standard reference in English for Marx's works. This is the Karl Marx and Frederick Engels, *Collected Works*, published by Progress Publishers in Moscow. Whenever possible I have referred to this source and indicated my references with the abbreviation *MECW*. When this has not been possible, since the later volumes of this edition have not yet appeared, I have used other widely available sources. In case of doubtful translations or translations of difficult passages I have used the *Marx Engels Werke* (Dietz Verlag, Berlin). I have also included within the text references to the *Grundrisse* which I have abbreviated as *Grund.*

Finally, I would like to acknowledge a number of friends and institutions that have contributed in various ways to the completion of this manuscript. For financial aid I am indebted to the generosity of the Alexander von Humboldt-Stiftung for a research fellowship that allowed me to work on this book during the academic year 1978-9 in

Frankfurt a.M. I also thank the University of Tennessee for financial support that helped to reduce concerns during the same period. My stay in the Bundesrepublik was made both enjoyable and fruitful due to the kindness and friendship of Norbert Hoerster, Werner Becker, Arend Kulenkampf, Harmut and Elke Kliemt. I am also grateful to William H. Shaw and Allen Buchanan who were kind enough to read various portions of my manuscript and provide helpful comments. To Barbara Moser I am indebted for her excellent typing.

Various passages and ideas in Chapters 4 and 5 have been taken from my article, 'Freedom and Private Property in Marx,' which appeared in *Philosophy and Public Affairs*, vol. 8, no. 2 (Winter 1979): pp. 122-47. Copyright © 1979 by Princeton University Press. Adapted by permission of Princeton University Press.

I have quoted extensively from the following books: Karl Marx, *Capital* (New York: International Publishers, 1967), vol. 1; Karl Marx and Frederick Engels, *Collected Works* (New York: International Publishers), vol. 3 (1975), vol. 5 (1976) and vol. 6 (1976). All these extracts are reprinted with the kind permission of International Publishers.

Part one
The ethical foundations

1 Marxism, moralism, and ethics

Our insipid, moralising Sancho believes . . . that it is merely a matter of a different morality, of what appears to have a new outlook on life, of 'getting out of one's head' a few 'fixed ideas', to make everyone happy and able to enjoy life. (*The German Ideology*, *MECW*, 5:419)

I

The nature of Marx's views on morality and ethics has long been a matter of considerable dispute. One widespread view is that Marx had no ethics, he rejected morality, and envisioned a communism beyond both.[1] Marx is supposed to have founded a science which sought in an objective, morally neutral manner to understand the origin, growth, and collapse of capitalism as well as the ultimate succession of communism. One only has to read in the history of Marxism to appreciate how generally this view has been defended. Comments such as the following are wholly common:

> Marxism is distinguished from all other socialist systems by its anti-ethical tendency. In all of Marxism from beginning to end, there is not a grain of ethics, and consequently no more of an ethical judgment than an ethical postulate.[2]

> The obsolescence of ethical ideology is a corollary of historical materialism as applied to the superstructure of a socialist society. Ethical laws come into being as attempts to solve social antagonisms, not by removing their basic causes, but through moral coercion. An appeal to ethical doctrine is a confession that the given standpoint does not enable social antagonisms found to be resolved.[3]

> Marx's revolution in philosophy explicitly renounced the normative tradition of philosophical ethics while affirming the heritage of positive science.[4]

3

Accordingly, it can be said without exaggeration that it has seemed to many that it is misleading at best, wrongheaded at worst, to speak of Marx having an ethics. He simply does not fit into the categories into which we expect those having an ethics and reflecting on morality to fit.

There are, however, relatively straightforward problems with this view. For example, many of those who hold this view attribute a rather empiricist notion of science to Marx. But it is doubtful that Marx used such a notion of science. Indeed, Marx's claims about science must be understood in light of Hegel's claims about science. Marx's views were significantly influenced by Hegel — and surely Hegelian science was *not* empiricist. Secondly, it is often noted that Marx was not, as one would expect a scientist to be, a neutral, dispassionate observer in his writings. This is as evident in his writings on political economy as it is in his newspaper articles. In *Capital*, for example, he condemns the egoism, exploitation, estrangement, degradation, etc. which capitalism brings in its train. Marx's writings are pervaded by a normative and partisan atmosphere. His commitment to the particular kind of social order which he sees his work as advancing is always obvious and constantly present. Further, this commitment is not simply a personal commitment, but one which he clearly believes that others should share. Finally, if Marx were a scientist without an ethics, it is unclear how we are to understand his many comments that communism will constitute a 'higher' plane of existence for humanity, that there is a 'progressive' nature to history, and that communism will institute a 'true realm' of freedom.

Problems of these kinds have led some to modify the above view of Marx. They claim, instead, that Marx did have some kind of ethical or evaluative view but that this was simply added on to his scientific views. The two together explain the above kinds of problems. His science remains non-normative, neutral, objective and descriptive. It was his own personal commitments which explain his partisanship, his condemnation of various aspects of capitalist society, and his talk of communism as a 'higher' stage of society. Thus we may read amongst those who interpret Marx in this manner:

> As theoretical abstractions employed for specific methodological reasons, the models of both the abstract labour process and the capitalist labour process are neutral. No moral recommendations are implied. On the one hand, we have the claim that if one examines all past societies, then certain general features of the labour process common to them all will be found; while on the other hand, we have the claim that if one examines the capitalist labour process, then

certain specific features of that process will be found. However, moral implications can be drawn from a comparison between these models, if, like Marx, we are committed to a position which stresses the desirability and, in a kind of society not yet known in history the possibility of the free, purposive activity of human beings.[5]

Marx undertakes to predict on the basis of what he sees happening . . . and he proposes to make his prediction come true by arousing the minds of other men − the proletariat − to a sense of their future role. . . . We cross the inner threshold of the Marxian temple and pass from the strictly materialistic and evolutionary purlieus of history to the inner sanctum where the revelation of class consciousness and class struggle makes right belief essential, intense propaganda imperative, and ruthless political action a moral duty. . . . But in this [latter] part of his system Marx is really not thinking of his economic and material laws. He has become an ordinary political writer with a strong moral bias.[6]

There are, however, also difficulties with this interpretation. It does not modify the notion of science underlying the previous view. It simply adds an ethics to that science. The two remain wholly external to each other. This is not what we should expect, given Marx's demands for a unity of theory and practice, or given his claim that he seeks to form a single, all-embracing science. Even more disturbingly, this interpretation suggests no basis for Marx's advocacy of communism other than that (a) it was his own personal view − i.e. an arbitrary ultimate commitment − or that (b) he simply opted to defend morally that which he saw as inevitable − i.e. a kind of moral futurism or fatalism. Both suggestions leave much to be desired. The former contends that Marx's ethics are ultimately personal and arbitrary, even though, throughout his life, Marx emphasized the social dimensions of life, and argued that communism would be founded upon a rational, non-arbitrary, basis. The latter leaves us wondering why, if it was bound to come, Marx worked for that moral future. Indeed, how could he − as he did − condemn some of those things which came to pass within his own lifetime?

I believe that both this and the preceding view of Marx are fundamentally mistaken. I shall argue instead that Marx has a moral theory and that this moral theory was integrally part of his 'scientific' views. This position (at least as so far minimally described) has had other defenders. Most notable are the accounts of Howard Selsam (Socialism and Ethics) and Eugene Kamenka (The Ethical Foundations of Marxism).

Selsam's account was written forty years ago. It was a broadly aimed, but not a terribly rigorous, attempt to formulate a Marxist ethics. Selsam lacked a number of crucial manuscripts of Marx (*The Economic and Philosophic Manuscripts*, and *Grundrisse*); he underestimated how radically different Marx's views on ethics were; and indeed, he was not particularly concerned with explicating Marx's ethics so much as using the writings of Marx and his followers down to Stalin to develop a new ethics. Kamenka's work was written twenty years ago. But whereas Selsam did not have Marx's early writings, Kamenka's work oftentimes gives the impression of being overwhelmed by them. This is understandable in that ready access to those manuscripts occurred shortly before Kamenka began his book. Nevertheless, a more balanced account is needed. The purpose of the present book, however, is not to criticize such predecessors as Selsam and Kamenka, but to continue the work of explicating and evaluating Marx's ethics. This is especially important in light of the considerable discussion of Marx's ethics which has occurred in the last twenty years.[7]

II

At the outset it should be clear that I do not maintain that Marx formulated a moral theory in a manner comparable to the moral theories which past or present moral philosophers have formulated. Marx did not write a treatise, any pamphlets, or even any essays on ethics and morality. At the most we have various sections in larger works, paragraphs, and scattered comments on ethics and morality which are interwoven with his reflections on history, economics, and politics. Further, on those occasions on which he does speak of ethics he does not engage in moral reflection as traditional and contemporary moral philosophers have. He does not pose for himself the question, 'What ought I to do?' as a way of entering into moral reflection. He does not set out, as Kant and others have, to search for and establish the supreme principle of morality by argument and consideration of the reasons and views of others. Thus, he does not, in any obvious way, urge the universalization of the maxims of our actions (as Kant did) or the calculation of the greatest good our actions might promote (as J.S. Mill did). Such individual questions are quite secondary to Marx's concern for the social system within which people raise such questions. Nor does Marx attempt to develop a theory of the meaning and purpose of moral statements as individuals make them. As such, Marx was not a moral philosopher. There are few, I think, who would deny this.

However, it does not follow that Marx did not have a moral theory. A person may be said to have a moral theory, even though he may never have explicitly formulated it. Whether one has a moral theory and whether one has formulated a moral theory are two different questions. The answer to the one question is not necessarily the answer to the other question. The latter question refers to a certain process that a person engages in, while the former question refers to a set of reasonably coherent and interrelated views which generally are but need not be the product of that process. For example, it has been maintained that to engage in the process of formulating a moral theory one must suspend one's commitments; one must make certain conscious decisions or choices to act on the basis of moral principles; and one must have been able to have chosen otherwise.[8] Whether or not these conditions for ethical inquiry are plausible, they are not plausible for determining whether or not one has an ethics or a moral theory. Suppose, for instance, I have been inclined to promote the pleasurable aspects of any situation and that I have not generally been inclined to do this simply for myself. I have tried to promote the pleasures of others as well. Still I have not myself given any thought to such matters, and do not always act or judge in the above manner. However, someone gives me Bentham's work, I read it and am convinced.[9] Now I did not suspend my judgment. I have always been inclined along Bentham's lines. I do make, I suppose, a conscious decision to act in these ways in the future, but it is unclear whether I could have chosen to do otherwise. In this case, I think we might well say that though I did not at first have a moral theory, I now do have a moral theory which underlies my actions and desires. Thus, those features which characterize the formulation of a moral theory, the engaging in ethical inquiry, need not characterize the having of a moral theory or an ethics. Because these two different questions are confused, it is concluded that since the answer to the first question is negative, the answer to the second question must also be negative. But this does not follow.[10]

What is it then to have a moral theory? Surely it is not sufficient that one simply speak in favor of various notions which one might identify as moral notions. Politicians, farmers, and the common man speak, on occasion, in favor of various moral notions, but we are not immediately inclined to ascribe moral theories to them.[11] As such they are, in one sense of the word, simply moralists.[12] If they are to be said to have a moral theory, their ideas about ethics must possess a certain unity, even if their statements of these ideas be scattered. Their ideas cannot simply be unconnected references to various moral notions. Consider, for example, a person who (almost) always acts consistently on his moral choices (we must allow for weakness of the will and other human failings). He praises certain ends and various ways of acting. He defends his choices and views by giving certain reasons which are connected both with the choices and views he advocates and other systematic views he holds and expounds on. He attacks opposing views and tries to show their weaknesses in ways which are both consistent with and a consequence of his views. Certainly, such a person is more than the moralist. He may also be less than a moral philosopher in that he has never brought all these ideas together, he has never shown their interrelations and connections. Nevertheless, though he may not have formulated the moral theory implicit in his views it is not strange to say that he operates on the basis of an implicit moral theory. Accordingly, I suggest that to have a moral theory it is sufficient that one expresses an (essentially) consistent body of ethical judgments, that one be aware of some sort of systematic connection between these judgments, and that one derive them in a more or less conscious way from some common foundation. It is in this sense that Marx can be said to have a moral theory.[13] The proof of this must wait upon the discussions in the remainder of this book.

My proof will take various forms. Firstly, it will consist in the formulation of that theory itself, together with supporting textual evidence. This part of my proof will have two parts. On the one hand, I will discuss the logical and methodological aspects of Marx's ethics. That is, I will consider what might be called Marx's meta-ethics. This I shall do in Chapters 2 and 3. On the other hand, the moral values and standards Marx defends and by which he criticizes capitalism must also be developed. This normative side of his ethics is developed in Chapters 4 to 6. If a consistent moral theory can be extracted from, and shown to be supported by, Marx's writings, my thesis will be substantially proven. Secondly, I shall consider, while discussing Marx's meta-ethics, a number of traditional objections to the view that Marx can have an ethics. By answering these objections my thesis will be further supported. Thirdly, if my thesis helps to integrate and explain other views of Marx, e.g. his views on punishment and violence, as well as indicating difficulties and problems which those who subscribe to Marx's views encounter, then my thesis will be yet further confirmed. Finally, I would point out that Marx did, throughout his life, engage in discussions which have the appearance of ethical inquiry and discussion. For example, he discussed the relation of morality and moral principles to their historical and material settings; he analyzed and criticized egoism, utilitarianism, bourgeois rights and liberty, as well as other notions such as charity. In addition, he seems to defend values such as freedom, brotherhood, solidarity, and community. Now these various discussions may not constitute the formulation of an ethical theory. However, if he does have the moral theory which is developed below, then it would not be surprising to find such discussions in Marx and they would be an additional confirmation of the underlying moral theory that is here identified.

III

At the outset, we must begin by reflecting on the fact that not only did Marx not formulate a moral theory but he also seemed to have opposed any attempt to do so. For example, his works reveal precious little use, in any traditional manner, of moral language. Certain concepts central to modern moral philosophy are rarely, if ever, used.[14] In addition, there is a significant body of textual evidence that Marx simply rejected ethics and morality and wanted to have nothing to do with them. Statements such as the following are exemplary of Marx's apparently anti-moral and anti-ethical views:

> It may be remarked in passing that German philosophy, because it took consciousness alone as its point of departure, was bound to end in moral philosophy, where the various heroes squabble about true morals. (*MECW*, 5:36)

> In a party one must support everything which helps towards progress, and have no truck with any tedious moral scruples. (*MECW*, 6:56)

> My standpoint, from which the evolution of the economic formation of society is viewed as a process of natural history, can less than any other make the individual responsible for relations whose creature he socially remains, however much he may subjectively raise himself above them. (*Capital*, I:10)

> I wrote *An Address to the Working Class*. . . . My proposals [in this Address] were all accepted by the subcommittee [of the Working-men's International Association]. Only I was obliged to insert two phrases about 'duty' and 'right' into the Preamble to the Statutes, ditto 'truth, morality, and justice,' but these are placed in such a way that they can do no harm.[15]

[I] t was, of course, only possible to discover . . . [the connection between the kinds of enjoyment open to individuals at any particular time and the class relations in which they live, and the conditions of production and intercourse which give rise to these relations] . . . when it became possible to criticise the conditions of production and intercourse in the hitherto existing world, i.e., when the contradictions between the bourgeoisie and the proletariat had given rise to communist and socialist views. That shattered the basis of all morality, whether of asceticism or of enjoyment. (*MECW*, 5:418-19)

These kinds of statements and the previously mentioned characteristics of Marx's work demand explanation. How can Marx be said to have an implicit ethics and yet make statements such as the preceding? Do not such statements simply reveal an antipathy towards and a rejection of morality and moral philosophy?

The problem is not as insurmountable as it may seem. Marx was indeed opposed to the morality and ethics of his time. They represented to him a kind of dream-like acquiescence in the face of the increasing degradation suffered by larger and larger numbers of people in modern society. Either they amounted to a kind of simple moralism in which moral conclusions were drawn, society was condemned or criticized, but (after all this) everything remained simply as it was. Or they amounted to an attempt to justify the status quo. Whatever evils they saw were rationalized away in one way or another. In either case, morality and ethics neither understood nor affected the problems of the time. Marx's comment on Max Stirner illustrates these views on morality and ethics: he 'arrives merely at an important moral injunction. . . . He believes Don Quixote's assurance that by a mere moral injunction he can without more ado convert the material forces from the division of labor into personal forces' (*MECW*, 5:342-3). Similarly, morality and ethics did not do or accomplish anything since they did not directly face the problems and conflicts of society. Their theory was separated from any practical consequences or reflections.

This opposition to the ineffectiveness, as well as the illusions, of morality and ethics can be found throughout Marx's writings — from his early essays and poetry, through *The German Ideology* to *Capital*. Needless to say, it is a criticism that he brings not simply against morality and ethics, but against all theories and social institutions. Religion, political economy, as well as the sciences in general were the objects of such criticism. With regard to moral philosophy, Marx's well-known eleventh thesis on Feuerbach captures his view perhaps most succinctly: 'The philosophers have only *interpreted* the world; the point, however, is to *change* it' (*MECW*, 5:5). As opposed to the moral philosophers and moralists of his time, Marx insisted that any creditable critical theory of man and society must clearly distinguish between appearance and reality. It must relentlessly pursue and analyze 'the common wisdom' for the realities it conceals. Furthermore, such an account must show how human society really operates, how it can be and must be changed. In short, any critical science must be illusionless and effective.

This twofold demand manifests itself in the following ways. Firstly, it manifests itself in his language, in his rhetoric. The language of the poet or revolutionary is just as much Marx's language as is the dry, sober language of the ethicist or economist. Even in his 'economic works,' vivid, forceful, persuasive language is mixed with dry economic analyses. However, more is involved here than an intention simply to state his views forcefully. Marx's language also reveals his views about the nature of argument and how readily people can be moved by cool rational argument alone. Marx recognized the obvious point – though one often forgotten by ethicists – that people are not wholly rational beings, that they cling to their views at times for various reasons which no strictly rational argument can alter. 'The real, practical dissolution of these [forms and products of consciousness], the removal of these notions from the consciousness of man, will . . . be effected by altered circumstances, not by theoretical deductions' (*MECW*, 5:56). Thus, though the rational argument behind Marx's views can be formulated, the statement of his views often takes the form of polemic, of ridicule, of indignation and denunciation. The Preface to *The German Ideology* exemplifies the point:

> The first volume of the present publication has the aim of uncloaking these sheep, who take themselves and are taken for wolves, of showing that their bleating merely imitates in a philosophic form the conception of the German middle class; that the boasting of these philosophic commentators only mirrors the wretchedness of the real conditions in Germany. It is its aim to ridicule and discredit the philosophic struggle with the shadows of reality, which appeals to the dreamy and muddled German nation. (*MECW*, 5:23-4)

This passage is quite typical of Marx – forceful, vivid language used to attack the illusions of certain philosophers and, not only by argument but also by ridicule, to work on those who would accept such shadows of reality. Surely Marx would admit that there is something which might be called 'the force of ideas.' But the mistake of ethicists and moralists has been to rely entirely on this 'force.' Thus, they have been ineffective. On the contrary, Marx insists, ideas are not simply disembodied mental entities with an existence all their own. Instead, they come bound up with the various aspects of individual, social, and historical existence. One's emotions, feelings, and sensitivities — as well as one's cognitive beliefs and reasoning abilities — play a role in determining the rational arguments one is able to accept. Thus, for one's arguments to be effective, one must direct one's argument and views not simply at disembodied minds. Accordingly, Marx uses his language to threaten, ridicule, and hound, as well as to denounce. 'Criticism appears no longer as an *end in itself*, but only as a means. Its essential sentiment is *indignation*, its essential activity is denunciation' (*MECW*, 3:177).[16] On the other hand, one's social and historical position may also affect the arguments one is able to accept. Then argument alone, even denunciation and ridicule, may be inadequate. 'Criticism dealing with this content is criticism in *hand-to-hand* combat, and in such a fight the point is not whether the opponent is a noble, equal, *interesting* opponent, the point is to *strike* him' (*MECW*, 3:178). In both cases, ethics and morality as traditionally conceived and practiced must be transcended.

Marx's opposition to the ineffectiveness and illusions of the moralists and ethicists of his time manifests itself in a second way. This is Marx's view that a critical account of man and society must start out from the various forms of practical consciousness or practical activity by which humans sustain and develop themselves. 'Where speculation ends, where real life starts, there consequently begins real, positive science, the expounding of the practical activity, of the practical process of development of men' (*MECW*, 5:37). Out of a study of this basic human reality the criteria and standards for evaluating human society must be drawn. Thus, in contrast to the ethics with which he was familiar, Marx did not see his task as the imposition on human society of a set of external or transcendent demands and obligations derived from religion, God, or Spirit. Rather, a critical science must develop out of the various forms of practical activity and consciousness 'the true reality as its obligation and its final goal' (*MECW*, 3:143). Nor was Marx prepared, as some moralists he knew were, to give 'final' answers to man's present and future problems. 'Constructing the future,' he insists, 'and settling everything for all times are not our affair . . . ' (*MECW*, 3:142). Finally, Marx held that only if we understand the nature of the social system within which people live can we then say something about the particular (moral) questions which individuals have. Hence, moral philosophers who place questions of individual morality first, who seek the supreme principle of morality so as to answer such questions, are attempting to answer abstract, impossible questions.

In this sense, Marx's views bear a resemblance to Hegel's views. Hegel too criticized the attempt to give answers to individual moral questions by establishing the supreme principle of morality. However, Hegel's and Marx's reasons for this shared view are different. Hegel claimed that moral philosophers simply could not give such advice. They always came upon the scene too late:

> One word more about giving instruction as to what the world ought to be. Philosophy in any case always comes on the scene too late to give it. As the thought of the world, it appears only when actuality is already there cut and dried after its process of formation has been completed. The teaching of the concept, which is also history's inescapable lesson, is that it is only when actuality is mature that the ideal first appears over against the real and that the ideal apprehends this same real world in its substance and builds it up for itself into the shape of an intellectual realm. When philosophy paints its grey in grey, then has a shape of life grown old. By philosophy's grey in grey it cannot be rejuvenated but only understood. The owl of Minerva spreads its wings only with the falling of the dusk.[17]

Marx, however, did not hold that the world could not be changed, or that thinkers (if not critical philosophers) always come upon the scene too late. Indeed, it was the view that philosophers could only interpret the world, not change it, that he criticized in his eleventh thesis on Feuerbach. Rather, Marx's refusal to deal directly with the traditional moral questions which occupied Kant, J.S. Mill, and other moral philosophers was due, in part, to his view that such individual questions are secondary to questions concerning the social systems within which people ask these questions. Only if we understand the nature of social systems — how they can and morally should be changed — can we proceed to answer concretely moral questions of a personal and individual nature.

It is this lack of attention to the basic human conditions of a morality which condemns moralists both to their illusions and ineffectiveness. The moralist assumes not only that we can be better than we can actually be, but also that we can significantly change our moral behavior within our present situation, even though we cannot.[18] Thus, the moralist 'preaches.' He assumes it is simply a matter of individual will, rather than deriving from human social reality the standards by which society and individuals may correctly be measured and effectively

13

changed. For Marx, that is, the criticism of society can only be effective if it is illusionless, and it can only be illusionless if it is effective. In any case, it must rest upon a study of practical human activity. The idea that an effective theory or movement could depend on 'the big lie,' that it need not be based on a clear, demystified view of reality is utterly foreign to Marx's thought. His views are rather traditional, if not classical, in these regards. Knowledge of truth, of reality, is a central, constitutive element of what makes one free. The distinction of reality from appearance is thus at the very center of Marx's endeavors. Consequently, Marx contends, one cannot begin with founding a social critique, as the morality and ethics of his time did, on God or Spirit, or in some idealistic manner. Ethics must be brought down to the ground. Once it loses its footing, it loses, like the Greek god Antaeus, all its force and power.

It is little wonder then that Marx was not enamored with the morality and ethics of his time. By and large they were moralistic, conservative, and founded on religious bases. It is little wonder, accordingly, that Marx disdained to express his views in terms which would suggest his sympathy with their views and general standpoint. To have used the (moral) language of those who merely moralized about the evils of capitalist society, but did nothing about it, ran the risk of confusing his theory with theirs. It is for such a reason that Marx attacks any presentation of 'communism as the love-imbued opposite of selfishness . . . [a presentation which] reduces a revolutionary movement of world-historical importance to the few words: love − hate, communism − selfishness' (*MECW*, 6:41; cf. 315, 318). Similarly, because moralistic radicals of his time had appropriated the word 'alienation,' Marx all but gave up using the word 'alienation' in his published writings after 1845, though he continued to use both the concept and the word in his unpublished writings − as the *Grundrisse*, for example, has made clear.[19] Marx was understandably cautious about employing the same language as moralists who were content to preach moral regeneration which the facts of the social situation rendered impossible.[20]

This kind of occurrence should not be thought to be limited to an explanation of Marx's views on the use of moral terminology. A similar thing also happens, for example, when the political Right seizes upon such phrases as 'law and order,' to state their views. Political views of the Left are not thereby to be understood as opposed to 'law and order,' advocates of lawlessness and disorder. Nevertheless, those of the political Left would be quite wary of stating their views in terms of 'law and order' to the extent that the political Right has pre-empted this phrase.[21] A similar consideration motivates Marx, in general, with regard to moral words. It is also, at least one of the reasons, why his works manifest the anti-ethical and anti-moral tenor that they do.

IV

Does the preceding show or suggest, then, that Marx did not or could not have an ethics? I do not think so. To begin with, the view that if Marx did not use a certain moral vocabulary, he cannot be engaged in moral evaluation or criticism presupposes that some words are particularly *moral* words. This view has often been held. People even speak of 'the language of morals' — as if there were some special set of moral words or vocabulary which is particularly moral. Still, this view is mistaken. 'Good,' 'right,' 'duty,' etc., are not simply and solely moral words. They can be used in many different contexts and in many different ways. But other words and expressions can take their place. We see this in Marx. Certainly, he did not evaluate capitalism using the traditional moral words of 'justice,' 'right,' 'duty,' etc. It is striking, nevertheless, that much of Marx's writings, for example the *Economic and Philosophic Manuscripts*, *The Communist Manifesto*, even *Capital* and the *Grundrisse*, sound very much like moral tracts — or at least significant parts of them do — even though little 'moral language' appears in them. Thus, though Marx does on occasion use the words, 'good,' 'bad,' 'right,' 'wrong,' etc., his main words, his central categories, of criticism of bourgeois society are quite different. They include the following: 'human,' 'inhuman,' 'exploitation,' 'freedom,' 'slavery,' 'dependence,' 'subjugation,' 'imperfection,' 'defect,' 'brutalization,' 'venality,' 'corruption,' 'prostitution,' 'money-relation,' 'self-interest,' 'despotism,' 'repulsiveness,' 'suffering,' 'impotent,' 'involuntary,' etc. These are clearly less general, more concrete words and concepts than such words as 'good,' 'right,' etc. However, it is not obvious that all of them are intended in some non-moral way, or that none of them have moral uses. Certainly, words such as 'freedom,' 'slavery,' 'self-interest,' 'despotism,' etc. suggest moral ideas and uses. Whether this suggestion is defensible depends on views of Marx which we will examine in subsequent chapters. The point here is, quite simply, that the absence of traditional moral terms does *not* prove Marx's antipathy to the whole of morality and ethics.

In fact, the degree to which Marx abandoned traditional moral language can well be over-stressed. That is, it is quite possible to find instances in which he does, in more or less traditional moral ways, criticize society. Thus, he speaks of the 'tainted morals' due to capitalism,[22] and condemns the *evil* of wages (*MECW*, 6:436); he also claims that the elimination of exchange value will do away with the *evil* of bourgeois society (*Grund.*, 134).[23] Similarly, Marx characterizes communism in terms which, at least, appear moral:

> When communist artisans associate with one another . . . the brotherhood of man is no mere phrase with them, but a fact of life, and the nobility of man shines upon us from their work-hardened bodies. (*MECW*, 3:313)

> The standpoint of independent morality . . . is based . . . on the consciousness of *human dignity*. [The] morality [of Rudolph, a character in a book Marx attacks], on the contrary, is based on the consciousness of human weakness. (*MECW*, 4:201)

> Only within the community has each individual the means of cultivating his gifts in all directions; hence personal freedom becomes possible only within the community. (*MECW*, 5:78)

> In place of the old bourgeois society, with its classes and classes antagonisms, we shall have an association, in which the free development of each is the condition for the free development of all. (*MECW*, 6:506)

> In a higher phase of communist society, after the enslaving subordination of the individual to the division of labor, has vanished; after labor has become not only a means of life but life's prime want; after the productive forces have also increased with the all-round development of the individual, and all the springs of co-operative wealth flow more abundantly — only then can the narrow horizon of bourgeois right be crossed in its entirety and society inscribe on its banner: From each according to his ability, to each according to his needs![24]

Such characterizations of communism should be kept in mind when one reads other statements of Marx which seem obviously anti-moral and anti-ethical.[25] Certainly, any decision as to Marx's views on morality and ethics cannot be based on various isolated quotations. On any particular occasion, Marx may have overstated his views or even misrepresented them, due to inattention or an attempt to gain a tactical advantage over opponents. The point to be stressed here is simply that it is mistaken to claim that Marx forswore all moral language. Indeed,

16

though he rarely uses 'right,' 'duty,' and the like, he quite commonly uses the terms listed in the preceding paragraph. The appropriate conclusion to draw, then, at least from such textual evidence, is not that Marx abandoned morality, in any wholesale fashion, but that he held a view of morality in which certain traditional words and concepts did not prominently figure, while others did. This moral view, to be explored in subsequent chapters, deserves initial comment here.

Discussion of Marx's moral views has hitherto been deficient because it has failed to recognize a common distinction between two different conceptions of morality. Because it seems apparent that he does not have a moral theory in one sense of the term 'morality,' it is concluded that he does not have a moral theory at all. But this does not follow if there is another sense of 'morality.' We must recognize, that is, that the notion of morality is not a simple and unambiguous notion. We must distinguish between an ethics of duty and an ethics of virtue.[26] On the one hand, morality has been viewed as centrally concerned with the duties and obligations one person owes to another. So viewed, morality is characterized by certain notions such as duty, obligation, guilt, justice, rights, etc. On this understanding of morality, to be moral is to act in accordance with certain moral laws and duties, or to be moved by a sense of moral obligation. It is the morality of 'thou shalt' and 'thou shalt not.' Failure to act in these ways is met with condemnation for moral corruption, for being recreant to duty. In this sense, it has already been suggested, Marx does not have a moral theory. He rarely uses the notions and vocabulary which are identified with this view of morality. If one then assumes that this view is the only (proper) view of morality, one will quite naturally conclude that Marx must have been a scientist. Accordingly, one might further conclude that he condemned capitalism either simply because it was self-destructive, or because it violated various non-moral reasons or values.[27]

However, there is another understanding of morality which should not be forgotten. This is the sense of morality in which morality is linked with certain virtues, excellences, or flourishing ways of living. In this sense, morality is not primarily concerned with rules and principles, but with the cultivation of certain dispositions or traits of character. This view has been expressed in this way: 'The moral law . . . has to be expressed in the form, "be this", not in the form, "do this". . . . the true moral law says "hate not", instead of "kill not". . . . the only mode of stating the moral law must be a rule of character.'[28] This, I believe, is quite close to Marx's views.

Accordingly, Marx avoids (certain) 'moral words' not only because their use has been appropriated by moralists (as noted above), but also

17

because he has different concerns than most modern moral philosophers. Usually morality tells us not to steal, kill, lie, cheat, commit adultery, etc. But what about the people to whom this is told? What if they have been transformed into commodities, into (say) the equivalent of hats (*MECW*, 6:125)? What if their labor or activity is itself treated as a commodity (*MECW*, 6:113, 125)? What if the crafts they learn are but forms of craft-idiocy (*MECW*, 6:190), and they are abased in the process (*MECW*, 6:201)? How do any of these things count in morality? Marx speaks, for example, of one's feelings towards the dwelling in which one lives — does one find it a natural or an alien environment which one can have only in so far as one gives up blood and sweat on it (*MECW*, 3:314)? He speaks of activity in direct association with others becoming a means for expressing one's own life (*MECW*, 3:301). He criticizes money for 'overturning and confounding . . . all human and natural qualities' (*MECW*, 3:324-5). In essence, Marx believes that it is crucial to push beyond the rules and principles of an ethics of duty to the underlying realities which constitute and form people's daily lives. Morality has tended to demand that we act in certain ways, whereas the daily life we really live has told us other things. What we are, the nature our characters and dispositions take in society, is, Marx suggests, what is crucial and of immediate (moral) significance. The rules of duty and obligation seem remote to such concerns. Indeed, even some who defend an ethics of duty have noted this remoteness. Thus, they have expressed their consternation 'that so many *admirable* people live by something other than a sense of moral obligation . . . that what takes primacy in the lives of such people . . . is not . . . a sense of moral duty . . . but an ideal of being virtuous. . . .'[29] That traditional morality, the ethics of duty, is separated from the underlying concerns of daily life is a crucial part of Marx's attack on ethics and morality. One basis for life and another for science is a lie, Marx claims. Marx does not seek a morality that is separated from other crucial areas of life, but a view of life which would unify our daily concerns and our moral concerns. In so viewing the subject of his concern, Marx looks at morality more broadly than is often done today.

   In this sense, Marx's approach to morality is akin to that of the Greeks for whom the nature of virtue or human excellence was the central question of morality. In contrast to the more restricted notion of moral excellence as the fulfillment of moral duty, the Greeks wanted to know what kind of life is best suited for a human being. What kinds and range of activities are required for a person to lead a flourishing life? To lead such a life would be to lead the moral life *par excellence*. Marx too, when he was not condemning the narrow, ineffective morality of

18

his time, thought in these broad terms. Thus, he comments that besides 'purely physical limitations, the extension of the working-day encounters *moral* ones. The laborer needs time for satisfying his intellectual and social wants, the extent and number of which are conditioned by the general state of social advancement' (*Capital*, 1:232, my emphasis).[30] As such, Marx's treatment of issues that relate to what we might understand as morality and ethics is broader and different from what we may expect. It is, essentially, an attempt to provide a characterization of the moral or flourishing life, which is not separated from its underlying bases and conditions. It is an attempt which, because it jettisons certain concepts traditionally identified with morality, challenges our conceptual prejudices.

Now if Marx is said to have an ethics of virtue then it might be that some of those who have denied that Marx's theory is a moral one merely meant to deny that it was an ethics of duty. Consequently, they might not actually disagree with the view that is defended here.[31] Unfortunately, it is not clear exactly what sense of 'moral' others have used in their interpretations of Marx. Almost without exception they have neither made the distinction invoked above, nor discussed the sense of 'moral' or 'morality' they use. Still, there is reason to believe that by and large previous commentators have denied that Marx's theory was a moral one in both of the two senses above. On the one hand, in either sense of the term, to speak of Marx's moral views is to speak of views which carry normative force — they tell us how we should live, they act as guides and directives to a different kind of life. This, however, is explicitly denied in the quotations with which this chapter begins. On the other hand, if they have admitted that Marx was centrally concerned with certain characteristics of life which have been linked above with virtue, they have denied that for Marx this was a matter of morality. Instead, such virtues and excellences were of a non-moral nature.[32]

It is impossible fully to discuss here which one of the two senses of morality noted above might be the one which most faithfully and correctly captures 'the' meaning of 'morality.' Indeed, it may be that both are legitimate. However, because of the preceding challenge to the propriety of considering Marx's concerns to be of an ethical nature, the following observations should be made. To begin with, if we see in morality only an ethics of duty, we restrict morality to a particular social and historical view. It becomes questionable, for example, whether the Greeks had a morality, since it is a matter of dispute whether Plato and Aristotle gave any significant place to the modern notions of duty and obligation.[33] Indeed, it has been argued that the

notions of duty, guilt, and the like are bound up with a divine com-
mandment — e.g. a Judaeo-Christian — view of morality.[34] But surely it
is historically and intellectually mistaken to impose the requirements of
such an ethics on all moralities. We may speak intelligibly of moral
codes which do not employ a variety of notions common to present
(bourgeois) morality. For example, it has been noted that

> there may be codes of conduct quite properly termed moral codes
> (though we can of course say they are 'imperfect') which do not
> employ the notion of *a* right, and there is nothing contradictory or
> otherwise absurd in a code of morality consisting wholly of prescrip-
> tions or in a code which prescribed only what should be done for the
> realisation of happiness or some ideal of personal perfection.[35]

Thus, the fact that Marx does not use certain traditional moral notions,
that he does not have an ethics of duty, does not imply that implicitly
he could not have what may legitimately be called a moral theory.
Those who raise this objection have an unjustifiedly restricted notion of
morality.

Further, to view Marx's thought as founded upon an ethics of virtue
has a number of other advantages. Firstly, Marx himself uses the word
'moral' in contexts in which it clearly has a broad rather than a narrow
nature.[36] That Marx held an ethics of virtue would be compatible — in a
way that an ethics of duty would not be — with both such usages of
'moral' as well as with his claim that communism will constitute 'the
most radical rupture with traditional ideas' (*MECW*, 6:504). Similarly,
the categories Marx uses to appraise and condemn capitalism (cf. p. 15)
themselves suggest an ethics of virtue much more readily than an ethics
of duty. Those words and categories are primarily connected with states
or conditions of being rather than the qualities of particular actions
which one may or may not be duty-bound to fulfill.

Secondly, Marx maintained that we must create a single science
which can act as a guide to revolutionary activity, i.e. one which has
normative implications. That is, he argued for a unity of theory and
praxis. If we take this claim to mean that the normative implications of
Marx's science are intrinsic to it and not simply appended to it, then to
view Marx's science as a moral science is enlightening and faithful to
Marx's own demands. But to do so is possible only if we view morality
in the broad sense of an ethics of virtue.

Finally, the relation of an ethics of virtue to social change is different from that of an ethics of duty. Inasmuch as an ethics of duty
concerns the duties and obligations one person owes another person

and/or society, it lends itself quite directly to formalization in a legal code.[37] 'Thou shalt do this or that' becomes a law requiring or forbidding this or that action. Thus, an ethics of duty lends itself easily to evolutionary change within present institutions. This is particularly so if it is correct, as it has been argued,[38] that an ethics of duty is conceptually linked with capitalism. An ethics of virtue, however, questions which ways of life are worthy of man. It seeks the virtues, excellences, the flourishing life. But judgments relative to these matters have no direct bearing on the law. They cannot so readily be translated into law as can judgments of duty. Rather, if such judgments are to be a vital part of people's lives, the entire social structure of society — formal and informal — will have to be in accord with its prescriptions. Thus, if an ethics of virtue is to have an effect, and not simply serve as a set of ideals to which people hypocritically aspire, and if it rejects as illusory the flourishing life that present (capitalist) society prescribes, then it must give itself to more radical change, change which will significantly alter the face of society and its institutions. Accordingly, if we understand Marx's implicit moral theory as an ethics of virtue, I think we shall more fully appreciate the dynamics of his thought which leads him to advocate the need for revolution.

V .

What, then, are we to conclude regarding Marx's unwillingness to use traditional moral terms and to engage in familiar moral reflection and evaluation? What we see here is Marx's disdain for moralism and an ethics of duty. We do not have evidence for a wholesale rejection of morality and ethics. Others who have also opposed traditional ethics for its ineffectiveness, illusions, and duty-bound nature have nevertheless developed ethical theories. Hence this opposition does not of itself exclude the possibility of developing a Marxist ethics, or reconstructing the ethics to which Marx adhered implicitly. Correspondingly, we have seen that the categories in terms of which Marx does criticize bourgeois society may be used in various moral and ethical senses.

Marx saw his task as that of providing a critique of existing society. The preceding discussion indicates some of the parameters within which this critique, or science, and the ethics implicit in it, must be developed. For one, an acceptable critique must be linked to material considerations. It must not be separated from the practical activity through which people sustain and develop themselves. The immediate object of study and critique, then, is social phenomena. Marx assumes that answers to individual questions will be dependent on this prior critique. Further, the critique of such social phenomena must be systematic — it must show how they are interrelated and what course of development they follow. Secondly, the criteria by which society is to be criticized do not lie beyond or external to that society, rather they lie within it. As opposed to previous ethicists and moralists 'who have had the solution of all riddles lying in their writing-desks' (*MECW*, 3:142), Marx sought to found his critique on an account of the 'real relations,' 'the true reality,' which constituted that society.[39] That is, one must derive these criteria from a study of human practical activity — not simply impose them on it. Over against the ethicists and moralists of his day, this was Marx's 'Copernican Revolution.' It did not mean that Marx ceased to see moral problems, it only meant he saw them from another perspective, which he wished to distinguish from the perspective he rejected. Thirdly, there must also be no separation of the proclamations of such an ethics from how people act and live. Moral theory and moral praxis must be joined. Ethics must concretely and practically show how society should be changed in light of the possibilities for such change. It is to a discussion of the methodological bases of this ethics that we now turn.

2 Ethics and historical materialism

> It has not occurred to any of these philosophers to inquire into the connection of . . . philosophy with . . . reality, the relation of their criticism with their own material surroundings. (*The German Ideology*, *MECW*, 5:30)

Marx's lifelong work was an attempt to understand and ruthlessly to criticize human society. This criticism, I maintain, was at least in part a moral criticism, as well as one which, Marx held, might play an active and effective role in changing society. To defend this claim we must examine Marx's views on the role which ethics and morality can play in society. Traditionally, it has been held that ethics and morality, through human consciousness, people's thoughts and wills, can play an important and significant role in directing human affairs. Accordingly, not only can the morality one espouses be a crucial determining force in society, but also individuals may be held morally responsible for the actions they perform and the relations in which they live. However, historical materialism, i.e. Marx's account of society, is usually taken to deny this view of morality and ethics. The mode of production of a society is said to be the determining force which dictates the course society will follow:

> Intrinsically, it is not a queston of the higher or lower degree of development of the social antagonisms that result from the natural laws of capitalist production. It is a question of these laws themselves, of these tendencies working with iron necessity towards inevitable results. The country that is more developed industrially only shows, to the less developed, the image of its own future. (*Capital*, I:8-9)

The various other elements of society, e.g. the state, political struggles, cultural forms, as well as ethics and morality, seem to amount to mere epiphenomena, i.e. impotent by-products of the economic juggernaut.

In any traditional sense, then, ethics and morality appear to be impossible. As a consequence, the individual does not appear to be morally responsible for his actions and relations. Marx himself seems to support this conclusion:

> But here [in *Capital*] individuals are dealt with only in so far as they are the personifications of economic categories, embodiments of particular class-relations and class-interests. My standpoint, from which the evolution of the economic formation of society is viewed as a process of natural history, can less than any other make the individual responsible for relations whose creature he socially remains, however much he may subjectively raise himself above them. (*Capital*, I:10).

Contemporary commentators, such as Kamenka, have been quick to agree:

> it was primarily on this ground that he [Marx] rejected the conception that ethics is concerned with 'guiding' human behavior in those realms where human beings are 'free' to act in a number of possible ways. It is for this reason that he rejects the notion that morality is concerned with 'obligation'. A person cannot be 'obliged' to act contrary to the course his character and circumstances inevitably determine him to take, and there is no point in obliging him to act in accordance with this course, for he will do so in any case.[1]

Consequently, we must carefully reconsider Marx's views on the nature of society, ethics, and morality. Unless the above apparent conflicts between historical materialism and ethics can be overcome and the various comments of Marx that people are not free but forced to act as they do can be explained, it would be silly to claim that Marx's criticism of capitalist society was a moral criticism. If we can resolve these conflicts and answer such comments, we shall have achieved new insight into the nature of historical materialism as well as Marx's views on the nature of ethics and morality.

I

Marx's famous, if not infamous, statement regarding the nature of historical materialism is to be found in the Preface of *A Contribution to the Critique of Political Economy*:

The general conclusion at which I arrived and which, once reached, became the guiding principle of my studies can be summarised as follows. In the social production of their existence, men inevitably enter into definite relations, which are independent of their will, namely relations of production appropriate to a given stage in the development of their material forces of production. The totality of these relations of production constitutes the economic structure of society, the real foundation, on which arises a legal and political superstructure and to which correspond definite forms of social consciousness. The mode of production of material life conditions the general process of social, political, and intellectual life. It is not the consciousness of men that determines their existence, but their social existence that determines their consciousness. At a certain stage of development, the material productive forces of society come into conflict with the existing relations of production or — this merely expresses the same thing in legal terms — with the property relations within the framework of which they have operated hitherto. From forms of development of the productive forces these relations turn into their fetters. Then begins an era of social revolution. The changes in the economic foundation lead sooner or later to the transformation of the whole immense superstructure.[2]

Needless to say, there have been many and varied interpretations of this passage. Since our purpose concerns the role ethics and morality can have in a society as well as the moral freedom an individual can be said to have, the following will concentrate on those interpretations of the above passage which might be taken to raise problems for attributing to morality a significant role in society and to humans the freedom required for morality. Accordingly, we must concentrate on those interpretations which emphasize the deterministic nature of Marx's views, the accounts in which necessity, inevitability, and the confining nature of social relations play the central role. Having done this and indicated the purported problems for morality which historical materialism is said to raise, I wish to show that such an interpretation of historical materialism is not the most plausible one. Viewed differently and more accurately, I believe it can be shown that historical materialism, morality and ethics are compatible.

The type of interpretation which must be the object of consideration here takes the above passage to hold that a society can be analyzed into three distinct and logically independent components: the forces of production (the material productive forces), the relations of production, and the superstructure ('the social, political, and intellectual life'). The forces of production are the basic forces in society, the engine of society. They are constituted by the means of production and labor-power. The former includes the instruments of labor, e.g. tools, machines, workshops, roads, canals — in short all objects necessary for carrying on the labor process — as well as the objects of labor, the raw materials and nature-given materials on which man works.[3]

It has sometimes been held that the ultimately determining factor of society was simply the machinery or tools of a society. After all, Marx did say, 'The hand-mill gives you society with the feudal lord; the steam mill, society with the industrial capitalist' (*MECW*, 6:166). This view is, however, wildly implausible. Machinery by itself can do nothing. One only has to reflect on how hand-mills and steam mills come about, as well as the conditions required for their operation, to recognize that more is required. Marx has given abundant evidence that he too was aware of this. Further, Marx's summary statement of his own views cited above does not suggest such a simplistic view — at the least it refers to productive forces, a much more complex concept.

The other aspect of the forces of production is labor-power, man's capacity to work for a certain period. Its characterization involves not only its strength and durability, but also its skill, talents, knowledge, training, experience, etc. It is not, in short, simply the capacity to provide dumb, brute force. Together, the forces of production determine the direction in which and the speed at which society runs. As such they are the explanatory basis of historical materialism. Two points should be noted concerning this interpretation. Firstly, the forces of production do not include morality, the judiciary, or the like. Such 'things' are part of the superstructure. They constitute the explanandum, not the explanans. The forces of production are limited 'to those elements which can actually be utilised in the labor process.'[4] Secondly, the forces of production also do not include human beings, their desires, or interests. Human labor-power is an abstraction; it is not simply an indirect way of referring to humans. Of course, labor-power only comes embodied in humans. But it is simply the capacity to labor for a certain number of hours — this abstract aspect of humans — which is part of the productive forces.

The relations of production consist of the relations in which people and productive forces stand in production. Examples which are traditionally given are those of master and slave, feudal lord and serf, and capitalist and worker.[5] These relations initially correspond to the forces of production of a particular epoch. Then the two are in harmony. However, not being dynamic in themselves, the relations of production tend to stagnate — they do not change with the times. Hence, from time to time they become fetters on the forces of production. When this occurs society must pass through a revolutionary period in which the relations of production are changed, brought up to date.

Lastly, resting upon the economic base is the superstructure. This is composed of morality, ethics, religion, the state, political struggles within society, as well as forms of consciousness corresponding to the preceding. These phenomena are themselves the result, or 'expression,' of the actual social relations of production. When the forms of consciousness mistakenly reflect in a systematic way the actual social relations, such consciousness is said to be false consciousness — ideological consciousness.

It is a common misinterpretation (one that gives rise to determinist problems) that the superstructure of a society plays no role in, has no effect on, the economic base. This is an understandable mistake, given various one-sided comments from Marx, but still a mistake. On many occasions Marx and Engels clearly indicated that they did think that the superstructure and the ideology of a time could influence the path of development of the mode of production. This point is made repeatedly in *The German Ideology* if the text is read closely. Thus, Marx and Engels write:

It shows that circumstances make men just as much as men make circumstances. (*MECW*, 5:54)

This conception of history thus relies on expounding the real process of production — starting from the material production of life itself — and comprehending the form of intercourse connected with and created by this mode of production, i.e., civil society — its various stages as the basis of all history; describing it in its action as the state, and also explaining how all the different theoretical productions and forms of consciousness, religion, philosophy, morality, etc. etc., arise from it, and tracing the process of their formation from that basis; thus the whole thing can, of course, be depicted in its totality (*and therefore, too, the reciprocal action of these various sides on one another*). (*MECW*, 5:53; my emphasis)

Industry and commerce, production and the exchange of the necessities of life in their turn determine distribution, the structure of the different social classes and are, in turn, determined by it as to the mode in which they are carried on. (*MECW*, 5:40)

27

Thus, quite clearly Marx thought that there were reciprocal effects between the mode of production, and the ideology and superstructure of any period. Morality, ethics, as well as the other parts of a society's superstructure, must, accordingly, be included in any account of the development of a society. And, indeed, given Marx's dialectical views, one should expect this. Marx's dialectics enjoins that in order to understand any social or human phenomenon we must see it in its essential and reciprocal interconnections with other phenomena. When we grasp the various connections amongst phenomena we see that they constitute organic systems or totalities. Society is one example of a totality, i.e. the various parts of a society, the mode of production and the ideology, are interrelated with and interact on one another. Consequently, it is most implausible that Marx explained the social forms of life solely on the basis of some narrowly conceived economic segment of society. This undercuts the more simplistic deterministic problems which have been attributed to historical materialism. Still, problems remain.

The technological determinist view sketched above may grant that the superstructure may have effects on the forces and relations of production. For example, it may note that Marx allows that laws, traditions, customs, etc., may play a stabilizing role in society. This certainly suggests that the superstructure may interact with the forces and relations of production. Nevertheless, the technological determinist still insists that the forces of production retain explanatory primacy. Any efficacy that the superstructure has is 'only because of the more fundamental pressure of the productive forces.'[6] As a consequence, there appears to be, according to such an interpretation, at least two aspects of historical materialism which are incompatible with ethics and morality. Firstly, though the above account allows for some interaction of base and superstructure, still it holds that the productive forces determine the nature and development of society. Inasmuch as the productive forces do not include human beings, their desires, goals, and/or interests, it would appear that things are in control and ride humanity. As such, people cannot be responsible for either the nature or course of development their society takes. We could not, seemingly, morally approve or condemn a particular historical stage or the transition from one epoch to another epoch. If historical movement is outside the hands of individuals, if they are simply transported along through history like a prisoner in a jail cell might be transported across the countryside, then, for example, we could not morally criticize the development of capitalism or morally approve the transition to socialism.

Secondly, the above account suggests that, to the extent an individual plays a certain role in a social formation, he must do certain things. For example, an individual *qua* capitalist *must* try to create more surplus value. A worker *must* try to sell his labor. Thus, within each social formation certain behaviors are necessitated by the role and relations constituting that social formation. Supposedly, it is for this reason that Marx said that his view 'can less than any other make the individual responsible for relations whose creature he socially remains, however much he may subjectively raise himself above them.' Accordingly, if the individual in the travelling cell *must* act in some prisoner-like manner (whatever that might be), then it would appear that he is not free. Thus, again historical materialism raises deterministic problems for morality.

Finally, it might be noted that the above account of historical materialism is developed on a level at some abstraction from the level of particular acts and events. On the above view, Marx is showing how various relational structures and ideological (super-) structures come about. He is not showing how particular things occur within these structures. Thus, it is said,

> Since the production relations comprising a certain mode of production would only determine the various superstructural relations compatible with it to different degrees and within varying ranges, other regularities and laws would have to be utilised if the precise nature and history of a particular society were to be scientifically explicated. The relations of production for Marx shape the social world in general, but alone they do not reveal what is unique to a given social formation. The analysis of a mode of production, although according to the 'Preface' it can be accomplished 'with the precision of natural science,' does not straightforwardly allow deduction of its particular manifestation in a specific social formation.[7]

Consequently, it might be claimed that historical materialism does not attempt to explain — or at least it is not an explanation of — particular individual and superstructural phenomena. This means that the determination of which Marx speaks in historical materialism is that of the structures within which people live, not directly of the people themselves.

Accordingly, with respect to historical materialism, people's actions and desires might be said to be free, though within certain broad bounds. That is, to the extent a person is more — or other — than simply a capitalist, proletarian, or prisoner, his actions might be free within the historical context in which he lives. To use the analogy suggested above, man would have the freedom a person in a jail cell might have as he and his cell were being transported across the country. Within the cell he could do what he liked; other people who shared his cell would have a similar freedom. But their actions and decisions would be limited by the cell itself and its movement across the countryside. Freedom to this extent would perhaps satisfy at least some of the demands of morality. Though such freedom is limited by social structures, certainly morality also recognizes limitations on what an individual can do. Even though the person, in the above analogy, is locked in his cell, to the extent he is free to do one thing or another to his fellow prisoners, to help or to hurt them, he remains a moral being. Thus, though a general view of historical materialism suggests that it is inimical to morality, a more particular view suggests that some room might be saved for morality. What historical materialism, as above interpreted, contends is that the structural changes from one moral form to another moral form rest on factors external to morality. But it allows that within any epoch and hence within any moral structure, people may make choices, decide between different actions, etc.

Nevertheless, though Marx's historical materialism as above characterized may not provide a complete deterministic explanation of human action, proponents of the above interpretation are quick to add that it is not implausible that Marx thought that such an account was possible:

> Marx and Engels, with a scientific optimism characteristic of the Victorian age, did believe that scientifically adequate explanation is in principle possible for the 'contingent surface of history' in all its nuance and detail; but it is important to see that some of the laws on which such a complete explanation of history would have to draw (individual psychology, for example) are not those which are the object of historical materialism's investigation.[8]

Accordingly, the deterministic knot is tied once again. The freedom required for morality is supposedly denied by Marx on both the general and the individual levels. The limited nature of historical materialism is no guarantee that people have the freedom that morality requires.

On the contrary, I believe that the preceding kind of account is fundamentally mistaken and that we need not, therefore, accept its implications. To arrive at an adequate answer to the question of freedom and historical materialism, however, we must examine the above account of historical materialism in light of the preceding three implications. I wish to show that the preceding interpretation of historical materialism is incorrect and that a more plausible interpretation allows for the possibility of morality.

II

There are a variety of different kinds of problems with the technological determinist account that might be discussed. I will concentrate in the following on but one kind, viz., those relating to the nature of the forces of production and their relation to the rest of society.

To begin with, the above account simplifies and falsifies Marx's views. The productive forces cannot be characterized as simply as is suggested above, nor do the productive forces as described above have explanatory primacy. It should be noted, that Marx at least *says* that amongst those 'things' constituting the productive forces are included not simply tools, machinery, labor-power, knowledge, skills, and raw materials, but also the revolutionary class (*MECW*, 6:211), the community (*Grund.*, 495), science (*Grund.*, 699), and the division of labor itself (*Grund.*, 765). He also mentions 'the mode of co-operation' (*MECW*, 5:43), the collective (productive) powers of the masses (*Capital*, I:326), the power of the state (*Capital*, I:751), as well as the growth of population (*Grund.*, 765), etc.[9] That is, Marx includes amongst the productive forces various productive relations and members of productive relations (i.e. the revolutionary class). The productive forces are not limited simply to technological forces. Thus, new technical inventions and instruments of production 'give us' a new social formation, but only together with a variety of other non-technological factors.

The mention of such additional productive forces which do not fit into the technological determinist's neat schema might be said to be simply a matter of Marx's pen slipping, or (more likely) a loose way of speaking. For instance, Marx does say:

> Capital which consumes itself in the productive process, or fixed capital, is the *means of production* in the strict sense. In a broader sense the entire production process and each of its moments, such as circulation — as regards its material side — is only a means of production for capital, for which value alone is the end in itself. Regarded as a physical substance, the raw material itself is a means of production for the product, etc. (*Grund.*, 690)

The ethical foundations

Surely it can be admitted that a machine in operation is productive, is a productive force, in a way in which a class or relation of production is not. Still, it is significant that even the latter are called productive forces. The significance is that Marx does *not* isolate or separate the productive forces (as the technological determinist does) from the productive relations. It is only the two together which constitute production. And though the technological determinist may agree to this, he or she will not draw the further conclusion I wish to defend, that, accordingly, the explanatory basis of historical materialism is not the forces of production but the mode of production which includes forces and relations of production. But this requires explanation and defense.

Firstly, it is simply implausible that Marx would or could attribute explanatory primacy to the productive forces as the technological determinist characterizes them. There are no contradictions built into the productive forces. As such, there are no contradictions built into the basis upon which Marx's explanation rests. That, however, is undialectical. According to Marx, phenomena are a 'unity of the diverse' — they consist of diverse, conflicting, and contradictory determinations. Thus, he speaks of the unity of opposites or the interpenetration of opposites. It is on the basis of the conflict between the contradictions which are essential to, or constitutive of, a phenomenon and yet which tend at the same time towards its destruction or transformation into a new phenomenon (i.e. dialectical contradictions) that Marx seeks to understand and explain that which he investigates (cf. *MECW*, 5:64, 74, 357). Accordingly, any explanatory basis to which Marx could appeal must consist of phenomena constituted by certain essential conflicts and contradictions. But any contradictions to which the technological determinist can point would be external to the elements of the productive forces. They would be between the productive forces and the relations of production. And though there are indeed contradictions here, they are not, as described by the technological determinist, dialectical contradictions. As such, it is difficult to imagine how there could be history. Society might just as well remain the same on the above basis. Accordingly, if we are to remain faithful to Marx's dialectical views, it would seem that we must reject the explanatory basis which the technological determinist describes. To do this would seem to have Marx's approval inasmuch as he explicitly notes that production necessarily involves a distribution of the instruments of production and a distribution of the members of society among the different kinds of production (*Grund.*, 96; *MECW*, 5:43). The technological determinist, of course, generally admits that production forces stand in various relations of production. Because of his non-dialectical views, however,

32

he refuses to see that it is the two together which explain society's course. If, as Marx says, it is the capitalist mode of production which assigns rank and influence to other kinds of production, i.e. capitalist production influencing agriculture, as well as medicine, law, the arts, etc., then it would seem that it must be the mode of production – the forces and relations of production – which explains society.

Secondly, though the technology of a society is crucial in sustaining and further developing each stage of production, it is not itself sufficient – and not even necessary in some cases – for the original development of a stage of production. Indeed, certain technologies may only be possible given the changed social conditions which a new stage of production brings about. Thus, Marx claims concerning the development of the feudal period out of the ancient period:

> if antiquity started out from the *town* and its small territory, the Middle Ages started out from the *country*. This different starting-point was determined by the sparseness of the population at that time, which was scattered over a large area and which received no large increase from the conquerors. In contrast to Greece and Rome, feudal development, therefore, begins over a much wider territory, prepared by the Roman conquests and the spread of agriculture at first associated with them. The last centuries of the declining Roman Empire and its conquest by the barbarians destroyed a considerable part of the productive forces; agriculture had declined, industry had decayed for want of a market, trade had died out or been violently interrupted, the rural and urban population had decreased. These conditions and the mode or organisation of the conquest determined by them, together with the influence of the Germanic military constitution, led to the development of feudal property. (*MECW*, 5:33-4)

It should be noted that this passage does *not* claim that due to the thrust of productive forces (in the technological determinist sense) a new mode of production is produced. Indeed, it suggests that a new mode of production may come about even though such productive forces have decayed or even been destroyed. In a similar vein Marx makes the following comment on the development of the capitalist mode of production:

> Capitalist production only then really begins . . . when each individual capital employs simultaneously a comparatively large number of labourers; . . . A greater number of labourers working together, at

the same time, in one place . . . in order to produce the same sort of
commodity under the mastership of one capitalist, constitutes both
historically and logically, the starting-point of capitalist production.
With regard to the mode of production itself, manufacture, in its
strict meaning, is hardly to be distinguished, in its earliest stages,
from the handicraft trades of the guilds, otherwise than by the
greater number of workmen simultaneously employed by one and
the same individual capital. The workshop of the mediaeval master
handicraftsman is simply enlarged. (*Capital*, I:322)

This passage, too, does not suggest the introduction of any new technology, or productive forces, at least as the technological determinist
understand them. It cannot be objected that merely the greater number
of handicraftsmen constitutes a new productive force since it is inconceivable that a greater number of handicraftsmen could have been
brought together without the introduction of new relations of production. Indeed, the essential difference between the guild and the
manufacturer suggested in the passage lies in the introduction of new
relations of production, but these, on the technological determinist's
view, are not productive forces. Hence, again, a new mode of production has entered upon the scene without new productive forces. Only
after capitalist relations of production were in place could the tremen-
dous forces of production and technologies which capitalism has
brought forth be developed.

It might be objected, however, that Marx only held that 'the instal-
lation of capitalist relations be a response to the existing level of the
productive forces.'[10] Thus, the above points are not contrary to a technological determinist interpretation. But to remain faithful to technological determinism it must be shown that the existing level of the
productive forces (in the technological determinist sense) has become
incompatible, due to their prior development, with the relations of production. However, this is not the case in the first passage cited above. In
the second passage it is not obvious that the forces of production are
incompatible with the then existing relations of production. The manufacturer is using the same forces of production that the guild master did
— he is only using them in greater numbers.

I do not deny that when Marx spoke generally and programmatically
he often asserted that an increase in the productive forces bursts the
bounds of the social relations within which they had been held. And
indeed he held that the productive forces of capitalism are superior to
those of feudalism, which were superior to those of ancient society. But
what must not be forgotten is that Marx's understanding of 'productive

forces' is broader and more complex than that of the technological determinist.

Thirdly, technological determinism claims that labor-power is one of the two main elements of the productive forces. Labor-power, Marx says, is 'the aggregate of those mental and physical capabilities existing in a human being, which he exercises whenever he produces a use-value of any description' (*Capital*, I:167). The technological determinist interprets labor-power to include skills, training, know-how, and experience. Scientific and technological knowledge are also part of, or an attribute of, such labor-power. The preceding list is supposedly acceptable because each member of it is directly used in production. Productive forces include only those things 'which can actually be utilised in the labor process.'[11] But if scientific knowledge and one's past training for a job will satisfy this condition, there is no reason not to think that a person's moral and value structures are not also directly relevant and do not themselves also play a direct role in one's performance of a job.

It is objected, however, that morality is not part of the productive forces:

There is no license in Marx's texts to incorporate within the 'productive forces' those things — such as morality or the judiciary — which may be necessary for production to continue; the term is restricted to those elements which can actually be utilised in the labor process. The distinction is between those things which occasion production or permit it to proceed and those things which are physically part of, and materially necessary for, production. Only the latter may be productive forces.[12]

But if only that which is 'physically part of, and materially necessary for, production' were the criteria for productive forces, then science, past training, and the like would not be part of the productive forces. Thus, this argument and its suggested criteria are implausible. Even if morality as a social institution does not play a role in production, certainly the moral values which are part of the worker do play such a role.

What technological determinism forgets is that not only must the laborer exercise his knowledge in production but also his judgment and will (*Capital*, I:361). But the exercise of judgment and will directly presuppose the person's moral and value structure.[13] Thus, Marx refers to political economy as 'the most moral of all the sciences' (*MECW*, 3:309). The worker must value saving his money, being on time, doing acceptable labor, earning more money, etc. Were such values to disappear the factory would have to be guarded and run by an army of overseers, rather than just a few. Similarly, the conversion of surplus value into capital requires that one accumulate the surplus value rather than simply consume it (*Capital*, I:580). But that one does this depends on one's valuing such accumulations, not despising or condemning them.

Are such values plausibly productive forces? We tend to have too simple a view of productive forces. Productive forces are not simply tools and raw materials. These alone can do nothing. It is only when labor-power is joined to them that we have productive forces. That is, in an important sense a tool by itself is not a productive force (just as a railway on which no trains run, Marx says, is not, in reality, a railway). It becomes a productive force only when conjoined with human labor-power. But again labor-power is not simply a burst of energy. It must be (self-) controlled, directed, and expressed in certain ways. However, to do this involves knowledge as well as values. A person who, though scientifically wise, had the values and needs of an ascetic prepared to starve to death before making anything would do nothing with his scientific knowledge. In this sense, then, knowledge and values are directly participant in the productive process and, as attributes of labor-power, are productive forces. Scientific knowledge as such is not a productive force — only when it is incorporated in human labor-power is it part of a productive force. So too are human moral and non-moral values! In short it is the totality comprising social production — labor-power, relevant values, knowledge, training, and tools, factories, etc. which Marx claims determines the rest of society.

Now the upshot of the preceding argument is that the productive forces — as identified by the technological determinist — are not the explanatory basis of historical development. Rather, it is the contradictions which exist in the mode of production constituted by the forces of production, relations of production, and related values. It is this complex dialectical totality which constitutes the explanatory basis of history. Secondly, it is important to emphasize that we find values, desires, and interests present in this explanatory — 'economic' — basis. These are included not simply in the labor-power of the individual, but in the objectified form labor takes, in machinery, etc., as well as in the individuals themselves as members of the relations of production. Furthermore, by including relations of production in the explanatory base, humans themselves and not simply their abstract labor-power are given a role in historical materialism. Accordingly, the development of a mode of production, both internally and in transition to another mode of production is not something which necessarily takes place independently of humans and their values. The dynamics of a society and even transitions to other forms of society take place because of the consequences and implications of certain forms of human activity. Such forms of activity inherently include values, goals, purposes, and needs. Thus, there is less reason to object that history is out of man's hands and that the pronouncements of history exclude moral considerations. To return to the jail cell analogy – though people are locked into certain historical epochs, their values as well as the values of previous generations have a role in determining the direction of the cell across the countryside. There is an interrelation of the two. Hence, those accounts of historical materialism, such as technological determinism, which have posed problems of freedom for morality can be rejected.

However, we must ask now about the nature of the relation between the mode of production and the rest of society. The former still remains the explanatory base on our view. And yet we have allowed for various relations which the technological determinist will now allow. What is the nature of the domination which the mode of production exerts over the rest of society and is the resulting view plausibly Marxist?

III

If the character of Marx's views on history, society and morality be the one ascribed to them by the argument of the preceding section, some have claimed that Marxism loses its distinctiveness.[14] That is, suppose we take Marx to hold

> that economic factors are important, but that others are important too. Now is there anyone who would deny that? One had imagined that [Marx's theory] . . . was a distinctive theory, which sharply separated Marxist from other philosophies of history. The separation seems now to disappear. [Other] . . . philosophers are quite ready to allow the importance of economic interests, and if Marxist philosophy allows that religious, patriotic and other interests can play free of the economic, does it any longer have a position of its own?[15]

Thus, a dilemma is forced upon Marx: either maintain that only economic factors in some narrow sense account for the intellectual, social, and political history of an epoch, or allow that other factors play a role as well. If he holds the former view, what he says is noteworthy but wrong. If he holds the latter view, what he says is correct, but obvious and not noteworthy.

I have argued that Marx does not maintain the first horn of this dilemma. Does it follow that what he says is uninteresting and common? Not necessarily, since Marx seemingly wants to say that though other factors may play a role in the development of a society, still the material bases of the society play 'an ultimately determining role.' The influence they exercise in the society is special. Engels stated the point as follows:

> According to the materialist conception of history, the *ultimately* determining factor in history is the production and reproduction of real life. Neither Marx nor I have ever asserted more than this. Hence, if somebody twists this into saying that the economic factor is the *only* determining one, he transforms that proposition into a meaningless, abstract, absurd phrase.[16]

In what way or sense, then, is the mode of production the 'ultimately determining element' over society? The answer involves the following two steps. Firstly, it has been argued that it is the mode of production — not simply the forces of production — which is explanatorily basic for the rest of society. As such, the explanatory basis of social change and development includes labor-power, tools, relations, consciousness, as well as various moral and non-moral values.[17] Yet if the mode of production is to influence or determine the rest of society, it should be separately identifiable — it is not simply itself the whole of society. When Marx speaks of the base influencing or determining society he is not simply saying that society influences or determines itself. How, then, can the mode of production as explicated above be identified separately from the rest of society?

Marx's answer to this question has two parts. On the one hand, with regard to the range of practical activities and relations which constitute the mode of production, Marx seems to suggest that, in general, they are the ones in which use value is created. Thus, employer/employee would be a productive relation, but father/son would not be a productive relation. Making shoes would be a productive activity, while reading a book simply for enjoyment would not. This is, admittedly, rather vague. It requires elaboration and would have to be made more specific for each historical epoch. For example, under capitalism, productive activities would be those involved in the production of use-values *and* surplus value. Nevertheless, such vagueness does not have to hinder us since it does suggest a certain (admittedly vague) set of activities and relations which are different from other activities and relations.

On the other hand, since values are also included in the mode of production we must suggest how these values can be distinguished from those in the superstructure. That is, we must distinguish the moral and non-moral values as they play a role in the base from the values as part of the ideology and superstructure. Values, as they play a role in the base, are lived values, those ways of choosing, those desires, which people actually have and which direct their behavior — without which there would be no behavior. They constitute man's social existence. Values in the superstructure, in man's and society's social consciousness, are values which have been codified, transcribed, theorized about, legislated, and legally enforced — in short, they are values which have become *institutionalized*. There is nothing problematic in holding that *these* values are determined by the *lived values*. Of course, during certain periods both sets of ideas and values will be roughly the same in content. But this is not to gainsay the fact that it is the latter which are vital and hence subject to change due to forces within themselves and the rest of the mode of production rather than receiving changes from without as do the institutionalized values and ideas. Accordingly, at the beginning of an historical stage, a new mode of production embodies values which are not part of the current ideology. This mode of production then modifies the present mode of production and the ideology which has developed in conjunction with it. Thus, this new totality spreads its influence — as capitalism spreads its influence to agriculture, and also over the moral, religious, and judicial ideology of the time.

We should remember here that when Marx claims that the mode of production determines the superstructure and its ideas and values, he is not claiming that the mode of production must be appealed to in every instance to explain every single idea or value that this or that person has. A person may have ideas which do not correspond to, and are not explicable by, a given mode of production. For example, throughout history numerous people have had the idea of a communist revolution, without this idea being part of their society's ideology, or intelligibly said to be determined by the then existing mode of production:

These conditions of life, which different generations find in existence, determine also whether or not the revolutionary convulsion periodically recurring in history will be strong enough to overthrow the basis of everything that exists. And if these material elements of a complete revolution are not present — namely, on the one hand the existing productive forces, on the other the formation of a revolutionary mass, which revolts not only against separate conditions of the existing society, but against the existing 'production of life' itself, the 'total activity' on which it is based — then it is absolutely immaterial for practical development whether the *idea* of this revolution has been expressed a hundred times already, as the history of communism proves. (*MECW*, 5:54)

Instead, Marx claims that it is the prevailing system of institutionalized ideas and values — not this or that idea or value of a particular individual — which is ultimately determined by the mode of production. The ruling class may have ideologists who spin out their own ideas and theories which may or may not correspond to the social system of ideas. Generally they do correspond. Sometimes they do not. When they do not, a crisis will indicate that the ruling ideas are the ideas of the ruling class — those determined by the mode of production — and not those formulated by such ideologists (cf. *MECW*, 5:50). Thus, it is the existence of a system of institutionalized ideas and values that obtains in a society which is ultimately explained — 'ultimately determined' — by the mode of production.

Secondly, then, what is the relation which exists between the mode of production and this superstructure? What does it mean to say that the former is the 'ultimately determining element' over the latter? One possible answer, which is suggested by the word 'ultimately,' is that Marx means that *in the long run* changes in society are determined by the economic conditions, but that *in the short run* these changes are determined by power relationships.[18] Such an interpretation would allow a place for political activism on the part of the proletariat, while at the same time securing Marx's claim for the role of economic factors.

Nevertheless, such a view is surely implausible. It robs Marx's views of their whole atmosphere of the ever-present weight of the mode of production. It puts off the effect of the mode of production until some distant, vague, indetermined (and probably indeterminable) future. It is true, of course, that changes in the productive forces and relations of production are not always immediately reflected in the ideology of the time. Indeed, some time may pass between such changes and 'official' recognition by the ideology. But it is also true that the mode of production exerts a contstant pressure on the ideology — sustaining it, as well as calling for modifications and being modified by it in turn. Finally, none of Marx's statements would seem to sanction such an interpretation. When he speaks of the effect of the mode of production on the ideology he speaks of its current effects, not some possible future effects.

Another way of understanding the 'ultimate' or special role of the mode of production is to take it to be the element which has 'the most force' in social development and change. Thus, one might imagine society as driven along by various different forces — the direction in which society goes is said to be ultimately determined by the mode of production because the mode of production contributes the largest vector to its direction. Analogously, the distance which bowling pins will fly when struck might be said to be ultimately determined by the force of the ball which strikes them. However, such an interpretation would also be inadequate. Marx does not think that the course of society is to be determined simply by adding up the various different and independent vectors which impinge on it. Such a mechanical view is opposed to Marx's dialectical views. Indeed, Marx would object that society is not something independent of these forces. More importantly, the present interpretation does not allow for Marx's distinction between the mode of production ultimately determining the course in which society goes and its playing the dominant role in that course of development. That is, Marx distinguishes between the conditions which determine the weight and force which the various aspects of society will have, and this or that aspect of society which might consequently have greatest weight or force. Considered more concretely, surely it is obvious that religion or political elements can be and have been dominant in present and past societies. However, whether the religious or the political elements will be dominant, and what form its dominance will take, is ultimately determined by the mode of production which exists in a society. Marx's comment in *Capital* is directed to this point: 'the middle ages could not live on Catholicism, nor the ancient world on politics. On the contrary, it is the mode in which they gained a livelihood that explains why here politics, and there Catholicism, played the chief part' (*Capital*, I:82). Thus, it has been correctly observed that:

> the economic is ultimately 'determinant' but it need not be 'dominant' in a given economic social formation. The Catholicism of the Middle Ages and the politics of the ancient world . . . could not have existed unless there was first provision for food, clothing, shelter, and the other necessities; but in these societies that basic and primordial fact was mediated by religion and politics rather than by economic forces acting in their own name. In capitalism, the society of *homo economicus*, one has the unusual situation in which the economic is both determinant and dominant. Most interpreters of Marx, his friends and foes, have unfortunately taken this historically unique case as valid for all times and places.[19]

Thus, for Marx, though the mode of production ultimately determines the form which a society will take, this does not mean that the mode of production plays the chief or dominant role in society.

As opposed to the preceding mechanical and temporal interpretations of the role of the mode of production in society, I wish to suggest an interpretation which makes full allowance for the nature of the base as laid out above. It is an interpretation compatible with Marx's more theoretical statements of historical materialism, his practical and concrete analyses of historical events, as well as (I will later argue) his advocacy of communism.

It is important to remember that the base is a complex totality – a contradictory, complex whole consisting of tools, raw materials, relations, people, labor-power, values, and needs. The difficulty is to give some sense to such a totality 'ultimately determining' the superstructure I have argued above. The issue to be joined here is how the former may be said to be ultimately determinative of the latter.

I would like to begin with an analogy, in which we have a similar problem. That is, a situation in which one set of experiences can plausibly be said to be ultimately determinative of a whole complex of other experiences. Having indicated by analogy the plausibility of such a view I will then go on to try to unfold some of the aspects of the situation that confronts us between base and superstructure.

Consider, then, a similar claim about the ultimately determining role which some element played in the formation and development of a person's character. There are clearly many forces and conditions which play a role in such a process. Still, it might be said that some early experience, or (more probably) set of experiences, played and continues to play an ultimately determining role in the person's character. For example, the death of a parent, toilet training, or a rule-bound upbringing might play a role of ultimate importance. In any case, this basic experience (or set of experiences) plays a role of ultimate importance not simply in the long run, but also here and now. Further, it is not simply another force, and need not at all times be the most strong force, in the person's life. Still it is a force which organizes all other forces about itself, subordinates them to itself, colors and gives the other aspects of the person's character the significance and meaning they have. It is like the theme in a piece of music which may at times come to the fore or at other times recede into the background, but which is at all times the organizing principle, that ties the work together. Finally, these other forces and conditions may clearly react on and modify this basic determining element. Nevertheless, this ultimately determining experience is the basic unifying thread which runs throughout the person's character and life and ties the various aspects of that person together. It is for this reason the person is a whole, is a totality, as it were, and not schizophrenic or mad. It is for this reason that we can understand such a person.

Now we might try to apply this kind of model to Marx's claim about the relation of the mode of production and the superstructure. There is certainly a closer fit here than with the previous suggestions. Just as we speak of the character of a person, so we might, analogously, speak of the character of a society, its nature and development. In both cases, this character arises out of the various elements which constitute the society or the person. However, not all these elements are of equal weight and significance. Just as with a person, some elements subordinate others to themselves — they 'assign rank and influence' to the other elements throughout the society. Furthermore, there is interaction and interdetermination amongst these various parts of the system. Finally, it is possible that certain elements in a person or society play, at various times, dominant roles even though these elements can play such a role only due to other aspects of the person or society.

It might be objected that there are two important dissimilarities which seriously weaken the above analogy. Firstly, we may say of a person, but not of a society, that it is conscious. Because a single consciousness constitutes the individual, an individual can or must integrate various experiences, and thus may be affected throughout his life by some experience(s). This can not be said in the case of a society or group of people. Hence, the attempt to use this model to render intelligible Marx's claim regarding the ultimately determining effect of the mode of production breaks down. Secondly, the above model might also be said not to fit a society since, whereas the ultimately determining elements in a person's character and life might be an early experience or set of experiences, it is not an early experience or traumatic happening which plays this fundamental role in the development of the character of a society. It is rather the mode of production which plays this role.

It must be admitted, of course, that the above analogy is not exact. Surely Marx did not view society as conscious in the way in which a person was conscious. Nevertheless, these objections should not blind us to the similarities which do exist here. Specifically, it should be clear by now that to speak of the mode of production is simply to speak of human praxis, that is, man's conscious attempt through productive activity to fulfill the needs, wants and desires he experiences. It is the experience of these needs, the necessity of fulfilling them, but especially the way in which man tries to do this that colors human society. This is not disanalogous to the instance of a person's experiences for surely it is not simply the experience(s) itself (themselves), but the way in which the person seeks to deal with them, which affects the rest of a person's life. Similarly with a society. It is the way in which a society fulfills its material interests which subordinates all other activities and relations to themselves:

> In all forms of society there is one specific kind of production which predominates over the rest, whose relations thus assign rank and influence to the others. It is a general illumination which bathes all the other colours and modifies their particularity. It is a particular ether which determines the specific gravity of every being which has materialised within it. . . . In bourgeois society . . . agriculture more and more becomes merely a branch of industry, and is entirely dominated by capital. Ground rent likewise. In all forms where landed property rules, the natural relation still predominates. In those where capital rules, the social historically created element. . . .
> Capital is the all-dominating economic power of bourgeois society. It must form the starting-point as well as the finishing point. . . .
> (*Grund.*, 106-7)

Thus, if we recognize that the mode of production is but the manner in which society's practical or material interests are fulfilled, the above analogy does not seem wholly inappropriate. Still, how is this model to be unpacked with regard to society?

The analogy suggests that to maintain that 'X ultimately determines Y' is to say the following: (a) X conditions the form which Y phenomena in Z (a person or society) will take, though Y phenomena may also influence the form that X phenomena may take; (b) X plays the organizing or ordering role which determines the relative importance, value, and/or degree of realization which Y phenomena have in Z; and (c) all other ways, W, of determining Y phenomena in Z would be given up, abandoned, before X would be given up. The significance, then, of maintaining that the base is ultimately determining is practical. The determination of a society's superstructure by its base or material interests, is a determination which would be held on to while all other determinations of the superstructure — both internally and externally — would be abandoned. Materialist interests, that is, are the last interests which a class — or social group (Marx does not say an individual) — would give up in their determination of their actions. Accordingly, Marx says that 'the Tories in England long imagined that they were enthusiastic about monarchy, the church and the beauties of the old English Constitution, until the day of danger wrung from them the confession that they were enthusiastic only about *rent*' (*MECW*, 11:128).

And in *Capital*, in a passage which echoes this one, Marx writes:

> in the domain of Political Economy, free scientific inquiry meets not
> merely the same enemies as in all other domains. The peculiar nature
> of the material it deals with, summons as foes into the field of battle
> the most violent, mean and malignant passions of the human breast,
> the Furies of private interest. The English Established Church, e.g.,
> will more readily pardon an attack on 38 of its 39 articles than on
> 1/39 of its income. (*Capital*, I:10)

It is the way in which a society (and its classes) seeks to fulfill its material interests, it is the activities in which it thereby engages, which
subordinate all other activities and relations to themselves.

This is not to say, as I have noted before, that the material interests
are always determinative of happenings in a society. For example, the
struggle between the republican factions of the bourgeoisie and the
loyalists, etc. in France was one in which the republican faction was *not*
'held together by great [material] interests and marked off by specific
conditions of production' (*MECW*, 11:112). Rather,

> it was a clique of republican-minded bourgeois, writers, lawyers,
> officers and officials that owed its influence to the personal anti-
> pathies of the country against Louis Philippe, to memories of the old
> republic, to the republican faith of a number of enthusiasts, above
> all, however, to *French nationalism*, whose hatred of the Vienna
> treaties and of the alliance with England it always kept awake
> (*MECW*, 11:112-13).

Further, Marx allows that 'in the case of the arts . . . certain periods of
their flowering are out of all proportion to the general development of
society, hence also to the material foundations, the skeletal structure as
it were of its organisation' (*Grund.* 110). Conversely, later periods may
return to earlier art forms and find in them means whereby to conceal
various truths from themselves (*MECW*, 11:104). Still, in each of these
cases, though this faction's influence or those art forms are not directly
linked to the material interests of the time, that they could have the
influences they do, that personal antipathies, memories, their myth-
ology, etc., play a role in this situation is due to the base, to the
material interests involved. Thus, Marx says regarding a different but
relevant situation:

> What kept the two factions apart, therefore, was not any so-called
> principles, it was their material conditions of existence, two different

kinds of property, it was the contrast between town and country, the rivalry between capital and landed property. That at the same time old memories, personal enmities, fears and hopes, prejudices and illusions, sympathies and antipathies, convictions, articles of faith and principles bound them to one or the other royal house, who is there that denies this? Upon the different forms of property, upon the social conditions of existence, rises an entire super-structure of different and distinctly formed sentiments, illusions, modes of thought and views of life. The entire class creates and forms them out of its material foundations and out of the corresponding social relations. (*MECW*, 11:127-8)

The mode of production has such influence, Marx maintains, because it is 'the point of departure,' it is 'the act through which the whole process [of production, distribution, exchange, and consumption] again runs its course' (*Grund.*, 94, cf. 95, 96, 99). As he says in *Capital*, production 'is a necessary condition, independent of all forms of society, for the existence of the human race; it is an eternal nature-imposed necessity, without which there can be no material exchange between man and Nature, and therefore no life' (*Capital*, I:42-3). This basic unavoidable requirement of human existence must daily and hourly be confronted:

But life involves before everything else eating and drinking, housing, clothing, and various other things. The first historical act is thus the production of the means to satisfy these needs, the production of material life itself. And indeed this is an historical act, a fundamental condition of all history, which today as thousands of years ago, must daily and hourly be filled merely in order to sustain human life. (*MECW*, 5:41-2)

Unlike the instance of a person (as characterized above) in which various experiences might play a basic role in his life, the necessity of fulfilling human needs and the manner of doing so unavoidably play the basic role in human society. However, in correspondence with our model, the way in which society fulfills its needs must not necessarily take the fulfillment of these needs themselves, the resolution of this urgency, as its open and conscious aim. Thus, under capitalism, the main purpose of the mode of production is the creation of surplus value – not (directly at least) the fulfillment of needs. It is in terms of this (former) purpose that the manner of production is characterized. It is this underlying purpose which characterizes the mode of production and influences all other relations and activities. Accordingly, Marx can allow, as we have seen, that the technique of production may (initially at least) be the same in two societies even though the social formations are distinct — e.g. capitalist as opposed to feudal. Marx's comment on capitalism is relevant:

> The reader will bear in mind that the production of surplus value, or the extraction of surplus value is the specific end and aim, the sum and substance, of capitalist production, quite apart from any changes in the mode of production, which may arise from the subordination of labor to capital (*Capital*, I:298).

It would seem, then, that it is possible to interpret Marx's views in a manner which renders them intelligible and allows them a distinctiveness. They retain a distinctiveness in that the mode of production is granted a fundamentally influential role in society. His views may be said to be intelligible in that we can interpret them with regard to a model which, even if not itself explicated here, is familiar and plausible. Certainly, if we were interested in an account of historical materialism itself, such an account would leave much to be desired. Marx himself is at fault for a good part of this situation. He simply did not analyze the relations, and interactions, involved in the above account. He states his views on numerous occasions but instead of analyzing them simply uses his views against those he would criticize and condemn.

Nevertheless, the above account is satisfactory for our purposes. Firstly, it allows for the active and effective role of superstructural elements such as morality and ethics. This role is set within the limits and restrictions of the material world, but so in fact is morality and ethics limited. Secondly, the preceding account is faithful to Marx's views in that it allows for various relations between the superstructure and the mode of production. Some are causal, others are logical, conceptual, teleological. Because many commentators have assumed the relations involved must be of *one* kind, they have tried to force all Marx's various claims into a causal, a logical, or a teleological mold. They did not see that the relations here could be of different kinds.[20] In essence, then, what we are confronted with in Marx's view is two intersecting sets of ideas, values, activities, and relations which do not stand wholly independently of each other but rather share certain elements as well as do not share certain elements. Together they constitute the totality we call human society. Still both sets of ideas, values, activities, and relations retain an identity of their own within this totality. Those which constitute the mode of production take their identity from the notion of

47

production or productive activity. Those which constitute the ideology are defined in terms of the prevailing, institutionalized ideas and values in society. Thirdly, the above account renders intelligible and distinctive, within the limits of Marx's own discussion and our present purposes, Marx's claim that the ideas, values, activities, and relations constituting the mode of production ultimately determine and color those ideas, values, activities, and relations which constitute the ideology.

Finally, though the preceding account contends that humans, their values and goals, do play an active role in history, it does not purport to show that Marx held that humans are wholly free and can shape society as they will. Far from it. As Marx says, they enter into relations independent of their wills, relations which shape and determine the course of actions they follow. As a consequence, people are determined both internally (i.e. their own nature is affected) and externally, by the relations and conditions of their society. What poses for the historical materialist's deterministic threat, then, has to do with the influence, the domination, which the productive activities, relations, and values play in the lives people lead. Just as behaviors in which a person engages may become rigidified and, in effect, dominate his life, so too, Marx claims, the activities and relations, which society creates to satisfy its needs, may become rigidified and restrictive of life in society. This means that the necessity under which people live derives from the particular kind of praxis which has developed out of other, earlier forms of praxis. It is Marx's claim that these forms of praxis, these activities, roles, and relations achieve an independence of individuals; they come to dominate people, rather than be dominated by them. This takes place in part because people objectify themselves in various objects and relations which both manifest or express their own needs and state of society, as well as continue to exist after them and determine the lives of those who come later.

> The sensuous world around him is not a thing given direct from all
> eternity, remaining ever the same, but the product of industry and
> of the state of society; and, indeed [a product] in the sense that it is
> an historical product, the result of the activity of a whole succession
> of generations, each standing on the shoulders of the preceding one,
> developing its industry and its intercourse, and modifying its social
> system according to the changed needs. Even the objects of the
> simplest 'sensuous certainty' are only given . . . through social devel-
> opment, industry and commercial intercourse. The cherry-tree, like
> almost all fruit-trees was, as is well known, only a few centuries ago
> transplanted by *commerce* into our zone, and therefore only *by* this

action of a definite society in a definite age has it become 'sensuous certainty'. . . . (*MECW*, 5:39)

One particular kind of relation which has been especially crucial in the above development is the division of labor. With the division of labor occurs a cleavage between the particular interests and the common interest. As a result, 'man's own deed becomes an alien power opposed to him, which enslaves him instead of being controlled by him' (*MECW*, 5:47). Having taken on lives of their own, man's products and relations play an essential role in the determination of people's lives. For example, in so far as a person is a capitalist and remains a capitalist, he must ever seek to increase the surplus value he derives from workers. In so far as a person is a worker, he must sell his labor-power to a capitalist and will try to do so for the highest price. Thus, 'worker' and 'capitalist' denote roles and relations which lead the people who occupy those roles and relations into deadly combat. The determination here is of a kind we are all familiar with: e.g. the parent who must say 'no' to a child because of the role he occupies; the teacher or manager who must demand or require certain things of students or subordinates because of his or her position. As long as a person can identify with and approve that which must be demanded or required, there are but few problems. However, when we come to despise, reject, question or doubt that which we must nevertheless demand or require, then we feel out of sorts, we feel determined from without, constrained, and coerced. Then we do not feel free. But in either case, that one must act in these ways, the determination and domination which one experiences, stems from the social relations which human activities and values have assumed. It is a self-imposed (in the sense that mankind is the 'self') domination. That is, the determination of which Marx speaks is that which is brought about by human action and the creation of human activities; it is not brought about by some agency or process external to humans. This is, however, often not understood. Indeed, because of the fetishism of commodities people tend to think that they are subjected to a natural necessity, whereas in fact it is but a necessity stemming from rigidified and mystified relations which they and their predecessors have created (cf. *Capital*, I:81-2, 352). As Marx comments, 'The relations of the producers to the sum total of their labor is presented to them as a social condition, existing not between themselves, but between the products of their labor' (*Capital*, I:72).

Mankind's situation, then, is analogous to the person who has built up a habitual way of acting to fulfill certain needs. Having continued in that manner of acting, it may be difficult to change the habit. If the habit is drug-based it may be extremely difficult and painful to change. In extreme cases of this sort, we may attribute a lessened responsibility to the person for his actions, though we may still morally condemn such a condition and seek ways to change it. A significant impetus which may involve conflict and struggle may then be required to change the behavior. Thus, the habit may outlast the needs it was originally meant to fulfill. Similar comments may be made about society as Marx views it. In both cases, the determination stems from forms of praxis in which individuals have been engaged. And in both cases, this determination may bring it about that individuals 'have' to act in certain ways. Further, we may say, as Marx does say, that we can attribute to individuals trapped by certain ways of acting only a lessened responsibility for those ways of acting. But this does not mean that we may not morally condemn those ways of acting, and seek to change them. And indeed most of Marx's condemnations are of various relations and ways of acting in which people find themselves. This is not, however, to say that he cannot or never does condemn or praise individuals. He can and does. Still, to the extent his focus of concern is on the social level he condemns the social conditions and relations in which people find themselves. Given this view, we may also expect that moral exhortation alone will do little and that people will continue to act in those ways unless and until the conflicts which their present habitual ways of acting generate become so great that they must be overthrown. Change requires action, understanding, and co-operation as well as other necessary conditions. When these conditions hold we may try, with some hope of success, to bring about a different and better set of human relations. In this manner, Marx's ethics is a most realistic ethics, one which details for us the ways in which we get trapped by the relations within which we live and the conditions required for us to change them.

The preceding would be a threat to the freedom required for morality only if Marx held that humans must always be dominated and coerced by their relations and roles in a way which could not be changed or overcome. If a person could never change a habit and that habit was such that it frustrated his very wants and needs, then we would hold that he was determined in a manner which would lessen his responsibility. So it is with the actions of people who have become addicted to certain drugs. But Marx clearly does not hold that this must be the case with society. He suggests that before the division of labor became established and/or elaborated, people had moral freedom — i.e. they were not dominated by their relations. He also clearly suggests that with communism, i.e. with the elimination of the division of labor, people will also be freed of this domination. Hence, the determination of which Marx speaks, though it may raise difficulties at particular times and epochs — e.g. during capitalism — is no insuperable barrier to the freedom required for morality.

But what are we to say about Marx's comments on the 'inevitability' of communism or on the laws of capitalism working with 'iron necessity?' Do not these comments suggest a situation in which people's wants, wishes, and desires (whether for or against communism) are impotent? I think not. Firstly, it is not clear how seriously Marx himself takes his comments on 'iron laws' or on 'iron necessity.' For example, Marx sarcastically comments on Lassalle's 'iron law of wages' that 'the word *iron* is a label by which the true believers recognise one another.' He adds, 'If I abolish wage labour, then naturally I abolish its laws also, whether they are of "iron" or sponge.'[21] Similarly, Marx thinks that the 'iron laws' of capitalism can also be abolished. Any suggestion that the laws of capitalism are unalterable because they are 'iron' is mistaken. Secondly, even when Marx does speak of communism as unavoidable, his comments have been greatly overplayed — at least in so far as the question of freedom and morality is concerned. It is true that Marx did indeed think, more than once, that a communist revolution was just around the corner and was not to be avoided. But it was not to be avoided *not* because the desires and needs of people had nothing to do with it. Just the opposite. He believed communism to be inevitable because he believed that the desires and needs of people were such that, given their current situation, people would indeed rise up and revolt against the present order. Finally, one must remember the context in which such remarks occurred. Marx sought, as noted in Chapter 1, to have an effect on society through his writings — not only in their content, but also in their form. His writings were intentionally polemical. However, in polemical writings one simply does not say, if one wants to have any impact on people, that 'maybe' or 'perhaps' a communist revolution will come about '*if* a great many people desire it.' That would be absurd. Instead, one says directly and firmly 'a communist revolution is coming — it is inevitable!' But, as already indicated, this kind of statement and the view behind it, absolves no one from the need and the freedom to act. Thus, such a view is not incompatible with morality and ethics.

IV

There remains a final problem of freedom and morality, viz., the determination of individual human actions (cf. p. 30), which can be rather briefly treated. To begin with, the whole atmosphere in which this question arises for Marx is quite different from those, such as Kant, who raise this problem in terms of the freedom of the will. Marx speaks of the will only infrequently. Instead, he speaks of human practical action which seeks to fulfill various desires and needs, as well as to develop human capacities and talents. Such actions, desires, needs, talents, etc., are said to be determined by personal, social, and natural conditions. When Marx does speak of the will, then, it is never in the Kantian sense. It is not unlikely that he would have accepted an account of the will along the lines of J.S. Mill's view that the will is a kind of habitual desire. As such, Marx's view constitutes an open rejection of the role that Kant and others have attributed to the will. That is, clearly, for Marx, the will is not free in the transcendental sense that Kant insisted was necessary for morality. Hence, it would follow for Kant that the Marxist view made moral principles impossible: 'Without transcendental freedom . . . no moral law and no accountability to it are possible.'[22] Accordingly, if freedom from material conditions is a requisite for morality and ethics, then surely Marx must deny the possibility of morality. However, instead of denying the possibility of morality he denies that such transcendental freedom is required for morality. In this way, it would be clear, Marx's views, *vis-à-vis* the problem of freedom and determinism, are no different from those of other philosophers, such as Aristotle, Spinoza, and Mill, who also denied that some kind of transcendental freedom from determinism was required for morality. Thus, the present question, though important for Marx to answer, is in no way peculiar to Marxism. Marx's approach to this question can briefly be sketched as follows.

Firstly, Marx has allowed that human activity is and can be significant in effecting changes in society. Not only can individuals make changes in society, they may also be creative, make inventions, discoveries, etc. However, such activities do not occur in a vacuum, but rather in a social or material context which poses the problems and tasks to them, as well as limits and ultimately dictates the extent of the success of such activities. To be creative in this context is to produce something valuable which has not been produced before, or to produce some such thing in a way in which it has not been produced before. It is not to be free from causes. Accordingly, Marx maintains that preceding moralists and moral philosophers have been mistaken to claim that change in society is simply a matter of will or creative consciousness. Marx has shown that such change is not simply a matter of consciousness, or of will, but must rest itself against other determinates. This is a conservative, but realistic, element in Marx's thought.

Secondly, the problem Kant struggled with — as well as other philosophers, theologians, and laymen — is misunderstood if it is taken to be a philosophical, a theoretical problem. Instead, it is a practical problem which can only be resolved in a practical way. Marx says, regarding this and other similar problems:

> we see how subjectivity and objectivity, spirituality and materiality, activity and suffering lose their antithetical character, and thus their existence as such antitheses only within the framework of a society; we see how the resolution of the theoretical antitheses is only possible in a practical way by virtue of the practical energy of man. Their resolution is therefore by no means merely a problem of understanding but a real problem of life, which philosophy could not solve precisely because it conceived this problem as merely a theoretical one. (*MECW*, 3:302)

This quote is relevant here since the antithesis of spirituality and materiality is but the antithesis of freedom and necessity as Kant and others have seen it. This antinomy Kant thought he could resolve only in a theoretical way — by positing various practical postulates. For Marx, this problem is not a theoretical problem, but a practical one.

The practical problem is one of what people can do voluntarily. One is free in at least a minimal sense required by morality when, if one wishes to do something, one can do what one wants. That is, the kind of freedom at issue is a freedom from the coercion or constraint of one's actions. It is not a freedom from causation or the lack of causation in the determination of the will. The history of man up to the present has been a history of man being subordinated, dominated, by nature, by other men, by his own creations and productions. This is not to say that people have not been able to act voluntarily so far. Rather it is to say that significant aspects of their lives did in fact dominate them and inhibit their activities. Communism is the attempt to overcome these forces. Thus, Marx claims that 'communism, as fully developed naturalism, is said to equal humanism. It is said to be the genuine resolution of the conflict between man and nature and between man and man — the true resolution of the strife between . . . freedom and necessity' (*MECW*, 3:296). Given freedom from coercion and constraint, then, morality should be possible. Indeed, in early forms of society people have not fully had this freedom. Nevertheless, they were members of moral communities, morality and ethics were part of their society, since they could (within certain limits) act voluntarily. In transforming the theoretical question of Kant into a practical question of the constraints of people's actions, Marx's answer is an example of his claim that 'when things are seen in this way, as they really are and happened, every profound philosophical problem is resolved ... quite simply into an empirical fact' (*MECW*, 5:39).

Accordingly, it is not apparent that anything which Marx maintains with regard to the fact that ideologies are not basically determinative or not independent, or that consciousness itself is tied to the material conditions, would show that morality or ethics would be or must be impossible under Marx's views. Marx speaks of various tasks, etc., which must be accomplished both before and after communism. This itself would seem to allow that something like a morality would remain possible. The fact that there are various bounds to what morality and ethics can possibly accomplish does not indicate their impossibility. There are, similarly, bounds to what any mode of thought or form of consciousness can accomplish. This does not show that any particular form of consciousness is impossible. Thus, it is not surprising at all when we find Marx chiding associates for refraining from criticizing others because they are 'only children of their time.' Marx comments, 'unfortunately everyone is only a "child of his time" and if this is a sufficient excuse nobody ought ever to be attacked any more, all controversy, all struggle on our part cease. . . .'[23] Marx's view is obvious. People, though the children of their time, though determined by the productive nature of society, may still be criticized and attacked.

Marx's answer to the problem of freedom and determinism, it must be admitted, is only roughly stated. It does not add, as such, to the discussions other philosophers have contributed to this problem. Where Marx's answer does offer something uniquely Marxian is in his discussion of the social conditions which have inhibited and continue to inhibit a more comprehensive voluntary activity for all people.

Accordingly, neither Marx's views on these matters, nor his views on historical materialism, exclude the possibility of a Marxist ethics. It is simply mistaken to say that, because of the preceding views we have considered, Marx could not hold either a normative conception of ethics or an ethics of duty.[24] It is true that he does reject the latter. But he does so for reasons unrelated to questions of determinism. Neither those reasons nor his views on historical materialism prevent him from holding a normative ethics.

There remain questions, however, about the logical and conceptual relations that exist between morality, ethics, and the mode of production. Specifically, we must next consider the kind of justification which morality or moral claims can receive on Marx's views. It is to this question we turn in Chapter 3.

3 Ideology and moral justification

> But the moment you present men as the actors and authors of their own history, you arrive ... at the real starting point. (*MECW*, 6:178)

Morality and ethics, we have seen, are not independent of the mode of production in which they are found. However, in general, moral philosophers have *not* denied that the morality which presently exists in a society — i.e. the moral relations in which people actually live — is causally influenced or determined by the mode of production, as well as the historical period, in which this particular morality is found. This has usually been all-too-obvious. Economic depressions may contribute to a higher rate of theft, the pill may encourage greater sexual contact, and natural disasters may precipitate looting. Moral philosophers may even admit that the theorizing about morality (i.e. ethics) is itself causally influenced and affected by the material and historical conditions within which it takes place. Thus, if Marx were to have thought that moral philosophers have held morality to be independent in these ways he would simply have been wrong. Moral philosophers have not claimed this kind of independence for morality and ethics.

It is a logical — or justificatory — independence of the mode of production which has traditionally been claimed for morality and ethics. Whatever the actual moral relations in a society are, whatever the present ethics says about those moral relations, there is supposed to be a justified set of moral principles and values, discoverable by ethics, which would be the proper measure of the morality of any society and time. This kind of independence has been held, by moral philosophers, to be essential to valid moral claims. And yet it is just this view which Marx also seems to deny. Here, then, we come to Marx's views on the nature of moral and ethical judgments. What kind of justification, if any, are such judgments capable of? Can moral claims be said to be valid or true? Can they be validated or vindicated for different classes, societies, and historical epochs? If so, in what ways? In considering these questions we shall be examining Marx's views on the ideological nature of ethics.

I

It is a traditional question in moral philosophy whether or not moral claims can be justified. Some have held that moral claims can be justified. Others have denied this. As evidence they note the lack of agreement over moral claims as opposed to the relative agreement over scientific and factual statements. Similarly, there is little agreement over the definition of moral terms, whereas we can achieve a significant amount of agreement over the definition of factual and scientific terms. Marx himself notes the difference between claims which can be determined with precision and other claims, such as in ideology (hence, morality and ethics) which cannot similarly be determined:

> In studying such transformations it is always necessary to distinguish between the material transformation of the economic conditions of production, which can be determined with the precision of natural science, and the legal, political, religious, artistic or philosophic — in short, ideological forms in which men become conscious of this conflict and fight it out.[1]

Nevertheless, we should not conclude that Marx thought that moral claims could not be justified in some manner. On the one hand, the mere fact that moral judgments cannot be determined with the same precision as judgments of natural science does not necessarily mean that moral judgments cannot be said to be justified in some sense. Aristotle wisely remarked that the claims made in various fields require proofs of different kinds and strengths. Surely, for Marx too, the claims of maths or chemistry are demonstrable in a stricter sense than those of the social sciences, e.g. when the proletariat of a society might revolt. Nevertheless, it does not follow that only the former claims but not the latter can be justified. Similarly, it may be that the claims of ethics and morality can be justified in ways appropriate to them. On the other hand, though there is, in general, greater agreement on the claims made in the natural sciences, it would be mistaken to think that there are not deep and significant differences over natural scientific claims. Nevertheless, few doubt that such claims can be justified in some manner. Hence, the simple fact of disagreement need not indicate that the claims over which there is disagreement cannot be subject to adjudication and justification. Once again, precipitous interpretations of Marx's views must be avoided.

Let us begin, then, with perhaps the most well-known statement of Marx regarding the justification of claims. This statement is quite general. Nevertheless, we shall see that it does apply to ethics and morality. In the second Thesis on Feuerbach, Marx states:

> The question whether objective truth can be attributed to human thinking is not a question of theory but is a practical question. Man must prove the truth, i.e., the reality and power, the this-worldliness of his thinking in practice. The dispute over the reality or non-reality of thinking which isolates itself from practice is a purely *scholastic* question. (*MECW*, 5:6)[2]

In order to understand Marx's views in this statement, three points should be noted. Firstly, Marx speaks here not about justification but about truth. There is, however, a distinction usually drawn between justification and truth. A statement, e.g. it is raining, can be true or false, but is not itself as such justified or unjustified. What is justified or not is the assertion or judgment that it is raining, e.g. if I were to claim 'I think it is raining outside,' then this assertion or judgment may or may not be justified. Whether it is justified or not would depend (at least in part) on whether or not it was true that 'It is raining.' Thus, to say that something is justified is to say that certain reasons or grounds can be given for holding or maintaining it; this usually involves referring to various facts, i.e. that which is true. However, to say that something is true is not to say that certain reasons can be given for it, but (usually and roughly) to say that it corresponds with reality. Accordingly, in the history of philosophy, people have commonly distinguished between the thinking in which a person engages and the content of that thinking, or perhaps the object of that thought, which might be expressed in some language or other. That which is required to evaluate the former is not the same as that which is required to evaluate the latter.

Now, in the above passage, Marx says that truth concerns the human process of thinking rather than the content of that thought. Not the content of the thought, e.g. 'It is raining,' but the thought or thinking that it is raining seems to be what Marx is talking about. It is concerning this thought process that Marx claims it is a practical question whether or not objective truth can be attributed to it. Stated in terms of the preceding paragraph, then, Marx's second Thesis actually concerns the justification of claims people make, rather than the nature of the truth which we may attach to that which they have claimed.

Secondly, the above Thesis on Feuerbach does not refer to individuals, so much as to 'man.' This, however, is not simply a circumlocution for this or that individual but rather Marx's way of speaking of humans as a group or species. Whether objective truth can be attributed to human thought, i.e. the thought which characterizes man in this or that historical period, is a practical question. Now surely this is related to the thoughts of individuals. Nevertheless, what Marx is primarily interested in, when he speaks above of the truth or the justification of human thought, are the conditions under which the thought that characterizes a particular historical epoch can be said to be justified. Contrariwise, why are other forms of thought or consciousness which may occur in certain historical epochs not justified?

Thirdly, though Marx is willing to follow philosophical tradition and to distinguish between thinking or consciousness and the objects or products thereof, he is disinclined to separate them when it comes to questions of their correctness or evaluation. To do so, he thinks is to take a first step in the direction of idealism — which he characterizes as maintaining that ideas rule the world. Instead, the truth of those ideas characteristic of some period is linked to the thought or the consciousness which people have of themselves. Whether such thought can be said to be justified or valid is a question of 'the reality and power, the this-worldliness of [such] thinking in practice.' Thus whether various moral claims can be justified or not is a question of their reality and power, their this-worldliness. But what does this mean?

Let us begin simply and intuitively, keeping morality and ethics foremost in our minds. It is a fact that various moral claims and beliefs have had a reality and power in past history. People have died for their beliefs in certain moral principles. If such moral claims and views have had such reality and power are they not thereby justified on Marx's views? Further, since people have believed in certain moral principles and values for thousands of years does not this also prove that these moral beliefs have a validity which spans various historical epochs, and hence that they might be taken as eternal truths? Finally, are not these two points confounded by the fact that contrary moral views have also had significant influence in world history? Racism, egoism, fascism, etc., have had their influence as have brotherhood, selflessness, and liberalism or communism. Thus, do not Marx's views, in fact, justify conflicting and contradictory moral beliefs? Far from indicating how moral beliefs are justified, his position seems to lead to moral scepticism. Hence, if Marx does hold these views, isn't his position simply untenable?

This rather simplistic interpretation of Marx's views is, in fact, a misinterpretation that many have made.[3] Rather, clearly, Marx did not hold such a view. Just because a particular situation obtains or institution practically exists and fulfills certain functions, does not mean that the views, the beliefs and values, on which one or the other is based are justified or true. Thus, Marx says that 'our estates have fulfilled their function as such, but far be it from us to desire to justify them on that account' (*MECW*, 1:262). Similarly, it is Hegel's 'restoration of the existing empirical world,' his defense of the *status quo*, which Marx condemns as 'uncritical positivism' (*MECW*, 3:332). In order to show, then, what Marx's views are we must first look more closely at his understanding of 'the reality and power' which various claims may have. The notion of 'reality' is most important here.

In general, by 'reality' Marx refers to things, activities, and relations considered variously as external to and independent of man, as modified by man, as well as the product of human activity. Thus, for example, he wishes to allow that, given his views, the priority of external nature remains unassailed (*MECW*, 5:40). Nevertheless, Marx maintains that it makes little sense to discuss nature or reality as something apart from the modifications which human activity has impressed upon it. 'The chief defect of all previous materialism . . . is that things [*Gegenstand*], reality, sensuousness are conceived only in the form of the *object or of contemplation*, but not as *sensuous human activity, practice*, not subjectively' (*MECW*, 5:3). These two sides of reality – the object and its modification through sensuous activity – are (as far as humans are concerned) inseparably related and intermixed. Somewhat ironically, Marx says that

> Nature, nature that preceded human history, is not by any means the nature in which Feuerbach lives, it is nature which today no longer exists any where (except perhaps on a few Australian coral islands of recent origin) and which, therefore, does not exist for Feuerbach either. (*MECW*, 5:43)

Instead, nature or reality, in short the sensuous world,

> is not a thing given direct from all eternity, remaining ever the same, but the product of industry and of the state of society; and, indeed, (a product) in the sense that it is an historical product, the result of the activity of a whole succession of generations, each standing on the shoulders of the preceding one, developing its industry and its intercourse, and modifying its social system according to the changed needs. Even the objects of the simplest 'sensuous certainty' are only given him through social development, industry and commercial intercourse. The cherry-tree, like almost all fruit-trees, was, as is well-known, only a few centuries ago transplanted by *commerce* into our zone, and therefore only *by* this action of a definite society in a definite age has it become 'sensuous certainty'. (*MECW*, 5:39)

Thus, when Marx speaks of reality in the context of man and society he is, in effect, speaking of human practical activity and the products of that activity. Several points should be stressed here. Firstly, note that Marx speaks of 'human activity,' not of 'individual activity,' as such. Surely the former consists of the latter, but still it is the collective, the general, character of the latter, not the individual characters, which creates that which we know as reality. This 'reality-creativeness' of human activity includes, then, not simply the modification of the sensuous world but also the creation of new objects, new forces, and the real relations in which humans live with one another. Secondly, Marx's claim that the activities in which man engages create both what he is as well as the particular character of the world relies on the notion of objectification, which Marx took over from Hegel:

> The product of labor is labor which has been embodied in an object, which has become material: it is the *objectification* of labor. . . .
> The object of labor is, therefore, the *objectification of man's species-life*: for he duplicates himself not only, as in consciousness, intellectually, but also actively, in reality, and therefore he sees himself in a world that he has created. (*MECW*, 3:272, 277)

In short, in his practical activity man objectifies himself and creates his world. He does this in the production and refashioning of objects, in the various relations within which he works and lives, and in the thought systems through which he understands himself and the world. Thirdly, human activity is characterized by the special way in which it seeks to fulfill its practical interests. Animals too produce in an attempt to fulfill their needs. But human productive activity is differentiated from animal activity due to the nature of the consciousness involved. Humans have an awareness of themselves and their relations to others and to nature that animals do not have (cf. *MECW*, 5:44). In addition, human conscious activity may also involve the creation of plans, designs, etc., to which humans may subordinate their will and activity in order to reach certain ends (cf. *Capital*, I:178). Because human practical activity involves the creation of plans before they are carried out, because humans may plan what to do in accordance with various desired objects and are not simply determined to live and to produce in certain biologically required ways, Marx often says that human conscious activity is free activity (*MECW*, 3:276). Nevertheless, it remains for him a naturalistic activity which arises from practical interests and finds expression through the manipulation of various natural or material means:

[Consciousness, Marx claims,] is not 'pure' consciousness. The 'mind' is from the outset afflicted with the curse of being 'burdened' with matter, which here makes its appearance in the form of agitated layers of air, sounds, in short, of language. Language is as old as consciousness, language *is* practical, real consciousness that exists for other men as well, and only therefore does it also exist for me; language, like consciousness, only arises from the need, the necessity, of intercourse with other men. (*MECW*, 5:44)

Finally, human activity is characterized by its ability to apply standards to itself and its world which are not limited simply to its own immediate needs. There is, consequently, a potential universality to human practical activity:

An animal forms objects only in accordance with the standard and the need of the species to which it belongs, whilst man knows how to produce in accordance with the standard of every species, and knows how to apply everywhere the inherent standard to the object. Man therefore also forms objects in accordance with the laws of beauty. (*MECW*, 3:277)

Since Marx connects the notion of reality with practical activity, and practical activity is characterized in the preceding manner, Marx often links the reality of things, activities, and relations with their fulfillment of human practical interests. A railway on which no trains run, hence which is not used up, since there is no need for it, is a railway only potentially, and not in *reality*. Similarly, a product becomes *a real product* only by being consumed. For example, a garment becomes a real garment only in the act of being worn. The product, unlike a mere natural object, proves itself to be, becomes a product only through consumption (*Grund.*, 91; cf. *Capital*, I:36). Thus, the reality of various objects is directly linked to their being used to fulfill human practical interests. Conversely, however, human interests which cannot be fulfilled lack reality. 'If I have no money for travel, I have no *need* – that is, no real and realisable need – to travel. If I have the *vocation* for study but no money for it, I have *no* vocation for study – that is, no *effective*, no *true* vocation' (*MECW*, 5:39, 40, 43). Because Marx allows that there are objects which are not dependent on human beings for their existence (at least in some ultimate sense) he takes himself to be a materialist, to be opposed to Hegel. Because he sees any objects with which humans are concerned as molded and changed by sensuous human activity he takes himself to have adopted the important insight

61

of idealism. In this way, Marx believes he has avoided any crude or purely mechanical materialism. To say, then, according to the first stage of this argument, that a moral claim is justified or valid is to say that that claim refers to a set of activities and relations within a society, i.e. forms of social existence, which play a determinate role in the effective fulfillment of its members' practical interests.

This clarifies but one part of the initial (mis-)interpretation (pp. 58-9) which we considered above. When we consider the justification, the reality and power, of a moral claim, Marx is *not* speaking of those situations in which this or that person feels 'compelled' to die for his moral beliefs. Rather, he is referring to those material and social conditions created by human activity which play a concrete and actual role in the fulfillment of human interests. Surely many objections to such an account of the justification of moral claims will occur to the reader. But the preceding is merely the first step in developing Marx's views.

II

The second step in explicating Marx's account of the justification of moral claims requires that we consider Marx's view that up until now, anyway, the interests which are fulfilled, the interests which form the basis on which moral judgments are justified, are the practical interests of the ruling class. Marx claims in an often cited passage:

> The ideas of the ruling class are in every epoch the ruling ideas: i.e., the class which is the ruling *material* force of society is at the same time its ruling *intellectual* force. The class which has the means of material production at its disposal, consequently also controls the means of mental production, so that the ideas of those who lack the means of mental production are on the whole subject to it. The ruling ideas are nothing more than the ideal expression of the dominant material relations, the dominant material relations grasped as ideas; hence of the relations which make the one class the ruling one, therefore, the ideas of its dominance. (*MECW*, 5:59)

Thus, it would appear that Marx's further specification of the conditions underlying morality implies that the claims of morality are justified or valid to the extent that they fulfill the practical interests of the ruling class. This is, indeed, the usual interpretation of Marx's views on the problem of the justification of moral claims.

Now this interpretation has a number of implications which, since this interpretation is so common, should be noted. Firstly, if the moral principles justified for a particular society are simply those principles adherence to which will fulfill the practical interest of the ruling class, one can understand why some have claimed that for Marx morality is simply an instrument of class oppression. What is moral, then, would concern (at least ultimately) the interests of the ruling class, not the interests of subordinate classes. Such a morality would (seemingly) justify or rationalize the *status quo*. It would keep subordinate classes in line since it would pre-empt any moral criticism of the ruling class other than criticisms of hypocrisy – i.e. that the ruling class is not living up to its own morality, which is, after all, a statement of those ways of acting which fulfill its interests. Indeed, such criticism would seem to be a favor to the ruling class, since it would make them again aware of what it was that fulfilled their interests.

Secondly, if morality and the justification of moral claims are tied to the interests of the ruling class, then, all moralities can only be relative to the particular epoch in which the ruling class finds itself. Thus, the validity of moral claims would be restricted to particular historical periods and particular societies. It should be noted that such a view is more extreme than what is usually meant by ethical or cultural relativism. The present view would restrict the morality of a claim to each particular society, regardless of whether it partook of the same culture. Indeed, moral claims would not only be relative but also a kind of self-serving propaganda on the part of the ruling class; morality would simply be a kind of rationalization of the ruling class's position.

There is a related consequence implicit here. In periods in which the ruling class is crumbling, being overtaken by another class or classes, moral questions would be up in the air. We might speak of different moralities within the same society, depending on which class had more power. Accordingly, in periods of transition from one form of society to another, or from one ruling class to another, moral questions would be undecidable. Or, in periods in which different classes had roughly the same power, even though no sharp transition was going on, one might have to say that either that society simply had different, conflicting but valid moralities, or there was no valid morality in that society. This would further relativize morality. If one were clever enough in drawing the lines of different classes ever more narrowly, one might claim either that there were dozens of different moralities in each society, or that no society had a valid morality. Scepticism regarding morality would be the result.

Finally, were all classes (the ruling class included) to be eliminated by communism, then it would seem that morality might itself disappear.

That is, under communism class oppression will cease. The tools of class oppression will no longer be needed — hence it might seem that morality too will no longer be needed.

Thus, the conclusion of linking morality to the interests and needs of class would seem to be either moral relativism or scepticism before communism, as well as the disappearance of morality with the appearance of communism.

Now these relativistic and sceptical conclusions about the nature of morality prior to communism and the end of morality with communism are unwarranted by Marx's views. They depend upon a too simple view of the relation of morality to the practical interests of a class and to the oppressive uses to which a class might put morality. For the preceding objections to have any merit or force there must be some inherent necessity that morality, by its nature, serves the interests of some particular class, that such class oppression is a necessary feature of any and all forms of morality and not just early and undeveloped forms of morality. Unless this can be shown the argument or the objections above carry no force. One might as well argue, analogously, that since horses are used to pull carriages, the replacement of the carriages by the auto in a modern society, will spell the end of horses. Certainly, horses will no longer pull carriages, but this hardly shows that horses will no longer be around or will not have other uses! Indeed, it does not show that horses will not continue to be used for the other purposes which they had before the auto. Similarly with morality. Morality, if we are to believe Marx, has been historically linked, at least so far, to the fulfillment of the interests of certain classes. This has been tantamount to the ruling class's use of morality for the oppression and exploitation of the subordinate classes. But unless some inherent connection can be shown between the nature of morality and the practical interests of a ruling class, then we surely do not need to conclude that morality cannot be disassociated from this or that class. Morality, then, could be relieved of its oppressive uses, of its link with this or that class, and still retain its essential nature.

Thus, we must ask: why has morality played this role of class oppression in the past? How is it that morality has served the interests of the ruling class, and not the interests of all people? In short, how is it that morality is linked to class interests? What is the nature of this connection?

Marx gives a genetic account in answer to these questions. In early society, due to differences in sex, 'natural pre-disposition (e.g. physical strength), needs, accidents, etc.' there is a natural division of labor (*MECW*, 5:44). Marx takes this as a given from which an account of the development of society must begin. Now the division of labor itself implies a division and separation of interests among individuals. With the increase in population, productive abilities and the like, this division and separation of interests becomes all the more exaggerated and increased. In short, with the division of labor among individuals and the division of interests, we have the foundations for the division of society into various classes with opposed interests. This betokens a number of other consequences in society.

Firstly, with the division of labor and the creation of classes, people are separated naturally, spontaneously into various activities from which they cannot escape. These occupations take on an existence independent of the individuals (*MECW*, 5:92, 93), just as the class of which one is a member takes on an existence independent of one (*MECW*, 5:77). The productive forces then appear as a world for themselves, quite independent of and divorced from the individuals whose powers they are. Further, due to this situation there appears a cleavage in the life of each individual, in so far as it is personal and in so far as it is determined by some branch of labor and the conditions pertaining to it. We get then the difference between the class individual and the private individual. Since individuals tend to see themselves essentially as private individuals, the conditions of their lives appear accidental to them. As a result, they come to false views about the nature of these conditions — about the nature and kind of freedom they have, the nature of commodities, of money, etc.

Secondly, with the division of labor there arises a contradiction between the interest of the separate individual, or the individual family, and the common interest of all individuals who have intercourse with one another. 'This common interest,' Marx claims, 'does not exist merely in the imagination, as the "general interest," but first of all in reality, as the mutual interdependence of the individuals among whom labor is divided' (*MECW*, 5:46). However, because individuals seek only their particular interests (*MECW*, 5:47), the common interest must be asserted over these conflicting interests. This takes the form of the state (*MECW*, 5:46, 47) — one of these classes is always said to dominate over the other (*MECW*, 5:46). Thus, an illusory community, a general interest, is formed, though it is based on real ties existing in every family, conglomeration, etc. (*MECW*, 5:46). In the state, in the ruling class, a subgroup is formed of the ideologists of this class. The ideologists formulate the ideas of the ruling class. The formulations of the ideologists of the ruling class can themselves come into conflict with the ruling ideas (*MECW*, 5:60); but in times of conflict the ruling ideas, and hence the ruling social relations, reassert their dominance.

Now is there anything in this kind of account which ties morality and moral claims to the interests of particular classes in such a way that there could not be moral claims and morality without such classes, or without one class which rules over other classes? Certainly, the answer, in the case of the state, would seem to be that Marx thought that the state was a necessary consequence of the division of interests, the conflicts of interests and needs, amongst the various classes. And if, indeed, this was the sole reason for its existence, then seemingly with the end of class conflict the state would become a superfluous entity. At least, as defined and characterized in the preceding, this would appear to be a proper interpretation of Marx's views.

But is there any similar necessary link between morality and classes? I can see no argument or reason on the part of Marx's account why we should or must believe that this is so. Before the creation of states, indeed before the existence of classes, there was morality in the primitive gens.[4] There was no state, no sense of nationality, or even law, but there was morality (as well as religion, art, etc.). History, as a matter of fact, has developed − and in a certain sense it had to develop − through the division of labor, classes, the state, etc. But the necessity which Marx perceives here is not a necessity which would require that with the abolition (the *Aufhebung*) of classes, the state, and the division of labor morality would also necessarily end. There is nothing, we might say, which logically links the fulfillment of interests to the fulfillment of the interests of a particular group or particular person (e.g. God). Thus, even though morality has throughout history been linked with the claims of some particular class, this does not seem to imply that it *must* be linked to the claims of some class − the only point which does seem to follow is that the claims of morality must be linked with the fulfillment of human practical interests.

III

If morality need not be, though in fact so far historically it has been, linked to the interests of a particular class, Marx's view would seem to be that moral claims are to be justified by appealing (in some way) to their effects on, or their fulfillment of, human interests. However, if this is Marx's view, he seems to be faced with a dilemma. On the one hand, how can Marx simply maintain that a moral claim is justified by appeal to the fulfillment of human interests and not thereby fall into the empty abstraction into which he claims that others fall? On the other hand, if he proceeds to tie interests to those present in a particular society, how can Marx's views avoid simply rationalizing the *status quo*?[5] The preceding argument would only seem to show that morality need not be linked to the interests of particular classes — and hence something along the lines of morality might survive the arrival of communism. The preceding argument does not indicate the nature of the appeal to interests or in what sense such an appeal is morally justified. The above account is in the right direction but it remains incomplete.

It must be allowed that that which is moral, according to Marx, is that which plays a determinate role in a particular mode of production. Marx comments, for example, that 'the positive expression "human" corresponds to the definite relations *predominant* at a certain stage of production and to the way of satisfying needs determined by them, just as the negative expression "inhuman" corresponds to the attempt to negate these predominant relations and the way of satisfying needs prevailing under them' (*MECW*, 5:432). That is, Marx's view avoids abstraction by continuing to link morality to the particular mode of production. What is moral in this way is valid or justified inasmuch as it plays its concrete role in the operation of that mode of production. It is important not to deny or prefer not to see this side of Marx's views. He insists on the connection of morality to the mode of production. In showing its 'reality and power' within that situation, moral claims show their justification.

However, it does not follow from this that Marx's ethical views end here. Nor does it follow that the views in the preceding paragraph commit him to a relativistic ethics. That is, the claim that what is moral in one society may not be moral in another society which has a different ruling class with different interests does not necessarily commit Marx to relativism. Though Marx is not very clear on these problems, it should be emphasized that Marx assumes that societies with similar ruling classes and, thus, with similar interests (e.g. the bourgeoisie in various countries), will have similar moral codes. Accordingly, Marx's ethics is *not* relativistic in the strong and important sense of ethical relativism which holds that 'what is right and good for one individual or society is not right or good for another, even if the situations involved are similar, meaning not merely that what is thought right or good by one is not thought right or good by another . . . , but that what is really right or good in one case is not so in another.'[6] Marx is *not* maintaining this. Indeed, he insists that the situations of societies with different ruling classes are significantly different. This is in contrast to the tradition of moral philosophy which takes the nature of the ruling class to be ethically irrelevant. But this view is fully in line with traditional moral philosophy in that it maintains that what is moral must be determined by reference to the morally relevant considerations of each situation. It is, Marx holds, because bourgeois and feudal societies have different morally relevant characteristics that they foster and demand different moral behaviors. It could still be that there are moral principles which unite them.

Now this possibility that there are moral standards which unite and apply to all societies, can only be entertained if the situations of societies with morally different characteristics are themselves connected in some way. If these various situations are unconnected, then the possibility the previous paragraph proffered would have to remain a possibility. Marx's ethics, though perhaps not relativistic in a strict sense, would have the same consequences as relativism. No cross-cultural moral judgments could be justified.

It is at this point, then, that it is important to avoid the error, to which many have unwittingly fallen victim, of interpreting Marx's views statically and abstractly. If one so views Marx's theories one is led to the problems of relativism, or perhaps scepticism, noted above; there could, then, be little basis for moral action against the ruling class — morality would simply be that which fulfills the ruling class's interests. However, Marx's views on morality and society are not abstract — they do not merely link morality with the interests of classes, but (more generally) with the practical activity in terms of which classes themselves must be understood. That is, to speak of society and its classes is to speak of the creations, the products, of human practical activity. Thus, Marx claims that 'M. Proudhon the economist understands very well that men make cloth, linen or silk materials in definite relations of production. But what he has not understood is that these definite social relations are just as much produced by men as linen, flax, etc.' (*MECW*, 6:165-6). Thus, class conflict, the conflict of the interests of different classes, must ultimately be seen as a conflict within human practical activity itself. As such, an account of the forms this conflict takes in different societies, of 'the ensemble of the social relations,' is simply an account of man.[7]

On the other hand, Marx's account of human practical activity is not static — it does not simply pertain to this or that class or society independently of others and their historical development. The history of man and society is not merely a series of disconnected but juxtaposed events. This may be the empiricist's view (or so Marx and Hegel might say), but it is not Marx's view. Marx views a society as a developing historical entity which has emerged out of the contradictions of previous societies and will, due to its own contradictions, be transformed into another form of society. Thus, Marx comments, these various conditions [of the productive forces and form of intercourse — i.e. of societies themselves] . . . form in the whole development of history a coherent series of forms of intercourse, the coherence of which consists in this: an earlier form of intercourse, which has become a fetter, is replaced by a new one corresponding to the more developed productive forces and, hence, to the advanced mode of the self-activity of individuals — a form which in its turn becomes a fetter and is then replaced by another. Since these conditions correspond at every stage to the simultaneous development of the productive forces, their history is at the same time the history of the evolving productive forces taken over by each new generation, and is therefore the history of the development of the forces of the individuals themselves. (*MECW*, 5:82)

The historical development of society and man, then, is one in which there is direction and meaning. Marx was, in these terms, a man of his age.

Now, to forestall misunderstanding, the preceding is not to say that Marx held that it was 'the plan or the destiny of previous generations' to create for later generations the particular kind of society in which they live. The development of history, Marx says,

can be speculatively distorted so that later history is made the goal of earlier history, e.g., the goal ascribed to the discovery of America is to further the eruption of the French Revolution. Thereby history receives its own special goals and becomes 'a person ranking with other persons' . . . , while what is designated with the words 'destiny,' 'goal,' 'germ,' or 'idea' of earlier history is nothing more than an abstraction from later history, from the active influence which earlier history exercises on later history. (*MECW*, 5:50)

Nor is earlier history to be seen as motivated by the attempt to realize a moral principle which characterizes a later society. Marx comments that:

of course, the tendency towards equality belongs to our century. To say now that all former centuries, with entirely different needs, means of production, etc., worked providentially for the realisation of equality is, first of all, to substitute the means and the men of our century for the men and the means of earlier centuries and to misunderstand the historical movement by which the successive generations transformed the results acquired by the generations that preceded them. (*MECW*, 6:173)

Thus, it is simply mistaken to think that Marx held that the goal of each historical epoch was communism, or indeed that history could have goals. Individuals, living in certain specific circumstances, have goals. And the practical working out of these goals within these circumstances constitutes history. It is man, or society in this sense, which is the subject of history. Further, since Marx's account is linked to human practical activity within particular circumstances, Marx does not maintain that every step in the development of human practical activity need be forward, or that every society need always be in step, let alone on the same level. Just as the development of an organism or individual may regress at certain points or slow down, so too may historical development. Still, Marx claims that there is in general progress in the development of human activity and the forms it takes. It is finally worth noting, here, that Marx's account is taken (at least in his later writings) to apply primarily to Europe or Western Society.[8] How other societies might develop must itself be investigated.

In order to explicate further the nature of the connections between the developmental stages of man or society, we must keep Marx's views on dialectics in mind. History is the development of man and society, through various stages of production. It is a development in which the contradictions in each society account for change and movement. Moreover, as an instance of dialectical change, it is the movement of man and society from being abstract and one-sided to being many-sided and concrete. In addition, it is a movement in which the later stages of development are the manifest expression of the latent characteristics or tendencies in the earlier stages. That is, these latter characteristics are not only preserved but, through various significant modifications, brought to a more full development in the later stages. In Marx's dialectical terminology, these characteristics are '*aufgehoben*.' With greatest brevity, Marx sees this historical development in the following terms.

In each stage of the development of man and society, one finds labor, differentiation of laboring functions, exchange, etc. In the earliest forms of society, the human relations corresponding to these notions are limited and undeveloped, even though personal. They are personal inasmuch as individuals, e.g. master and slave, must depend on each other, rather than the market: 'Relations of personal dependence (entirely spontaneous at the outset) are the first social forms, in which human productive capacity develops only to a slight extent and at isolated points' (*Grund.*, 158; cf. *Capital*, I:77). These relations are limited and undeveloped in that the forces and relations of production restrict the possibilities of the self-activity of individuals. This applies not simply to those who work, but also to those who rule. Within each society, Marx claims, the 'restricted character of development consists not only in the exclusion of one class from development, but also in the narrow-mindedness of the excluding class, and the "inhuman" is to be found also within the ruling class' (*MECW*, 5:432; cf. 438, 51). Furthermore, people are generally one-sided and limited with regard to other societies as well, since each society is set off from other societies.

Now the history of man has been a history of the development of these social forms of life through different stages. This transition from one stage to another, as well as the development within each stage, are a working out of the latent characteristics contained at the beginning. Marx claims, 'nothing can emerge at the end of the process which did not appear as a presupposition and precondition at the beginning' (*Grund.*, 304). Thus, he claims of exchange that:

> the historical progress and extention of exchange develops the contrast, latent in commodities, between use-value and value. The necessity for giving an external expression to this contrast for the purposes of commercial intercourse, urges on the establishment of an independent form of value and finds no rest until it is once for all satisfied by the differentiation of commodities and money. At the same rate, then, as the conversion of products into commodities is being accomplished, so also is the conversion of one special commodity into money. (*Capital*, 1:86-7)

Further, with regard to exchange value and money he maintains 'that already the simple forms of exchange value and of money latently contain the opposition between labor and capital, etc.' (*Grund.*, 248). Hence, the characteristics of later historical stages are the unfolding and manifest expression of the earlier characteristics of social life. This is true not simply of exchange, exchange value, money and the division of labor, but also, more basically, of human practical activity itself.

This process of development, however, is not a simple optimistic one. Other and new forms of dependency, abstraction, and mystification are created in the process. Thus, though people are freed from the personal dependency they have had on former masters, they become dependent on social laws and relations, on the market, which they also cannot control. 'Personal independence founded on objective [*sachlicher*] dependence is the second great form, in which a system of general social metabolism, of universal relations, of all-round needs and universal capacities is formed for the first time' (*Grund.*, 158). People's lives are abstract in different ways inasmuch as all human and natural

71

properties are reduced to indifferent common denominators. Their lives are mystified due to the relation of exploitation in which they stand.

In spite of this, successive stages of development are progressive according to several criteria connected with human practical activity. Firstly, there has been a development in the power of human productive forces − in the wide sense Marx gives to this term. Human practical activity which ultimately aims at the fulfillment of man's practical interests is increasingly able to fulfill those interests through greater control of nature. Advances in machinery, in the organizaton of labor, and in social organization permit this. The development of man's ability to design courses of action to attain individual and social ends is part and parcel of this development. Secondly, there has been a twofold development in the universality of human practical activity. On the one hand, historical development has witnessed the simplification of the class struggle, the expansion of class interests to encompass the interests of other classes (*MECW*, 6:60-61). Thus, in contrast to medieval or feudal life, Marx speaks of 'the more general outlook of the bourgeoisie, based on the more general conditions of existence of this class' (*MECW*, 5:47). On the other hand, with the development of productive forces the standards that man in fact applies to himself and to the world need not be limited simply to his own immediate needs. Instead, man comes to apply standards inherent to the object itself. Thus man forms his world in response to the concrete nature of objects in that world. Finally, human practical activity develops from conditions which require mystification, false consciousness, and fetishism to conditions which do not. In short, there is development towards greater and more accurate self-consciousness, towards more rational and accurate forms of knowledge.

What we see, then, in the development through which human practical activity has hitherto gone is an interconnected series of social forms of life, or simply, of man. The nature of their interconnections is not simply that one form merges into, changes into, another form. This would be true on other views as well. Rather, the interconnection is such that earlier forms develop into later forms which are said to be 'higher,' 'more mature,' forms of society, or man, than the earlier social forms. Our ability, then, to understand and to judge our society, as well as other societies, depends upon the extent to which we are able to see in earlier societies the latent characteristics which receive their manifest expression in later societies. Thus, Marx claims:

> bourgeois society is the most developed and the most complex
> historical organisation of production. The categories which express

its relations, the comprehension of its structure, thereby also allows insights into the structure and the relations of production of all the vanished social formations out of whose ruins and elements it built itself up, whose partly still unconquered remnants are carried along with it, whose mere nuances have developed explicit significance within it, etc. Human anatomy contains a key to the anatomy of the ape. The intimations of higher development among the subordinate animal species, however, can be understood only after the higher development is already known. The bourgeois economy thus supplies the key to the ancient, etc. But not at all in the manner of those economists who smudge over all historical differences and see bourgeois relations in all forms of society. One can understand tribute, tithe, etc., if one is acquainted with ground rent. But one must not identify them. Further, since bourgeois society is itself only a contradictory form of development, relations derived from earlier forms will often be found within it only in an entirely stunted form, or even travestied. (*Grund.*, 105-6)

Accordingly, human practical activity creates various forms (e.g. societies, classes, their relations) which, though distinctive from each other, still find an underlying unity in that they represent various stages in the development and manifestation of the latent characteristics of that practical activity itself. Human labor is the ultimate touchstone upon which this historical process rests. History is but a record of the various forms of development which it goes through.

It is on the basis of this organic model of social and human development that Marx is entitled to make moral judgments of different societies in various epochs. As sketched above, Marx indicates quite clearly that the direction of the particular historical developments is towards a many-sided and concrete development of human practical activity and, hence, of man. Stated otherwise, we might say that Marx sees the forces of man and society working towards that condition in which man would truly flourish. Now if morality concerns those relations and conditions of life which are most basic for the good of human life, then, Marx's theory is at this point an ethical or moral theory. I do not deny that there are those who would take exception to this view of morality. But, as I have argued earlier, this is not only a plausible view of morality but also one which characterizes the views of other thinkers who are nevertheless, recognized to have moral theories. It is hardly illegitimate, then, to interpret Marx's views here in light of such a conception of morality.

Indeed, that a theory concerning the basic conditions of life might be called a moral theory seems even to find support in Marx's own characterization of the wants and needs of a worker as a 'moral element' determining the value of his labor-power:

> [The laborer's] means of subsistence must therefore be sufficient to maintain him in his normal state as a labouring individual. His natural wants, such as food, clothing, fuel, and housing, vary according to the climatic and other physical conditions of his country. On the other hand, the number and extent of his so-called necessary wants, as also the modes of satisfying them, are themselves the product of historical development, and depend therefore to a great extent on the degree of civilisation of a country, more particularly on the conditions under which, and consequently on the habits and degree of comfort in which, the class of free labourers has been formed. In contradistinction therefore to the case of other commodities, there enters into the determination of the value of labour-power a historical and *moral* element (*Capital*, I:171, emphasis added).

That is, Marx allows, the discussion of those basic needs and wants one must fulfill in order to live the normal life of the laborer is a discussion of the moral elements of life. There is no reason why this cannot be extended simply to include those elements which are basic for the good or flourishing human life. Indeed, later in *Capital*, Marx links 'time for education, for intellectual development, for the fulfilling of social functions and for social intercourse, for the free play of [one's] bodily and mental activity' with 'the *moral* . . . bounds of the working day' (*Capital*, I:264-5; emphasis added).

It is this view, then, of morality and of man and society, which entitles Marx to make moral judgments regarding other, as well as earlier societies. Because such societies constitute an interconnected series in the development of man towards that condition in which humans will truly flourish, Marx can justifiably use the moral principles characteristic of that flourishing condition to evaluate earlier and other social conditions. However, though in this claim we have now arrived at the foundations of a Marxist ethics, the nature and implications of this view still need to be elaborated.

IV

To begin with, the preceding interpretation indicates that there are bounds to the kinds of moral judgments Marx is entitled to make of other societies. In so doing, it renders intelligible Marx's claims about earlier and more primitive societies. Consider, for example, Marx's reference to the Greeks as 'normal children' (*Grund.*, 111), or to 'the childish world of antiquity' (*Grund.*, 488). By such comments Marx indicates that it is illegitimate to apply strictly a more developed morality (or theory of art, etc.) to an earlier form of society. Just as children cannot be morally condemned for various actions they commit, and cannot even begin to partake of other moral actions due to their lack of development, so too Marx claims with regard to earlier less developed forms of society that they lack the development of the bases which would allow them to partake in a fuller and more developed sense of morality.

Still, this does not mean that such children or societies fall outside the moral pale. They are to be raised, or we are to view their development, in light of a fully developed morality. Thus, Marx approves of various actions taken by the British against Indian traditional society, inasmuch as their actions will bring about a basis upon which a more fully developed and mature society can arise: 'The devastating effects of English industry, when contemplated with regard to India, . . . are palpable and confounding. But we must not forget that . . . the bourgeois period of history has to create the material basis for the new world.'[9] That is, there is a morality which does hold valid for other, and undeveloped, societies even though it cannot be applied in all its particulars to them. Its validity stems from the fact that this is the moral condition towards which the forces and characteristics of these societies themselves are developing. To 'the German reader who shrugs his shoulders at the condition of the English industrial and agricultural laborer,' Marx was fond of saying, '*De te fabula narratur*' — i.e. 'This story is about you' (*Capital*, I:8). There is, of course, a disanalogy here. Children can be expected to mature into adults, but the members of ancient Greek society did not have the possibility of maturing into individuals who might live under a communist ethics. This disanalogy, however, only indicates that Marx is centrally concerned with the stages of development of various forms of society and morality.

Secondly, it is important to note that the later development of man and society cannot be foreseen by earlier societies. Indeed, concerning 'everything living, everything which is immediate, every sensuous experience, any and every *real* experience,' Marx claims that 'the "Whence" and the "Whither" . . . one never *knows* beforehand' (*MECW*, 4:23). One might say that Marx takes seriously the fact that moral judgments cannot be made under conditions of full knowledge. This has a number of implications for Marx. The most crucial one is

that Marx does *not* presuppose a moral principle or ideal which could
be known and applied even in the first stages of human development.
What communist morality is, i.e. what constitutes the mature form of
human development, only appears after man and society have already
proceeded through various forms of life.

It is clear from the preceding that Marx's views are related to Aristotle's in a number of ways. That is, for both Marx and Aristotle, to
know how man ought to live it is crucial to understand what human
beings are. Further, in their accounts of what humans are, both emphasizes the importance of activity. Nevertheless, the present discussion
indicates that Marx radically differs from Aristotle in that man is not,
according to Marx, a being whose nature is given and complete outside
of history. Instead, what man is and can be is only revealed in and
through history — indeed, it is only a development of history. Thus, the
moral standards which Marx uses to measure man and society are those
which appear later in history. These standards speak directly to man's
fully developed condition, but also, as indicated above, to the earlier
less developed conditions in which man finds himself.

Another implication of the above point is that at each step in the
past, people have taken themselves to be living full and many-sided
lives. They have taken themselves to be living, more or less, by the correct morality. Their one-sidedness only appears to later societies, which
then project their awareness of the development of their more advanced
form of morality back onto the earlier societies:

> The conditions under which individuals have intercourse with each
> other, so long as this contradiction [between productive forces and
> productive relations] is absent, are conditions appertaining to their
> individuality, in no way external to them; conditions under which
> alone these definite individuals, living under definite relations, can
> produce their material life and what is connected with it, are thus the
> conditions of their self-activity and are produced by this self-activity.
> The definite condition under which they produce thus corresponds,
> as long as the contradiction has not yet appeared, to the reality of
> their conditioned nature, their one-sided existence, the one-sidedness
> of which only becomes evident when the contradiction enters on the
> scene and thus exists solely for those who live later. Then this con-
> dition appears as an accidental fetter, and the consciousness that it is
> a fetter is imputed to the earlier age as well. (*MECW*, 5:82)

Thus, Marx does not seek to place moral guilt on the shoulders of individuals living in past societies, or even (to a lesser extent) in capitalist

society. To the extent they do not and cannot know future forms of social and moral development, to the extent they must live in their present social conditions which do not allow this further, fuller development, individuals cannot be morally condemned. It is for this reason that Marx says that 'my standpoint, from which the economic evolution of the economic formation of society is viewed as a process of natural history, can less than any other make the individual responsible for relations whose creature he socially remains, however much he may subjectively raise himself above them' (*Capital*, I:10). Still, from this point it does not follow, as we have seen above, that Marx does not or cannot make moral judgments about previous societies and individuals.

The preceding point also implies the guardedness with which Marx theoretically must speak of future communist society and ethics. The details and concrete nature of this stage of human development can no more be foreseen by Marx, than bourgeois society and morality could be foreseen by medieval man. Thus, as we have argued before, it is not out of laziness, unclarity, etc., that Marx did not lay out more clearly the nature of future communism. His theoretical premises did not permit it. The most he could do was to indicate those characteristics which, presently considered, would apparently define communist society and morality.

Thirdly, we must be careful and explicit about the justification which can be given to moral standards. We indicated at the beginning of the previous section that Marx, indeed, wants to claim that those moral standards which characterize a particular mode of production are justified for that mode of production. Inasmuch as they play a role in the operation of that mode of production they evidence their 'reality and power,' and hence their validity. Now if one is looking for a Marxist moral standard (or set of moral standards) which is basic and valid in this way for all time, that is to say, a moral standard which is and has played an actual role, and the same role, in all present and past societies, a force actually determining their development, then one simply is not going to find it. However, this does *not* undercut moral philosophy. Indeed, in *this* sense of validity, most all previous ethical philosophers and moralists would say that there has not been a valid moral standard. Marx emphasizes this sense of validity, not because standards, ideals, or laws which do not have it are not to be accepted as valid in some other sense, or are not to be used as normative criteria of human activity, but because he does not want to allow others to claim that such standards are by themselves the ultimate determinates of historical development.

It is important to note, then, that Marx himself allows that there are other senses of 'validity' or 'justification.' For example, we can pick out certain common characteristics, standards, and values with regard to morality, as well as with regard to systems of production and distribution, which can be identified in all societies and cultures. Thus, Marx claims it is possible to identify certain 'general human laws' of production as well as of distribution (*Grund.*, 85, 87). Similarly, with regard to morality, Marx allows that the social consciousness of past ages moves within certain common forms, or general ideas. Now, what is important here is that there are certain common forms and ideas for all present and past epochs not only with regard to production and distribution, but also with regard to morality. Further, and more importantly for present purposes, Marx claims that these ideas and values have a validity inasmuch as they apply to all these various societies and epochs (cf. *Grund.*, 105). Marx says this explicitly with regard to the categories of bourgeois economics, or of political economy. But there is no reason not to believe that the same holds for moral views. For example, Marx claims that property involves juridical relations (i.e. ideological elements) and is yet itself a concept or notion which is valid for all epochs (*Grund.*, 87, 88, 102).

Now even though Marx is willing to grant that various general moral ideas and standards possess a validity for all epochs, he also maintains that the validity they possess is less than the 'full validity' possessed by the particular moral standards which characterize different modes of production. Indeed, Marx is inclined to speak of such general ideas as empty phrases (*Grund.*, 100) and chaotic concepts (*Grund.*, 100). It is important to note that he makes these claims with regard to ideas and concepts of political economy as well as with regard to moral concepts and ideas. Thus, the occasions on which Marx is attacking moral concepts in this way should not be taken as indicating that he is solely opposed to moral concepts for these reasons. These reasons also apply to the concepts of political economy. Concepts, principles, ideas of political economy and ethics, then, may have different kinds of validity or justification depending on their nature.

One of the main problems with such general ideas and standards is that they tend to reduce to a few simple claims which though valid are relatively uninteresting. Thus, regarding production we might end up with the claim that appropriation is a precondition of production (*Grund.*, 87). Similarly, with morality we might end up with the claim that one ought to do good and avoid or prevent evil.

Now what is missing in these cases and in this sense of 'validity,' but which is present in the former sense of 'validity,' and the standards characterized by it, is a direct connection or linkage with the actual mode of production, with the basic human practical activities involved.

But it is just this that the moral standards which characterize communism have − and in a twofold sense. Firstly, they are themselves directly
linked with the mode of production under *communism*. That is, these
moral standards play an active and concrete role in productive activity
under communism. And secondly, they are the dialectical development
or result of the particular moral standards and human activity of earlier
stages. As certain moral standards are the expression of this or that particular, but incomplete, mode of production, i.e. this or that stage in
the incomplete development of human activity, communist moral
standards are the expression not merely of the mature development of
human activity but also of the entire historical process which leads to
the development of that mode of production in which individuals
flourish. It is this connection of communist moral principles with the
practical human activity, the material bases, of communist as well as
previous societies which justifies the application of communist moral
standards to non-communist societies.

Communist moral standards, then, are not simply abstractions. They
do not have the empty validity which mere abstractions have. Inasmuch
as they are the development of the inherent features of previous
societies which played a role in the functioning of those societies, communist standards are not abstract. And since they also look to a wider
context than this or that particular previous society, let alone the needs
of a particular class, they are not rationalizations of the *status quo*. It
may not be correct to say that they have the same kind of validity that
the particular moral standards of a particular society have. Nevertheless,
it is clear that they possess their own important sense of validity or
justification. Unfortunately, Marxists, as well as others, have taken
Marx's view that the moral standards functioning in this or that society
are valid to mean that this is all that can be said about the problem of
justification. But, as we have seen, from the fact that we cannot know
or apply more advanced moral standards in less developed stages of
human development in the same strict sense that we can under communism, it does not follow that there are not more advanced, valid
moral standards which indicate the limitations and inadequacies of the
earlier moral standards. It is just this universalist view of morality which
Marx defends.

Finally, in light of the preceding elaborations, the question might be
raised: suppose that history does develop in the way that Marx thought
it did; further, suppose morality is connected with the development of
practical activity and the mode of production as he says it is; still, why
should the moral claims and standards to which human society actually
comes be said to be justified? History might develop in a certain way,

and yet this not be morally acceptable.

Marx's answer to this is that such a challenge is an empty, abstract, and meaningless challenge. the moral principles by which humans live do not come from some transcendental sphere, or from God. There is no such source. They stem from man himself. They are connected with his basic productive, practical activities.

What kind of connection is involved here? Does Marx simply define the moral uses of 'virtue,' 'good,' etc., in terms of the kinds of practical activity which will characterize communism? If he so proceeded, then, the behavior of people who engaged in this particular kind of activity would be *ipso facto* justified. However, Marx does not do this. He is not out to define terms. Further, as Frankena has correctly pointed out, even if one proposed such a definition, then, the question would arise — why should we accept this definition? Marx is not, that is, simply defining the activities which will characterize communism as morally 'virtuous,' 'right,' 'good' activities.

Instead, Marx is showing us the forces involved in the historical development of man and society. These forces, it should be recalled, involved moral standards which may affect and modify this historical development. Thus, Marx does not claim (cf. Chapter 2) that the historical development of man and society is blind. It is malleable. Moral standards may have their effect. They do not simply describe how people behave, but indicate how they should behave. In short, they carry normative force. Thus, it makes sense to engage in moral reflection. Still, moral standards do not operate in a social and historical — in a material — vacuum. There are limits and conditions to human actions. These must be recognized. On the one hand, they provide for the possibility of a communist society. As Marx says, 'if we did not find concealed in society as it is the material conditions of production and the corresponding relations of exchange prerequisite for a classless society [i.e. the moral society Marx envisions] , then all attempts to explode it would be quixotic' (*Grund.*, 159). On the other hand, given Marx's account of the nature of human activity, these limits and conditions indicate the direction in which man must go. That is, we see not merely the possibility of exploding the conditions of present society, but also the necessity that man explode them, and create a communist society. Of course, one may always *say* that society and history ought to have gone in some other direction, or followed some other moral standard. But such claims made without regard to the limits and conditions of human action are merely empty phrases. Were we to ape Kant's well-known saying, Marx's claim would be that values independent of the factual, historical development are empty, while facts independent of the value development of man and society are blind.

Thus, in showing us how the moral and material development of human activity are bound up Marx is showing us why we should accept certain moral standards rather than others. The dialectical characterization of human, material reality contends that humankind develops from an abstract, one-sided existence into a many-sided, concrete, flourishing existence. To accept Marx's account of this historical development of society and man, then, is to accept his moral theory. The two are not and cannot be separate. In this way Marx has collapsed facts and values. And, in this way Marx has fulfilled his demand that there be 'one science.'

V

In conclusion, the present chapter has argued that Marx's views on ideology and the justification of moral judgments also allow for a Marxist morality. This morality is not simply relativistic but one which is applicable to communist society as well as to previous societies. Nevertheless, because of the material conditions required for the application of this morality it cannot be applied at all times in the full and rich sense in which it is under communism. It is clear, further, that the justification of moral claims necessarily requires reference to the fulfillment of human practical interests. The fact that hitherto the fulfillment of human interests has been the fulfillment of the interests of the ruling class is to be explained historically in terms of the existing material conditions. Early society could not have developed otherwise than in ways which led to the creation of classes, division of labor, and private property — all of which restricted the fulfillment of practical interests to those of a particular class. Nevertheless, there is nothing which logically links the fulfillment of interests to the fulfillment of the interests of a particular group or person. Indeed, the dialectical account of the historical development of man and society indicates that fulfillment of interests under communism will occur in and through a form of practical life activity characterized by universality, concreteness, and rational self-consciousness. This universal ethics of man's flourishing condition is the basis upon which moral judgments of communist and non-communist societies can be made. However, the standards which would constitute this morality are themselves the products as well as expressions of historical development. There is no question, then, of Marx applying moral standards to this or that society which are not linked to their material bases. In effect, then, Marx allows for the moral standards of each epoch as well as for the moral standards of communism

which are their 'mature' development. The latter may be used to criticize the former; hence, Marx's moral views do not simply justify or
rationalize the *status quo*. But the former are the forms through which
the latter must go. The application of the latter moral standards to
societies characterized by the former moral standards must take this
into account. Hence, the application of communist moral standards is
possible without falling into the empty abstraction for which Marx
criticizes the moral standards that others have proposed.

This section also concludes Part one of this book. A few comments
are, then, also in order with regard to the general theme of this Part.
The unifying theme throughout the last three chapters has been 'the
ethical foundations of Marxism' — i.e., Marx's meta-ethics. From various sides I have argued that it makes sense to speak of Marx's ethics.
The objections to the contrary are not convincing. It is true that Marx
speaks with hostility of the ethics and morality of his time. But this is
due to the moralism, the abstraction, the other-worldliness into which
they consistently fell. Marx's concern is ever practical as well as theoretical. Unless ethical theory ever seeks its link with its practical conditions it will produce hopeless demands and claims. It is to be
regretted that Marx himself did not treat these topics with greater rigor
and directness. As a consequence, one can hardly say that Marx himself
advanced ethical theory. The situation is more that he provided certain
insights with regard to which ethical theory might be advanced. An
ethics today which would call itself Marxist would have to explore and
greatly develop these insights and directions. The present account has
brought them together in such a form that the ethical theory they constitute can be readily seen. Still, Marx's normative views themselves
have not yet been developed. The kind of normative standards which
the preceding discussion would sanction or exclude has not yet been
determined. Nevertheless, by the nature of the ethical views Marx has,
certain clear intimations of his normative views have already crept out.
It is to these views which we may now turn.

Part two
Marx's ethics

4   The ethics of freedom

> In place of the old bourgeois society, with its classes and class
> antagonisms, we shall have an association, in which the free develop-
> ment of each is the condition for the free development of all.
> *Manifesto of the Communist Party*, *MECW*, 6:506

An ethics encompasses questions about what is morally good and/or
right as well as questions about the methodology used to justify those
moral beliefs. So understood, the preceding chapters have accomplished
a twofold ethical purpose. Firstly, they have argued that it is plausible,
despite such apparent obstacles as Marx's language, and his views on
determinism and ideology, to speak of his ethics. Secondly, they have
developed the methodological aspect of that ethics. They have shown
us the nature of the justification which Marx can offer for normative
moral values and beliefs. Thus, the preceding chapters do not simply
serve as the preface to a discussion of Marx's ethics, which is only now
to come. If we distinguish between the normative and the meta-ethical
aspects of an ethics, then the preceding chapters have discussed Marx's
meta-ethics.[1] The answers to meta-ethical questions are, accordingly,
part of ethics. They are not external to ethics, merely interesting but
essentially unnecessary questions and answers to developing an ethics.
Rather, the answers given in Part one provide the foundation for Marx's
normative views which shall be treated in this and the following chapters. I wish now to show what Marx's normative moral views are and to
contrast them with other possible moral views which some commentators have attributed to Marx.

I

The main focus of Marx's thought was to formulate a critique of capitalist society as the latest in a series of historically developed social forms
of life. What is wrong with capitalist society is stated by Marx in a

85

variety of ways. Such a society presupposed the antagonistic interests of different classes as well as different individuals; the lives of individuals under capitalism are one-sided and deformed; people are impoverished, both physically and spiritually, by their work; personal relations are dissolved into money relations; neither individuals nor their classes (not even the bourgeois class) are in control of developments in society — the products of industry as well as social relations have acquired lives of their own which dominate and determine the course society blindly follows.

Various moral values and principles have been claimed to underlie the preceding criticisms. Some suggest that Marx's criticism of capitalist society was that it was unjust — it exploited the workers by robbing them of the products of their labor. Others claim that Marx objected to capitalism because it denied and corrupted human dignity. That capitalism did not promote the greatest good for the greatest number of people is also said to be Marx's central moral critique. Yet others argue that the following moral notions are important or central to Marx's normative ethics: security, equality, brotherhood, and love.[2] There is some truth to each of these claims. However, I believe that there is a more basic moral perspective from which to view Marx's criticism of capitalism. This is the view that Marx's central objection to capitalism is that, under it, people are not free. This objection not only underlies the criticisms of capitalism listed in the preceding paragraph, it can also be seen to encompass some of the different moral views, just noted, which have been attributed to Marx. Where this is not plausible, e.g. in the case of justice, I will argue that Marx did not, in fact, bring that criticism against capitalism.[3] Thus, at the center of Marx's condemnation of capitalism lies an ethics of freedom. His early as well as his later writings are filled with references to the lack of freedom, the illusory freedom, the slavery, that constitutes and results from capitalism. This chapter will show how these various comments fit together to form the basis of Marx's ethics of freedom.

The importance of freedom in Marx's thought has been recognized by others. For purposes of classification we can say that current interpretations of Marx's views on freedom divide into two camps. On the one hand, there are those who interpret freedom to be some form of self-realization. For example, it has been said that

> Marx calls man's freedom 'the positive power to assert his true individuality.' This 'true individuality' is man at the height of his powers and needs, thoroughly and intensively cooperating with his fellows, and appropriating all of nature. Free activity is activity that

fulfills such powers, and freedom, therefore, is the condition of man whose human powers are thus fulfilled; it passes beyond the absence of restraint to the active unfolding of all his potentialities.[4]

On the other hand, there is a rougher, less coherent group of interpretations, largely united by the fact that they do *not* give a self-realizationalist interpretation. In this latter group, some view freedom to be an ethical quality bound up with the co-operative working of goods;[5] others take it to be the rights of an individual to choose among various actions within limits determined by social necessity;[6] and yet others claim it is a mental or spiritual condition.[7] This twofold classification is useful inasmuch as the predominant interpretation of Marxian freedom is self-realizationalist in nature. There are, however, significant difficulties in rendering such an account of Marx. Indeed, I believe that none of the accounts of freedom which have so far been given have succeeded in giving us a plausible and detailed account of freedom as a moral notion, which is identifiable across the whole of Marx's writings.

To anticipate briefly the central aspects of the account I will offer, I will first contrast Marx's view of freedom with what Marx might call the bourgeois view of freedom. Though in comparison with his own views, the bourgeois notion of freedom looks thin and meager, Marx's notion of freedom is, nevertheless, related to this common, bourgeois sense of freedom. Secondly, I will state Marx's view summarily and identify its three main aspects. I will then note other central features which distinguish it from self-realizationist accounts. Since the self-realizationist interpretation of Marx's concept of freedom is, by far, the prevailing interpretation it is particularly important to distinguish from it the account which follows. My differences with other non-self-realizationist accounts will become clear in the course of this chapter.

According to the bourgeois sense of freedom to be free entails that one may act or live as one wants, independent of coercion or compulsion, in so far as one does not harm others.[8] A person who may so live, we say, is free since he himself determines his own actions and style of life. Marx's ethics of freedom, I believe, is the relentless, dogged, passionate development of this notion of freedom as self-determination. As such it reveals to us implications and consequences of our seemingly plain view of freedom which many may not like to see, but which hover about us.

There are two crucial directions in which Marx's notion of freedom is broader and richer than the bourgeois sense of freedom. Firstly, the bourgeois notion of freedom is a political, individual, and negative notion. Individuals are free to the extent that they are not coerced by others or the state. Their freedom is a negative freedom in that it consists solely in *not* being coerced or compelled to do or to be certain things by their society. In contrast to such political freedom or emancipation, Marx characterizes his notion of freedom in terms of human emancipation or human freedom. In Marx's eyes freedom requires not simply the lack of social coercion, but also a life of self-development within rational and harmonious relations to others. Accordingly, Marx's concept of freedom is social, collective, and positive. As such, Marxist freedom includes various aspects which the bourgeois notion has not traditionally included. Consequently, it has different implications. For example, the manner in which one objectifies oneself in working, even when one works as one desires, may nevertheless *not* be an instance of freedom. In particular, the wage laborer who is content in his job and who may change his place of employment if he wants, does not thereby enjoy freedom in Marx's sense.

Secondly, Marx's notion of freedom is a broad one because he interprets the notions used to characterize bourgeois freedom in a much more comprehensive fashion than is usual. For example, Marx comments that

> By 'external compulsion' the true socialists do not understand the restrictive material conditions of life of given individuals. They see it only as the compulsion exercised by the *state*, in the form of bayonets, police, and cannons, which far from being the foundation of society, are only a consequence of its structure. (*MECW*, 5:479)

That is, not simply may institutions, e.g. the state, exercise compulsion over a person, and hence rob him of his freedom, but also the material conditions in which one lives may do the same. This is an extension of the notion of compulsion far beyond that which traditional analyses of bourgeois freedom have employed. Consequently, even though Marx's notion of freedom directly draws on traditional (bourgeois) views of freedom, it goes beyond them.

What, then, is it to be free in Marx's sense? Stated most concisely, it is for one to live such that one essentially determines, within communal relations to other people, the concrete totality of desires, capacities, and talents, which constitute one's self-objectification. Naturally, the conciseness of this formula conceals most of its meaning. Nevertheless, it does suggest that there are three different, though interrelated, aspects of Marx's view of freedom: (a) self-determination requires self-objectification through one's desires, capacities, and talents; (b) one's self-objectification must be a concrete self-objectification with regard to other people and nature; and (c) self-determination is only possible within harmonious, communal relations to others. In short, for Marx freedom is self-determination of a particular kind. Each of the three aspects of self-determination will be discussed below. For the present, however, a number of additional features may be noted which characterize the account to follow and, as such, distinguish it not only from self-realization accounts of Marx's view of freedom but also from bourgeois freedom.

Marx's account of freedom is not an account of a principle of freedom such as Mill, for example, offered, but rather an account of freedom as the basic virtue by which people ought to live. As such, Marx's ethics of freedom is an ethics of virtue. By this I imply two things. Firstly, Marx is concerned with a certain state of being, a set of dispositions and character traits, which a person must have to be free. His pronouncements on freedom are not simply the demand that we act in certain ways according to some principle which may serve as the criterion for those acts. Secondly, Marx does not understand freedom to consist in a set of rights (and obligations) which its acceptance imposes on people. Freedom is not to be understood as an ethics of duty (cf. Chapter 1). Thus, his ethics of virtue differs from self-realizationist interpretations of freedom which may hold that we have a moral obligation to determine the rules by which we live or that the imperative to realize ourselves involves the fulfillment of various moral duties. Similarly, Marx's view of freedom differs from non-self-realizationist interpretations, such as Schaff's, which also explicate freedom by means of rights and obligations.[9] Moral obligations, duties, and rights are not part of Marx's ethics. Indeed, he condemns them as central and deficient features of bourgeois morality. Thus, an ethics of virtue has an advantage over other interpretations of Marx's moral views in that it does not imply an acceptance of those moral concepts which Marx explicitly rejected. An ethics of virtue does not, that is, tell us: 'You have a moral duty to do X!' or 'He has a moral obligation to do Y!' Rather, it says something more along the lines of 'Be Z!' It is primarily concerned with character traits, dispositions, and ways of being, rather than with ways of acting or doing.

The development of one's powers and talents is important for Marx's ethics of freedom. The self-realizationist view is so far correct. But Marx's view does not require, as at least some self-realizationist views assert, the realization of literally all of one's powers and talents. To such romantic and exaggerated interpretations Marx is not committed. As such, his view of freedom escapes problems into which self-realizationist views often fall and seldom recover. Neither does Marx's view imply the existence within us of two different selves, a false one and an ideal one, only the latter of which we are to realize. Such self-realizationist themes are foreign to Marx's position.

Marx's view remains, it should be clear, a normative theory. Simply because it is not an ethics of duty it does not become an empirical theory or a non-normative theory.[10] Amongst those offering a self-determinist interpretation of freedom there is a basic division between those who view freedom as an empirical or descriptive notion and those who treat it as a moral or normative notion. Part one has shown that Marx may treat freedom normatively and morally. This does not imply, however, the complete irrelevance of non-normative self-realizationist accounts. It could be that the content they suggest for freedom might be taken over and treated morally. In fact this does not, as we shall see, work out. But how this content should be morally treated would remain a problem. It is here that those self-realizationist accounts which allow that freedom for Marx is a moral notion do not help us. They do not tell us in what manner self-realization is a moral notion. Is such self-realization a moral duty or obligation? Is it an intrinsic good which our actions are to promote? Are our actions morally right/permissible/obligatory in so far as they accomplish self-realization? Such relevant questions for the self-realizationist view are not answered by its proponents. In contrast, the present account maintains that Marx was not concerned with detailing which particular action a person ought or ought not to perform. His answer would, instead, be 'Be free, and then do what you please!'[11] Such an interpretation can take into account Marx's condemnation of rights, moral obligations and duties, and yet still show how a moral thrust lies behind Marx's critique of capitalism.

Other ways in which the present interpretation of Marx's concept of freedom differs from previous accounts will become obvious in the following. The preceding, however, should give the reader an idea of some of the more important general features which distinguish the present account. The more specific differences must await the particular discussions now to follow.

II

The first aspect of Marx's view of freedom as self-determination is that one is free to the extent that one essentially determines the concrete totality of desires, capacities, and talents, which constitute one's self-objectification. This view, that freedom is characterized as self-determination, the self-determination of one's own objectification, is a plausible view. Stated in non-Marxist terms, it is the view that a person essentially determines for himself what he will be. As we have seen, it is related even to bourgeois freedom. Marx does, however, develop this notion in a unique way. Marx's views on self-objectification are crucial here.

Self-objectification, for Marx, signifies that man, given his various desires, capacities, and talents, objectifies or creates himself in his (productive) activities, his relations, and in the systems of thought he constructs by which he understands himself. That is, neither an individual nor mankind itself is, in the beginning, a finished product. Man is not at birth programmed to live in certain ways, only requiring some time to unfold and passively reveal these various characteristics. Rather, humans are various collections of needs, desires, and capacities which require activity and contact with others and nature in order to create the characteristics each person manifests. In Hegelian fashion, man only comes to know himself for what he is, and only comes to be what he can become through his active interrelation with other people and nature. This active interaction creates both himself and his world. Thus, Marx comments that 'the history of industry and the established objective existence of industry are the *open* book of *man's essential powers*, the perceptibly existing human *psychology*' (*MECW*, 3:302). This kind of intimate interrelation of man and his surroundings is not typical of bourgeois freedom. It implies for Marx the much greater and different significance for human freedom of one's relations to other people and to nature. Indeed, if one's work and relations to others are part of the process by which a person is created, then one can understand the importance Marx attaches to the nature of one's work and human relations.

The preceding comments on self-objectification should not be taken to mean that at any moment individuals or mankind can create literally any form of life which might suddenly be conceived. To be creative, we have said, is not to be free from causes or determination. Rather, within determinate conditions individuals (and mankind) create themselves by maintaining and reproducing the conditions within which they find themselves, as well as by creating new conditions and new forms of life for themselves. This process of self-creation is self-objectification.

Most frequently Marx emphasizes that self-objectification occurs in productive labor. To a great extent, then, Marx's discussion of self-objectification is concerned with human labor and work, with factories, farms, and the like. The reason for this emphasis, it should be obvious, relates to Marx's views on historical materialism, not to his views on objectification. That is, Marx's concept of self-objectification is not limited to productive labor in this narrow economic sense. Thus, on the one hand, Marx holds that a life is possible in which people will be significantly freed from labor for necessary economic ends. In such a life they could work on other projects which would be more immediately connected with that objectification of themselves they would choose. On the other hand, Marx seems willing to expand his notion of productive labor so that it and objectification become essentially the same. Accordingly, he notes that 'religion, family, state, law, morality, science, art, etc. are only *particular* modes of production' (*MECW*, 3:297).

Self-determination, then, occurs when a person essentially directs and controls the form his self-objectification takes. Self-objectification, we have seen, is the development of individuals (and mankind) through the active fulfillment and development of desires, capacities, and talents. As such, one's desires are not inherently opposed to one's self-determination or freedom. Accordingly, Marx's view differs from a number of other thinkers and movements. Marx himself contrasts his views with Christianity which has held that the determination of a person by his desires may be considered a fetter or constraint on a person:

> The only reason why Christianity wanted to free us from the domination of the flesh and 'desires as a driving force' was because it regarded our flesh, our desires as something foreign to us; it wanted to free us from determination by nature only because it regarded our nature as not belonging to us. For if I myself am not nature, if my natural desires, my whole natural character do not belong to myself — and this is the doctrine of Christianity — then all determination by nature — whether due to my own natural character or to what is known as external nature — seems to be a determination by something foreign, a fetter, compulsion used against me *heteronomy as opposed to autonomy of the spirit.* (*MECW*, 5:254)

There are other views that might also be contrasted with Marx's view. Plato saw the desires as rapacious and dangerous, as forces ever in need of restraint and limitation. Even Bradley, who held a self-realizationist ethic, spoke of 'the crude material of the natural wants, affections, and impulses, which, though not evil in themselves, stand in the way of good, and must be disciplined, repressed, and discouraged.'[12]

Marx, on the contrary, ever insists on the positive role which desires, capacities, and talents play in man's self-objectification and self-determination. Man's desires and needs are in themselves neither alien nor compulsive forces, nor are they forces standing 'in the way of good.'

Thus, the fact that in self-objectification, one acts to fulfill certain desires and needs does not compromise one's self-determination.

Nevertheless, Marx does allow that in certain circumstances our desires may become fetters on us, powers over us:

> Whether a desire becomes fixed or not, i.e., whether it obtains exclusive [power over us] . . . depends on whether material circumstances . . . permit the normal satisfaction of this desire and, on the other hand, the development of a totality of desires. This latter depends in turn, on whether we live in circumstances that allow all-round activity and thereby the full development of all our potentialities. (*MECW*, 5:255)

Thus, one's freedom may be diminished or restricted by various imperious and rigid desires. Marx's claim is that one's desires act as constraints on one's self-determination when their normal satisfaction is frustrated as well as when they are not part of the development and fulfillment of a totality of desires, capacities, and talents. Thus, Marx holds that destructive or imperious desires are the result of frustrated or impeded normal desires. In this way Marx may be said to have recognized the negative implications which unconscious desires, etc., have for one's self-determination. Abnormal desires not only are themselves instances of frustrated self-determination but also may inhibit other aspects of one's self-determination.

Now clearly no hard and fast lines can be drawn here as to how often a desire must frustrate the fulfillment of one's other desires and purposes before that person is no longer self-determining. Nor is Marx clear on the extent to which one's desires must be satisfied or the degree of development required of the material conditions in order to prevent one's desires from dominating oneself. What general guidelines can be given we will discuss below when we consider the relation of self-objectification and nature. Two points, however, should be urged here. Firstly, self-determination is not necessarily compromised by the fact that we act according to our desires or needs. The ends or purposes of such desires and needs are *ours*, not alien intruders. Only when such desires or needs become 'abnormal' due to insufficiently developed material circumstances would one's self-determination be compromised. Secondly, Marx does not conclude from the preceding as some self-realizationist theories have concluded, that we must speak about a false or bad self against which our good or ideal self must struggle. The mere fact that we may find ourselves struggling against an imperious desire of ours does not imply that we must distinguish two antagonistic selves in a person.[13]

III

Self-determination and self-objectification, or the fulfillment of one's desires, capacities and talents, are, thus, inherently connected for Marx. However, freedom as self-determination requires more than a person's control and direction of his self-objectification. It also requires that in self-objectification one develops his desires, capacities and talents. An appreciation for the plausibility of this requirement can be gained by again comparing Marx's views with the bourgeois view of freedom. It is compatible with bourgeois freedom that one did nothing, that one remained alone, tranquilly sitting on a stool looking at a blank wall. Such a person would be doing what he wanted — which was doing absolutely nothing — and would not be harming anybody. The question is whether he is free. Of course he is free, if one judges solely by the bourgeois definition. The point of the example, however, is to place this definition in question. What if that person wanted to do nothing else at all? What indeed, if the person were chained to his chair but loved his chains and simply wanted to keep looking at the wall? This is all rather implausible, of course, but nothing in the bourgeois definition makes it implausible. He is still free because he is doing exactly what he wants while not harming anybody. It is the implausibility of calling a person in such situations free that Marx's view of freedom responds to. Surely a person who does nothing which can be said to develop or fulfill his capacities, who is content to live in leg-irons, harming no one, has restricted his desires and the fulfillment of his potentialities to the bare minimum. What explains, we immediately wonder, this self-imposed restriction or confinement of his self-objectification? How is it, to use Marx's terms above, that this one desire to stare at a blank wall, to remain a prisoner or slave, has obtained such exclusive power over him that he wants nothing else? That we raise these questions and have these doubts about such behavior indicates that we believe that the self-determination of such a person is somehow impaired. Accordingly, if freedom is indeed linked with self-determination as the bourgeois concept of freedom itself allows, then the development of one's desires and capacities does seem plausibly to have a place in an account of freedom. Marx's notion of freedom openly recognizes and incorporates this point. It is for this reason that we find passages such as the following in Marx:

> 'Tranquility' appears [to Adam Smith] as the adequate state, as identical with 'freedom' and 'happiness.' It seems quite far from Smith's mind that the individual, 'in his normal state of health,

strength, activity, skill, facility,' also needs a normal portion of work, and of the suspension of tranquility. Certainly, labor obtains its measure from the outside, through the aim to be attained and the obstacles to be overcome in attaining it. But Smith has no inkling whatever that this overcoming of obstacles is in itself a liberating activity — and that, further, the external aims become posited as aims which the individual himself posits — hence, as self-realisation, objectification of the subject, hence real freedom. (*Grund.*, 611)

Freedom, or self-determination, then, is not incompatible with the fulfillment of one's desires, capacities, and talents. It is, however, incompatible with their non-fulfillment.

But which desires and potentialities is the free person to fulfill as part of his self-objectification? Further, to what extent or degree must they be developed or fulfilled? The bourgeois view is that the free person may fulfill whichever desires and potentialities he wants, and to the extent he wants, in so far as fulfilling them does not harm others. Marx rejects this view. Not only is such a view compatible, as we have seen, with one who would limit his desires to those of an oyster, but also the desires a person has may in fact degrade, demean, and impoverish him mentally and physically. The self-realizationist account of Marx is quite different. Its answer seems to be that we must 'fully' develop *all* our desires and potentialities. And doubtlessly it is correct that Marx himself never tires of urging man, as part of his self-determination, to develop fully all his desires, capacities and talents. Accordingly, Ollman, for example, claims that in communist society 'man's productive activity engages *all* his powers and creates ever widening opportunities for their fulfillment.'[14] But is this possible or even plausible? Ollman and many others, at least, write as if it were possible. According to Ollman, Marx holds that under communism, i.e. when man is free, he will be able to concentrate harder and longer, he will do all work with the ease of an expert, and he will be the master of all trades.[15] Surely, however, such a view is preposterous, romantic and silly. Even if one could really maintain such a view with a straight face, there are a number of obvious problems. One such problem, it would seem, which such a view must confront is that no one can develop 'fully' *all* his desires and capacities, since some of them will conflict. Further, simply the time and energy which the development of some potentialities requires will exclude the development of other potentialities. It is hard to imagine a person *fully* developing not only his potentialities as a pianist, but also his potentialities as a nuclear physicist, underwater explorer, not to mention those of father or mother and community leader. Finally, since one cannot develop all of one's capacities and talents one would have to employ some (moral) criterion to determine which ones to fulfill. It was just such a task, however, that the self-realizationist criterion was supposed to supply. Hence, the self-realizationist interpretation of Marx's view of freedom is not to be embraced.

Marx does not, however, have to be read as urging us to perform the contradictory and impossible tasks to which self-realizationist interpretations commit him. Clearly, he does not believe that each person should indiscriminately develop simply any and every desire, capacity, or talent he has. For example, one's capacity to harm others is not to be developed. Thus, Marx must indicate the basis on which we may decide which characteristics of humans are or are not to be developed, as well as how we may interpret the notion of 'fully develop' so as to be a plausible notion.

What general guidelines Marx uses to determine which desires, capacities, and talents are to be fully developed as part of one's self-determination we shall see later (cf. sections V to IX). Supposing the success of these guidelines, that is supposing we could determine which desires and potentialities are compatible with freedom, there remains the problem of interpreting 'fully develop' in some plausible manner. Marx does not, I believe, have to be understood as claiming that each person must develop whichever desires and potentialities our criterion will pick out to the same 'full' or complete extent. There are two steps required to explicate the way in which Marx might restrict, or envision limits to, their development.

Firstly, Marx might object to the implicit understanding of 'fully develop' which has been used in the preceding discussion. It has been assumed that 'fully develop' implies the unending, ever extendable, fulfillment or development of a desire, capacity, or talent which one might have. It was because of this interpretation of 'fully develop' that Marx's view was said to require impossible feats of development. But why assume that Marx held such a view? It would be more in line with the Greek and Hegelian influences on Marx's thought, as well as other aspects of his view of freedom, to assume that by 'fully develop' he meant the greatest development or realization of one's desires, capacities, and talents which was compatible, or harmonious, with certain limits set by one's own determination of the hierarchy of one's needs and interests. Plato, for example, maintains that each aspect of oneself is to be developed only within certain limits. Just as the good musician does not ever continue to tighten the strings of his lyre, so the fully moral person knows that there is a certain limit or measure which must be striven for in each of the aspects of his life.[16] Similarly, Hegel condemns as 'bad infinity' the notion of endless development. Surely Marx too did not mean by 'all-sided development' that one endlessly developed one's desires and potentialities. He may well recognize that people differ in their desires, capacities, and talents in various ways. Individuals may have certain talents and abilities which may be of predominant interest to them. Thus a person might wish to concentrate on these, relating his other abilities and talents to those which are more central to himself, or more highly valued by himself. Just as a piece of music can be wholly developed and worked out in which some themes are more developed than others, so too certain aspects of a person may be more developed than others in a person who has fully developed himself.

Marx opposes, it is true, the narrow development of humans due to the division of labor. He did expect that people when freed of the coercion, the lack of freedom, which typified their lives would develop themselves more widely and more generally than they previously had been able to do. Marx's comments on the all-sided development of individuals are directly correspondent with this point. However, since what he was primarily opposed to was the *forced* or *coerced* narrowness of past human development, the lack of self-control one had over one's self-objectification, it would be compatible with his views if one concentrated on certain areas in which one was particularly talented, gifted, or in which one had particular desires. This is the point which the following notorious passage makes:

> For as soon as the division of labour comes into being, each man has a particular, exclusive sphere of activity, which is forced upon him and from which he cannot escape. He is a hunter, a fisherman, a shepherd, or a critical critic, and must remain so if he does not want to lose his means of livelihood; whereas in communist society, where nobody has one exclusive sphere of activity but each can become accomplished in any branch he wishes, society regulates the general production and thus makes it possible for me to do one thing today and another tomorrow, to hunt in the morning, fish in the afternoon, rear cattle in the evening, criticise after dinner, just as I have a mind, without ever becoming hunter, fisherman, shepherd or critic. (*MECW*, 5:47)

The concrete totality of one's desires and potentialities which are realized in one's self-objectification is to be one's own determination. Thus, that which counted as 'fully developed' on the above interpretation (i.e. endless development) might be counted as 'over-developed'

97

on Marx's actual view. Consequently, Marx need not be understood as urging the impossible (the limitless) development of the various aspects of a person.

A second consideration indicates not merely other ways in which Marx is not committed by his concept of freedom to the limitless development of human desires and potentialities, but also why he does require a certain level of development of one's desires, capacities, and talents. As we have noted, the bourgeois concept of freedom is a political concept. As such one is free or not independently of questions about man's relation to nature. Marx's concept of freedom, we have noted, is much broader. One cannot be free, according to Marx, independently of certain relations to nature. According to Marx, nature 'first confronts man as a completely alien all-powerful and unassailable force' (*MECW*, 5:44). Because of man's undeveloped mastery of nature, his undeveloped material conditions, nature dominates man. It overawes him and determines him like a capricious tyrant. Thus, nature has constrained human life and action in two ways. Firstly, nature's powers and resources, either by their overwhelming presence or by their woeful lack, have inhibited the fulfillment of human purposes. Secondly, nature's powers and resources have also constrained human life by their fortuitous occurrences. Fortuity, or chance, has particularly characterized the early stages of human development. The fixing and the fulfillment of human purposes and ends waited upon the whims of impersonal forces. Accordingly, Marx maintains that individuals can be self-determining only after they have mastered the forces of nature. Man must develop his desires, capacities and talents in this basic realm in order to be self-determining and free. Thus the extent of one's self-objectification is not simply a matter of capricious desire. The implicit criterion is one of the determination and control of one's objectification.

Once again, however, some have held that, for Marx, self-determination implies that nature must be 'wholly tamed and humanised.'[17] Surely, however, it is implausible that man's desires and potentialities must be developed to the extent that man can tame the tides, control the wind, and direct all natural forces which impinge on him. Otherwise, Marx's own expectations that communism, and hence freedom, might be established even in the nineteenth century, would hardly be intelligible. And indeed, Marx does *not* insist that some 'total mastery of nature' is necessary for freedom, or self-determination. Instead, he claims 'a great increase in productive power, a high degree of development' is needed (*MECW*, 5:48). Later he claims that communism requires 'the advanced stage of modern productive forces' (*MECW*, 5:80). Nowhere does he claim that the self-determination, or

98

freedom, which will characterize communism requires extravagant, impossible, advances in the mastery of nature. Nevertheless, it remains true that the development of the forces of production (and hence, mastery of the forces of nature) was absolutely crucial to Marx's views. Without such a basis communism is a hopeless ideal, a mere phantasy.

What, then, does Marx's notion of self-determination imply for man's relation to nature? To begin with, I do not believe it is possible in any specific way to say how much control over nature Marx thought was needed in order to say that man was self-determining. Surely Marx does not have to say that the frustration by nature of any idle wish which an individual or even a society might have implies a lack of self-determination and consequently a lack of freedom. Man has always wished to fly exactly like the birds — but the fact that nature cannot be so manipulated that individuals grow wings and fly is not a constraint on human or individual self-determination. Self-determination, if it is to be anything more than an empty phantasy, must allow for distinctions between what it is possible and what it is not possible to determine or control.

We can, however, in general indicate the degree of control which man must be able to exercise over nature by pointing to several conditions of self-determination (and hence freedom) which such control would fulfill. Marx clearly assumes that fulfillment of these conditions does not require a total mastery of nature. On the other hand, he also assumes that fulfillment of these conditions would require a significant development of each individual's desires, capacities, and talents. Firstly, man must be able to control nature to the extent that his basic needs may be satisfied (cf. *MECW*, 6:353). Self-determination and freedom do not rest well on an empty stomach. The lack of normal satisfaction of desires we have seen to be one reason for desires becoming imperious and dominating a person. Indeed, a fundamental reason for the social, political — as well as religious — constraints which have until now restricted human freedom and self-determination relates to the lack of satisfaction of basic human needs. Secondly, freedom requires that man must be able to control nature to the extent that he can reduce to a minimum the labor he must perform to fulfill those needs. Thus Marx refers to 'the free development of individualities, and hence . . . the general reduction of the necessary labor of society to a minimum which then corresponds to the artistic, scientific, etc. development of the individuals in the time set free, and with the means created, for all of them (*Grund.*, 706).

Thirdly, man must have that degree of control over nature which would allow the abolition of social institutions such as private property,

99

the division of labor, the state, and classes — institutions which have hitherto acted as constraints on human action (*MECW*, 5:438-9). In short, Marx also employs a social criterion as a standard to determine how much control man must exercise over nature. There are two implications to this point which require emphasis and elaboration.

On the one hand, the close relation between individual self-determination and the self-determination which groups of individuals (or man) may be said to have should be emphasized here. Obviously, a society may control nature in a way that a particular individual could not. This indicates the importance of the group, in Marx's eyes, for the individual and explains why he speaks of 'man' as often as particular individuals. Individuals can be self-determining only within a community, since it is only within a community that nature may be controlled and directed to individual purposes. Only within the community can the wide range of alternatives be created which would allow individuals effectively to realize their various purposes and ends. Self-determination, then, cannot be simply an individual matter. However, to ensure that the wide range of possibilities for individual self-determination which social control of nature creates are extended to individuals, self-determination requires joint determination and control of human relations and productive forces with others. Self-determination is not at the expense of the self-determination of others. Indeed (as we will see in section VII) the necessary relation of one person to another is an important part of Marx's views on community.

On the other hand, self-determination requires that we distinguish between natural forces and those forces or powers which are social, even though they appear to be natural and beyond human control. Marx ever emphasizes his view that our relations with other people tend to become independent of our control and viewed as unalterable natural forces. Social relations take on a life of their own; as such, they determine the individuals who live under them, rather than are determined by those individuals. As a result, in such relations individuals are subservient to chance (cf. *MECW*, 5:438) rather than self-directed. A typical formulation of this view is Marx's claim that people often take the relations in which they exist with other people as kinds of natural relations, that is, they take them to be given by nature. Master-slave, lord-serf, capitalist-proletarian have each, in its own epoch, been proclaimed 'natural relations.' Consequently, people have viewed them as relations over which they have and can have no control or say. Similarly, the relation of supply and demand is said to be a natural relation which allots to some, but not to others, the very means of existence. As such it is a relation which determines humans, but cannot be determined by them. Likewise, with the system of private property one's life activities are not 'voluntarily, but naturally divided;' 'the cooperation of individuals is not voluntary but has come about naturally, not as their united power, but as an alien force existing outside them, of the origin and goal of which they are ignorant, which they thus cannot control' (*MECW*, 5:48). Accordingly, when Marx claims that people take various relations to be 'natural' or that a good many human relations have come about 'naturally,' his use of 'natural' differs from the current or popular use of 'natural,' which has positive connotations. Marx's use of 'natural' or 'naturally' in such cases is negative. It connotes an unconscious, involuntary – or at least not a rationally planned – occurrence. As a consequence, Marx holds that life within such relations is subject to chance and is not under individual control. Thus, the invisible hand and the impersonal forces of the market, as well as many other institutions of bourgeois society, are condemned by Marx as affronts to one's self-determination, to one's freedom. Far from being natural and uncontrollable, such forces and institutions are historical, human constructions which are amenable to change and control. Accordingly, Marx holds that one is self-determining only to the extent one overcomes such 'natural' conditions and gains control over them. Such conditions must 'lose their character of mere natural necessities and [be] established as purposes which the individual himself fixes' (*Grund.*, 611).

Self-determination, or freedom, then, requires identifying those forces and relations which are amenable to human control and direction – whether they are truly natural forces or relations but still capable of being mastered, or whether they only seem to be natural and as social or historical forces and relations can be mastered. Thus, self-determination implies a knowledge and understanding of the nature of one's life conditions and relations, how they arose and how they operate. Self-determination cannot be measured in terms of just any purposes the individual might fix for himself, since the individual might be falsely conscious of himself and his relations. Accordingly, self-determination involves individual control of one's affairs in light of a rational understanding of the situation in which one lives and the nature of the processes underlying that situation. Those who live under capitalism may believe that they are self-determining and free, but in reality they are not. This is true not only of the proletarian but also the capitalist. Since communism, on the other hand, will supposedly offer to people practical everyday relations which are 'perfectly intelligible and reasonable relations with regard to his fellow men and to Nature' (*Capital*, I:79), communism allows for individual self-determination.

101

Further, since under communism social relations will be under the joint control of the members of society and since nature will be controlled to the extent this is necessary, man will be self-determining and free.

IV

Now freedom and self-determination are realized within different segments of one's life, e.g. within one's production and daily concerns as well as at times when one is released from such considerations. During the former, one 'must wrestle with Nature to satisfy wants, to maintain and reproduce life' (*Capital*, III:819). As such, life — and this is true under all possible modes of production — remains rooted in necessity. Freedom in this portion of one's life

> can only consist in socialised man, the associated producers, rationally regulating their interchange with Nature, bringing it under their common control, instead of being ruled by it as by the blind forces of Nature; and achieving this with the least expenditure of energy and under conditions most favorable to, and worthy of, their human nature. (*Capital*, III:819)

Accordingly, one's self-determination and freedom in this realm are limited in a way in which they are not when one is released from the determination 'by necessity and mundane considerations.' In this latter realm, which Marx calls 'the true realm of freedom,' that development of human energy which is an end in itself (*Capital*, III:819) may occur. This does not, however, introduce a new sense of 'freedom,' rather it simply identifies a realm in which the freedom which people enjoy under communism is realized in a 'purer form.' An animal, as Marx notes in the *Economic and Philosophic Manuscripts*, 'produces only under the dominion of immediate physical need, whilst man produces even when he is freed from physical need and only truly produces in freedom therefrom' (*MECW*, 3:276). The fact that man partakes of both realms does not mean that he is divided between two senses of freedom. In both realms one is free to the extent one is self-determining. It simply is the case that such self-determination can be more fully realized in certain periods of one's daily life than at other times.

This view is not only plausible but compatible with other aspects of Marx's views on self-determination and freedom. Popper, on the contrary, uses the passages cited in the preceding paragraph as the basis for his claim that Marx 'identifies the realm of freedom with that of man's mental life.'[18] This interpretation is wholly implausible. On the one hand, the above passages would have to be twisted beyond recognition to support such a view. On the other hand, Popper's interpretation is incompatible with Marx's other basic views, e.g. his notion of self-objectification discussed above. Freedom, Marx is quite clear, is not to be identified with 'the emancipation from the flesh;'[19] rather, it is to be identified with one's self-determination — something one may realize more or less completely in different parts of one's daily life. Is it regrettable that this characterizes human life?[20] I suspect that Marx would simply say it is a fact of human life which cannot be avoided and as such is neither to be regretted nor condemned. One achieves self-determination and self-objectification in *both* realms. Indeed, one can only speak of such a 'true realm of freedom' to the extent one abstracts from the whole of one's daily life and considers only those parts in which we are not engaged in necessary labor. Realistically (and holistically) considered, we remain free and self-determining even when we consider ourselves within the 'limitation' of necessary labor in a communist society. 'The true realm of freedom . . . can blossom forth only with this realm of necessity as its basis' (*Capital*, III:819) — but the tree which supports the blossom (to use Marx's metaphor) is itself a tree of freedom. The point to insist on, then, is that the kind of freedom, or self-determination, which constitutes communism is attainable even without the ever greater extensions to which that kind of freedom and self-determination are susceptible.

Marx's account of self-determination, then, so far as we have proceeded, is uncommon, or particularly Marxist, in a number of ways. Firstly, its broad view of those things which may impinge on one's self-determination, e.g. nature, the division of labor, and private property, distinguishes it from the bourgeois concept of freedom. Secondly, though freedom, for Marx, has connections with traditional views of freedom from constraint or coercion, it differs from such accounts in that it emphasizes the importance of self-control, of rational self-control, over one's affairs. The usual account of bourgeois freedom is stated in terms of being able to do what one wants. Questions of one's understanding of one's relations, thus, do not so readily arise. Thirdly, Marx's account of freedom is richer than other accounts in that it goes beyond the requirements that there be no obstacles to doing what one wants. It implies the development of one's own peculiar totality of desires, capacities, and talents. There is simply no credible evidence in Marx to suggest that he identified freedom with one's mental or spiritual life or with 'the emancipation from the flesh.' Fourthly, freedom also requires one's participation in a community and hence the joint determination of what it is that one does. Freedom, that is, is not simply a personal matter but also a social affair. Thus, Marx's account of self-determination is, at the same time, part of his account of the concept of democracy. The social relations and relations of authority which are part of such an account do not compromise one's self-determination or one's freedom. Thus, certain 'limits' on one's self-determination must be accepted. Specifically, the ever-present necessity of material production and the organization of society's forces for material production act as justified limits to one's self-determination. However, to the extent that these limits are encountered within a community and are themselves rationally defensible, they are not so much limits, or restraints, on one's self-determination as conditions for it. In short, self-determination does not require setting one's own purposes without any conditions or bounds. The non-fulfillment of idle wishes, we have indicated, does not hinder self-determination. Nor does the fact that one lives within a society or community with other individuals which involves following certain rules. The notion that the hermit or savage is truly self-determining is an idle, romantic notion. Fifthly, freedom is *the* cardinal virtue of Marx's ethics. It is not simply a power or an ability to do certain things, nor is it a principle of action or set of rights. Rather, Marx's treatment of freedom is best understood as the characterization of a kind of life, a way of being, which we morally ought to realize. He urges us, at this historical juncture, to 'Be free!' This requires one's self-development or self-objectification to an extent determined by one's own desires within the constraint that this development enables one to rationally and essentially direct one's activities with and relations to other people, social institutions, and natural forces. As such, it seems mistaken to regard Marx's ethics as a self-realizationist ethics.

Finally, how significant is the preceding account of self-determination as an aspect of freedom and Marx's ethics in general? Might someone not object that the preceding (partial) account of freedom 'is empty for it fails to provide [a person] with guidance as to how he ought to act?'[21] Those such as Ollman and Kamenka who hold that freedom is a descriptive notion for Marx would supposedly not be disturbed by such an objection.[22] However, Chapter 3 has argued that Marx's ethics may be of a normative nature. Accordingly, one would expect his moral views to offer some guidance. Now, in one sense, it is true that the present account of freedom as self-determination does not provide one with guidance how one should act. That is, *assuming* the situation is such that one may rationally direct one's acts, etc., then the self-determination aspect of freedom does not tell one further what one should do or how to decide that question. But this is quite in line with the view defended here that Marx's ethics is an ethics of virtue.

Nevertheless, it does not follow that the preceding account of freedom is therefore empty. Far from it, for it tells one to change situations in which this is not the case — and this is significantly not the case under capitalism. Indeed, much of Marx's argument is to reveal how people are captives of their own relations and activities, so that they cannot fulfill the above directives. Marx's accounts of exchange-value, private property, the division of labor, etc., are all attempts to show how the relations within which people live constrain and force them to live in the way that they do — that they cannot freely choose how to live because of these relations. It is no empty directive then to be told to change these relations! The acceptance of Marx's account of self-determination would have significant implications for most societies.

V

The discussion of freedom or self-determination has so far emphasized the relation of these notions to one's own self-objectification. Other people and nature have only played the role of means to the end of one's self-objectification and self-determination. However, Marx insists that to be free, one's self-objectification must not treat other people and nature simply as means or as indifferent, abstract objects of one's will. Rather, one must live in concrete, communal relations with others and with nature. There are two aspects to this claim. Firstly, Marx claims that a person is free only when his interactions with other people and nature take place in terms of the concrete and individual qualities of oneself as well as the other people and nature involved. Secondly, one's relations with other people must be characterized by a harmony of interests. The first point we will consider in the present section; the latter point we will consider in sections VII to IX. Both these aspects of the above claim provide content to Marx's views on freedom as self-determination. They impose various limitations or conditions on a person's self-objectification for it to be an instance of self-determination.

Marx states the first point in various ways and places. For example, he urges that 'every one of your relations to men and to nature . . . [be] a *specific expression* corresponding to the object of your will, of your *real individual* life' (*MECW*, 3:326). Again, he urges that 'the *manner* in which they [i.e., various objects] become *his* depends on the *nature of the objects* and on the nature of the *essential power* corresponding to *it*; for it is precisely the *determinate nature* of this relationship which shapes the particular, *real* mode of affirmation' (*MECW*, 3:301). In contrast, capitalist society culminates in a set of relationships which concern not the concrete qualities, the use-values, produced or owned, but the amount of human labor in the abstract (the exchange value) which is embodied in whatever is produced or owned. Under capitalism, the (exchange) value of objects appears to be yet another property quite like the other natural properties they possess as use-values. It is not seen that the exchange values of products are not natural relations of one object to another, but social relations of producers to producers. As a consequence, personal relations between individuals become disguised and separated from them under the shape of the social relations between their products. Further, personal relations are understood in terms of abstract, symbolic characteristics. Thus, activities and relations in which one objectifies oneself are not understood or judged in terms of their own concrete qualities but in terms of secondary, abstract qualities.

How are we to understand this aspect of freedom? What does it mean to claim that in one's self-objectification one should treat other people and things according to their concrete and individual qualities? What is it for one's relations to men and nature to be a specific expression, corresponding to the object of one's will, of one's real individual life? Further, how is it that such relations are part of freedom? These questions are rarely asked in accounts of Marx's view of freedom.

To begin with, it might seem strange that freedom and Marx's moral views concern not simply the relations of oneself to others but also to things. However, this should not be so strange if one recalls (cf. section III) that nature or things may, according to Marx, dominate a person's life, as well as that (cf. Chapter 3), for Marx, 'the thing itself is an *objective* human relation to itself and to man, and vice versa' (*MECW*, 3:300). That is, objects or things are not to be seen as simply dumb objects, indifferent to humans. Not only may they dominate man, they are also reflections of individuals and their relations to other individuals: 'the object being the direct manifestation of his individuality, is simultaneously his own existence for the other man, the existence of the other man, and that existence for him' (*MECW*, 3:298). Accordingly, when Marx speaks of man's relation to nature he does not speak of some primitive, untouched nature to which man must become attuned. Nature is, at one and the same time, both independent of man and a manifestation of the development of mankind's powers and relations. Thus, man's relation to nature is part and parcel of his relation to man. The two are ultimately inseparable. The answer to the question, then, 'What kind of relation to things or nature is Marx urging as crucial in the objectification of oneself?' is essentially the same whether nature or humans are involved. However, since the relation to humans is more complex, I will look first to his comments on nature.

We have already discussed the issue of man's control or mastery of nature. Rational control of nature is a crucial aspect of human freedom. The issue at stake here is related but different. One is not supposed simply to control nature, but to manifest in one's relation to nature some expression of oneself which corresponds in some sense to nature. Now obviously Marx does not mean that if one wishes to develop mineral deposits one must make oneself mineral-like; nor is he saying that one has to be tree-like if one is to harvest the forests. Marx's idea, though somewhat obscurely stated, is not simply silly. Rather, he holds that the proper relation of oneself to an object, to nature, involves 'relat[ing] oneself] to the *thing* for the sake of the thing' (*MECW*, 3:300). Marx means by this that we are to grasp, in our relations, the aesthetic qualities of objects and nature. Marx claims in a well-known passage:

> The *sense* caught up in crude practical need has only a *restricted* sense. For the starving man, it is not the human form of food that exists, but only its abstract existence as food. It could just as well be there in its crudest form, and it would be impossible to say wherein this feeding activity differs from that of *animals*. The care-burdened, poverty-stricken man has no *sense* for the finest play; the dealer in minerals sees only the commercial value but not the beauty and the specific character of the mineral: he has no mineralogical sense. (*MECW*, 3:302)

That is, to relate properly to objects or to nature involves relating to them aesthetically, for the aesthetic relation considers the sensuous, concrete, and individual aspects of the object. The world of objects, of nature, is not merely to be related to as an object of utility or for various abstract characteristics it might have acquired. That this is how people presently view things is a result of private property: 'Private property has made us so stupid and one-sided that an object is only *ours* when we have it — when it exists for us as capital, or when it is directly possessed, eaten, drunk, worn, inhabited, etc. — in short, when it is *used* by us' (*MECW*, 3:300). Marx's view, though it condemns those relations to things which are merely utility relations, surely does *not* exclude the use of objects for various purposes. Marx is quite clear in these matters. 'Nature,' he says, 'has lost its *mere* utility by use becoming human use' (*MECW*, 3:300).[23] The point is that such utility relations are not the only ones our self-objectification is to realize in our relations with objects and nature. The point is not, as some have suggested, that for Marx freedom is simply an aesthetic state or realm.

One who objectifies himself in his activities on various objects and only sees in those objects their utilities or abstract characteristics has not objectified himself as he should. Man's objectification requires the development in him of sensibilities which make the specific characters of objects stand out for him:

> Just as only music awakens in man the sense of music, and just as the most beautiful music has *no* sense for the unmusical ear — is [no] object for it, because my object can only be the confirmation of one of my essential powers — it can therefore only exist for me insofar as my essential power exists for itself as a subjective capacity; because the meaning of one object for me goes only so far as *my* sense goes . . . — for this reason the *senses* of the social man *differ* from those of the non-social man. . . . The *forming* of the five senses is a labour of the entire history of the world down to the present. (*MECW*, 3:301-2)

However, what is to be the relation between this aesthetic relation to objects and other relations to objects, e.g. those emphasizing the use to be made of objects? Would Marx's view be satisfied if one cast a brief glance at the aesthetic qualities of an object and then proceeded to use or treat that object as before? Obviously not. Since Marx is concerned with the objectification of humans in certain ways, he is concerned with the creation of certain attitudes, dispositions, and ways of seeing reality — not simply with momentary occurrences or individual actions. His concern, rather, is that man's daily and hourly approach to nature and its objects should include an appreciation, an awareness, of the concrete, of the aesthetic, aspects of objects. Such an attitude or approach to reality is an on-going and constant concern.

How this is to be worked out in practice, in an industrial society, is clearly no small question. Certainly, it is a question Marx did not answer in any detail. In general he believed that overcoming bourgeois society's penchant for possession, competition, and the domination of nature for profit or surplus value would constitute important steps towards creating the conditions within which man could live in such a relation to nature. That is, modifications in man's relation to man are an essential condition for promoting the kind of relation Marx envisions between man and nature.

> The eye has become a *human* eye, just as its *object* has become a social *human* object — an object made by man for man. The *senses*

have therefore become directly in their practice theoreticians. They relate themselves to the *thing* for the sake of the thing, but the thing is an objective human relation to itself and to man, and vice versa. Need or enjoyment has consequently lost its *egotistical* nature, and nature has lost its mere *utility* by use becoming *human* use. (*MECW*, 3:300)

There are, that is, reciprocal and mutually supporting relations here. As noted above, man's relation to objects and things is at the same time his relation to other humans. The relation of man to objects, then, not simply for their use but also for the objects themselves means that other humans are not for one simply means to one's own ends, but also beings whose own qualities and demands are appreciated for themselves. Contrariwise, when man relates to objects simply for his use, simply as his private property, man is related to others in an egoistical and in-human manner (*MECW*, 3:298). There is, then, in the aesthetic (or human) relation to objects and nature, and hence to humans, a univer-salizing element which overcomes the one-sided and egoistic relation which the utility, or private property, relation suggests to Marx. The manner in which one relates to objects, and thereby humans, depends on the specific characters of those objects and humans. They are not merely seen but perceived, not simply heard but listened to. There are granted a voice, as it were, in the determination of one's activities and self-objectification. They are not simply indifferent material on which one imposes one's will. One who objectifies himself in this manner con-cretely develops his own qualities and characteristics.

VI

One's self-objectification occurs directly in one's relations with other people as well as through their mutual relations to objects and to nature. What do Marx's claims about self-objectification mean in the former case? What does it mean to say that your relations to other people should be 'a *specific expression*, corresponding to the object of your will, of your *real individual life*?' To begin with, the normative import of such passages must be insisted on. Marx's statements do not merely relate how man's qualities do, in fact, exchange for each other. He is not simply saying, matter of factly, that (for example) 'if an indi-vidual wants love — if love is the object of his will — then he must exchange for it a specific expression of his personality which corre-sponds to what he wants, namely love.'[24] His point is not simply that 'it is possible to be loved only if one loves,'[25] since surely that is false. There are occasions when one is loved even though one does not love.

Rather, Marx is saying something about how human qualities should, morally should, exchange for one another, how human beings should relate to one another in their self-objectification. A better interpretation of Marx's comments above would be that he is claiming that one should treat others as one would have others treat oneself. Thus viewed, Marx's comments that 'one can exchange love only for love, trust for trust, etc.' would be intelligible. The problem with this interpretation is that it says nothing about the nature of one's own qualities or the qualities which characterize the other person with whom one interacts in one's self-objectification. It would be compatible with this interpretation that people related to one another on the basis of abstract, symbolic qualities such as money, etc. However, Marx is not suggesting this. As such, he is not simply giving an up-dated version of the Golden Rule.

Marx himself indicates that his central concern here focuses on the 'general confounding and confusing of all things . . . the confounding and confusing of all natural and human qualities' (*MECW*, 3:326) that takes place due to various institutions, such as money and private property. Under the influence of such institutions people do not relate to themselves and each other in terms of their own real, concrete qualities. Instead, they relate to each other in terms of powers which are unrelated, essentially, to those qualities and even nullify the significance of such particular qualities.

> Thus what I *am* and *am capable of* is by no means determined by my individuality. I *am* ugly, but I can buy for myself the *most beautiful* women. Therefore I am not *ugly*, for the effect of *ugliness* — its deterrent power — is nullified by money. I, according to my individual characteristics, am *lame*, but money furnishes me with twenty-four feet. Therefore I am not lame. I am bad, dishonest, unscrupulous, stupid, but money is honoured, and hence its possessor. Money is the supreme good, therefore its possessor is good. Money, besides, saves me the trouble of being dishonest: I am therefore presumed honest. I am *brainless*, but money is the *real brain* of all things and how then should its possessor be brainless? (*MECW*, 3:324)

Now Marx is not saying here that the lame must remain lame, that the ugly shall do nothing to change their appearance. It does not follow from this passage that individuals could not take advantage of science and technology to overcome physical, as well as other, handicaps. Marx was ever quick to praise the importance and value of science, industry, technology, and machinery. He repeatedly claimed that development of the forces of production, new developments in machinery and technology, positively advanced man's self-objectification. Thus, he claimed that 'the history of *industry* and the *objective* existence of industry and the *open* book of *man's essential powers*, the perceptibly existing human psychology' (*MECW*, 3:302). Accordingly, Marx distinguishes between such universal abstract powers as money and the powers inherent in technology and machinery which are extensions of man's own characteristics. The latter but not the former may be used to change one's situation. What, then, is the point of the above passage?

The thrust of the above passage is that what a person is and is capable of should be determined by his individuality. Marx mentions, in this passage, the following as characteristics of one's 'individuality:' a person's looks, his individual (physical) mobility, integrity, and intelligence. 'Individuality' is used here in the sense of what makes one particular, i.e. different from others. It is not simply used in the sense of one's personality or character. It is, rather, the whole complex of characteristics that define a person as this particular person to whom Marx is referring. Marx is concerned that these specific characteristics in their relations to other people are mediated by something such as money which has the power of nullifying them, of transforming them into their contraries.

As in the case of man's relation to nature, Marx holds that one objectifies oneself properly only if one develops one's own individual qualities correspondent to those which one seeks in others, or which one claims to possess in one's relations with others. However, in the case of humans, one is not simply to give regard to the aesthetic qualities, but to the personal and moral qualities of the person to whom one seeks to relate. If I want trust from another, then I should myself be trustworthy; if I seek helpfulness, love, kindness, I myself should be helpful, loving, kind. If I seek to influence other people, I must myself have a stimulating and encouraging effect on others. On the other hand, if I seek to be accepted as clever, intelligent, brave, or honest, then I must develop in myself these qualities and not simply possess them vicariously by other powers or means. On the basis of my own individual characteristics I must develop myself such that my relations to others express my real individual life as it relates to the object of my will.

Now the intuitive idea here is fairly clear. Marx holds that people ought to relate to each other on the basis of their own individual

111

characteristics, rather than on the basis of characteristics and powers which do not essentially relate to them. We object to the person who flaunts his money or property, and seeks to relate to others on such a basis. We want to know what others are like behind their extravagant masks. We do not want to be offered, in our personal relations, money for our thoughts, but to share thoughts. We do not want a stand-in servant's help as an expression of someone else's helpfulness, but that someone else's own efforts. We want our attempts to secure relationships in which we offer our own individualities to be met with corresponding offers of the other's individuality. When the relations between people are such that the people involved do not manifest in themselves, or reciprocate, the qualities they seek in others, but attempt to command the qualities of others by other abstract means, such as money, the relation is felt to be wrong, mistaken, imperfect. Thus, Marx demands that a person be what he claims to be, that he has in himself qualities correspondent to those he seeks in others.

But what is the relation of such views to freedom? Marx's position is that the one who mediately objectifies himself by abstract powers does not have to develop his own qualities, as required by the object of his will. Instead, a universal and abstract power (e.g. money) is invoked which eliminates the need for one's actions and relations to be bound to one's individuality or take cognizance of the specific nature of the other person. In that situation, I am like the master in Hegel's master-slave dialectic. I do not essentially experience the realization or objectification of myself. Rather I know the realization of something else. There is no longer self-determination, but other-determination of the self. That which does my bidding becomes more fully developed than I do because of its actions on the world and with others.

> Everything which the political economist takes from you in life and humanity, he replaces for you in *money* and in *wealth*; and all the things which you cannot do, your money can do. It can eat and drink, go to the dance hall and the theater; it can travel, it can appropriate art, learning, the treasures of the past, political power — all this it *can* appropriate for you — it can buy all this: it is true *endowment*.

Why is this situation to be condemned? Marx continues: 'Yet being all this, it *wants* to do nothing but create itself, buy itself; for everything else is after all its servant' (*MECW*, 3:309). That is, Marx holds that if I do not objectify myself in terms of my own individual qualities, but in terms of abstract, universal powers, I lose control of my objectifications and relations with others. A person who lacks money finds that his demands or needs are ineffective: 'No doubt the *demand* also exists for him who has no money, but his demand is a mere thing of the imagination without effect or existence for me, a third party, for the [others], and which therefore remains even for me unreal and objectless' (*MECW*, 3:325). Indeed, if money (or other such powers) mediates my relations with others, *it* becomes the bond between people, not the particular needs and characteristics of the people related. 'The need for money,' says Marx, 'is therefore the true need produced by the economic system, and it is the only need which the latter produces. . . . [It] reduces everything to its abstract form' (*MECW*, 3:307). Thus, one person does not need another person, but needs money. Hence, that which is the bond between people does not so much unite them as separate them. The effect of objectifying oneself on the basis of money, then, is that money becomes the bond between people, a bond which takes on a life of its own, separating people from each other and rendering them incapable of determining their own affairs and activities. Objectification through such abstract powers, thus, negates the realization of one's own individual characteristics or the determination of one's relationships on their basis.

Accordingly, in one's relations to one's work, others, and nature, one's self-objectification must ever proceed from one's concrete and individual qualities. If one wants or desires, for whatever reason, someone or something, one must either be or develop oneself such that one's own qualities are correspondent to those qualities one seeks or demands in another person or thing. Certainly, this does not guarantee that one's wants or desires will always be fulfilled. One can love and not be loved: 'If you love without evoking love in return − that is, if your loving as loving does not produce reciprocal love; if through a *living expression* of yourself as a loving person you do not make yourself a *beloved one*, then your love is impotent − a misfortune' (*MECW*, 3:326). Marx does not claim that communism will solve the problem of unrequited love − though it is not unlikely that he would claim that communism would reduce this problem. However, to live such that one's qualities correspond to those one seeks in others and other things would guarantee the elimination of one of the major 'bonds' between people which render people's demands, based on their needs and passions, ineffective. It would also eliminate the abstract, imperfect realization of one's desires and potentialities. Thus, objectification of oneself on the basis of one's own qualities is not only itself characteristic of freedom, but is one way to ensure that one's objectification does not escape one's control. Hence, such self-objectification is but another way of characterizing one's freedom.

There is yet another connection between Marx's views on one's relations to nature and to people and his views on freedom which should be noted. Knowledge of the truth and being free have been closely related historically. For Marx, however, it is not simply knowledge of the truth, but a relation to other people and things in light of their real or true qualities which freedom requires. When one objectifies oneself on the basis of one's own needs and powers, as well as those of other people and objects, one's objectification is one's own, and not that of some other power or thing. 'It is only when the objective world becomes everywhere for man in society the world of man's essential powers — human reality, and for that reason the reality of his *own* essential powers — that all *objects* become for him the *objectification* of himself, become objects which confirm and realise his individuality' (*MECW*, 3:301). Now the relation of both (or all) members of a relation on the basis of their own, real qualities is a relation in which reality does not give way to image, in which the characters or individualites of the relata are not distorted. As we saw in Chapter 3, Marx characterizes truth in terms of the notion of reality. Thus, to the extent one objectifies oneself on the basis of one's own real characteristics and those of the objects of one's will, one has 'truly' objectified oneself; one's relations to others and to objects are 'true' relations. And to this extent, one is free — one is free from mystifying powers which negate and transform one's qualities into what they are not. One is free from bonds with others which do not depend on oneself and others. More importantly, one is free in the sense that oneself essentially determines the concrete totality of desires, capacities and talents which constitute one's self-objectification. One's self-objectification is not the realization of the powers and abilities of something else.

Finally, what kind of guidance does this aspect of freedom provide? As characterized above, self-objectification does not prescribe any particular objectification, let alone any specific action. Marx is not out to tell each person what particular life they ought to lead. One of his criticisms of those who attempted to impose censorship on newspaper publications is relevant:

> You admit the delightful variety, the inexhaustible riches of nature.
> You do not demand that the rose should smell like the violet, but
> must the greatest riches of all, the spirit, exist in only *one* variety? I
> am humorous, but the law bids me write seriously. I am audacious,
> but the law commands that my style be modest. *Grey, all grey*, is the
> sole, the rightful colour of freedom. Every drop of dew on which the

sun shines glistens with an inexhaustible play of colours, but the spiritual sun, however many the persons and whatever the objects in which it is refracted, must produce only the *official colour*! (*MECW*, 1:112)

The implication is, I believe, that it would be mistaken, it would be a violation of one's self-determination, if Marx did try to tell each person what particular life he should lead. Marx is not out to prescribe an official color.

Nevertheless, Marx does prescribe the manner in which any instance of objectification should be carried out so that 'the inexhaustible riches of nature' come to light. One must seek to make one's will, one's activities, not only an expression of one's own concrete qualities, but also open to, receptive to, the qualities of the person or object one encounters. As such, some simple directives (which have already been noted) do seem to follow from Marx's position. If I seek love, I have to make myself a loving person; if I seek to influence others, I must make myself interesting and stimulating; if I seek to enjoy art, I must make myself artistically sensitive. However, beyond these rather simple directives Marx also thought that other directions for action followed from his views. For example, the moral necessity of eliminating money, exchange value, wage labor, as well as, in general, private property, he also believed to follow from the preceding account. I do not discuss here either the particular grounds for these beliefs of Marx or the ways in which Marx's views differ from others. Clearly, Marx's views are opposed to the conclusions which others have drawn concerning the implications of freedom for private property, etc. Hegel, for example, held that property was the embodiment of personality,[26] and hence the prohibition of holding private property violated the right of personality.[27] Since freedom, for Hegel, is bound up with the full development of (the human) Spirit, the prohibition of private property also is an encroachment on freedom. However, the differences between Marx and Hegel ought not to be over-emphasized. Marx was not simply opposed to all and any forms of private property. He was opposed to those forms which gave one power and control over others. He was opposed to the several attitudes which were connected with such property, e.g. the attitudes of greed, lust for power, and concern only with those qualities of people and things which were useful for dominating them. Since I am concerned here to display the general value structure which lies behind Marx's condemnation of a variety of features of capitalism, I do not discuss any particular features of Marx's view, for example as they concern private property. Instead, I wish here simply to indicate that the present aspect of Marx's view of freedom does have significant social and individual implications.

Finally, one need not claim or believe that the directives which follow from the above discussion respond to all problems which a person might morally encounter. Other aspects of Marx's account of freedom may be drawn on to answer such problems. However, the above directives, it is clear, do carry significant implications for man and society.

VII

There is a third (and final) aspect of freedom to be considered. Freedom requires the harmonious co-operation and association of one individual with others — it requires the community.

> Only within the community has each individual the means of culti-vating his gifts in all directions; hence personal freedom becomes possible only within the community. In the previous substitutes for the community, in the state, etc. personal freedom has existed only for the individual who developed under the conditions of the ruling class, and only insofar as they were individuals of this class. The illusory community in which individuals have up till now combined always took on an independent existence in relation to them, and since it was the combination of one class over another, it was at the same time for the oppressed class not only a completely illusory community, but a new fetter as well. In the real community the individuals obtain their freedom in and through their association. (*MECW*, 5:78)

Freedom, that is, stands in a twofold relation to the community. On the one hand, the community provides each individual with the means of cultivating his gifts in 'all' directions. The community makes possible, in short, the self-development of individuals which we saw to be an important part of self-determination. The community, accordingly, stands as a means to the end of individual freedom. This aspect of the community we discussed in section III. On the other hand, life in the community is itself part of the realization of freedom. The communal life is, as such, not simply a means to freedom, but also part of the end, part of freedom, itself. The notion of community, then, plays a significant role in Marx's notion of freedom. It is important to determine what Marx meant by 'community' and what connections he saw between community and freedom.

Marx uses the word 'community' in two different senses. Firstly, there is a neutral or descriptive sense in which Marx refers to feudal or primitive communities. Sometimes he refers to the latter as 'the natural community' (*MECW*, 5:90). In this sense 'community' is simply a collection of people living together with various social, historical, and economic bonds. Secondly, there is a normative sense of 'community' to which Marx occasionally refers as 'the real community' and which he contrasts with 'the illusory community' (cf. *MECW*, 5:78). It is this 'real community' which constitutes part of Marx's account of freedom and which is at issue here.

Marx indicates what he means by the 'real community' on two different levels. On the one hand, he tells us a number of things about the nature of personal relations with a (real) community.[28] These features elaborate on the kind of character traits, dispositions and the like which a person would have who was self-determining and hence free. On the other hand, he indicates both positively and negatively various (structural) features of a community. These features appear to be, in part, an implication of his views on the kinds of personal relations which constitute a community. Since the first set of features is basic we will first look to Marx's comments concerning the personal relations of people in a community.

In one set of comments Marx suggests that for a community to exist is for the relations of its members to be such that for each person 'the *other* person as a person has become for him a need' (*MECW*, 3:296; cf. 304). Marx elaborates on the meaning of this claim when he notes that 'the need of a thing [or another] is the most evident, irrefutable proof that the thing belongs to *my* essence, that its being is for me, that its *property* is the property, the peculiarity, of my essence' (*MECW*, 3:218; cf. 228). In short, freedom involves treating others as a necessary part or aspect of one's own nature. By this Marx apparently intends that the other person, and one's society with others, becomes an end, and not merely a means:

> when communist *artisans* associate with one another, theory, propaganda, etc. is their first end. But at the same time, as a result of this association, they acquire a new need — the need for society — and what appears as a means becomes an end. In this practical process the most splendid results are to be observed whenever French socialist workers are seen together. Such things as smoking, drinking, eating, etc., are no longer means of contact or means that bring them together. Association, society and conversation, which again has association as its end, are enough for them; the brotherhood of man

117

is no mere phrase with them, but a fact of life, and the nobility of man shines upon us from their work-hardened bodies. (*MECW*, 3:313)

Such comments, however, do not carry their meaning on their face. The problem is to understand such claims as explications of Marx's notion of community.

One possible interpretation of the above comments is that Marx is suggesting that this communal relation to others entails respecting other's desires, where this means that a person 'regards it as a reason for his doing some action that another would benefit and against his doing it that another would be harmed.'[29] Or, stated more fully and correctly, this might mean that, in respecting the desires of another, one respects 'the desires which the other would have, given full knowledge and reflection, which might not be the same as his actual desires.'[30]

This interpretation of Marx's views on community, however, is inadequate inasmuch as it is fully compatible with a bourgeois sense of community. That is, on this interpretation, the community could simply consist of a kind of altruistic balancing of conflicting and opposed interests. Though one would regard the fulfillment of another's desires as a reason for acting, one might also have contrary reasons for acting due to the conflicting interests of both parties. Thus, we might well simply continue to have civil or bourgeois society, with its conflicting or antagonistic interests and desires. As a consequence, the above suggestion is compatible with a society in which people continued to be members of different classes. The state, then, would be called on to mediate individual interests through various general ends. However, it would not in this way secure freedom for individuals, or constitute itself as a community. Indeed, 'the communal relation into which the individuals of a class [enter], and which [is] determined by their common interest as against a third party, [is] always a community to which these individuals belonged only as average individuals . . . a relation in which they participated not as individuals but as members of a class' (*MECW*, 5:80). The Marxian notion of community, then, is much stronger than the view of community suggested above in which the separate interests of individuals are made compatible by finding ends which maximally fulfill these interests. For the same reason, this aspect of Marx's view of freedom could not be interpreted to require simply that one not harm others. A 'community' of individuals related in such a meager fashion would not be a community of free individuals. It would simply be a collection of atoms which avoided bumping into each other. Marx's notion of community requires much more than respecting the interests of others in either of the above senses.

Instead, the notion of treating others as an end, or as a necessary part of one's own nature — i.e. Marx's view of community — has much more to do with the harmonization or unity (*MECW*, 5:81) of desires and interests among people in the first place — the overcoming of the separation and antagonism between individual interests. It concerns 'the extent to which [a person] in his individual existence is at the same time a social being' (*MECW*, 3:296). A community exists, that is, to the extent that the separateness of individual interests is overcome in the self-conscious realization of individuals that their lives as particular beings reflect and are essentially part of, a larger social and rational order.

> Only when the real, individual man re-absorbs in himself the abstract citizen, and as an individual human being has become a *species-being* in his everyday life, in his particular work, and in his particular situation, only when man has recognised and organised his '*forces propres*' as *social* forces . . . only then will human emancipation have been accomplished (*MECW*, 3:169)

— then does a community, a harmony of interests, exist. How are we to understand these views?

To say that man, as a free or human being, is a social or communal being and, as such, treats others as an essential part of his nature is to indicate a certain harmonious relation which is supposed to exist between people within a community. It is mistaken, however, to think that this implies that there must be the same, intense relation among all people for a community to exist. This harmonious relation would seem to exist on various levels and to various degrees. Thus, on one level Marx emphasizes the identification which may occur between people in human affective relations such as love, mutual enjoyment and delight. For example, Marx claims that under communism 'the senses and enjoyment of other men have become my *own* appropriation' (*MECW*, 3:300). Again, he says that 'insofar as man, and hence also his feeling, etc., is *human* the [sensuous] affirmation of the object by another [e.g., eating, drinking] is likewise his own gratification' (*MECW*, 3:322). On another level, there may be an identification between people in the objectification and expression of themselves in production. That is, my creative or productive activities may not only objectify and affirm myself but also others. Thus, Marx claims:

> Let us suppose that we had carried out production as human beings. Each of us would have *in two ways affirmed* himself and the other

person. 1) In my *production* I would have objectified my individuality, its specific character, and therefore enjoyed not only an individual manifestation of my life during the activity, but also when looking at the object I would have the individual pleasure of knowing my personality to be objective, visible to the senses and hence a power beyond all doubt. 2) In your enjoyment or use of my product I would have the direct enjoyment both of being conscious of having satisfied a human need by my work, that is, of having objectified man's essential nature, and of having thus created an object corresponding to the need of another man's essential nature. 3) I would have been for you the mediator between you and the species, and therefore would become recognised and felt by you yourself as a completion of your own essential nature and as a necessary part of yourself, and consequently would know myself to be confirmed both in your thought and your love. 4) In the individual expression of my life I would have directly created your expression of your life, and therefore in my individual activity I would have directly confirmed and realised my true nature, my human nature, my communal nature. (*MECW*, 3:227-8)

Quite often the above comments from Marx's early writings are held to constitute his final views on human communal relations. Thus, Schacht maintains that Marxian sociality is 'direct and personal.'[31] Ollman too romanticizes human communal relations in his multiple suggestions that such relations are solely characterized by the most intense and personal interrelations.[32] However, if this were the correct interpretation of Marx's views on community, they would surely be, even at the outset, rather implausible. Some people under the proper conditions might be able to relate in the above ways, but that all people even strangers could and would relate in these ways is rather difficult to believe. However, I do not believe that Marx must be said to hold such a romantic view of communism. What we see in the various comments above is Marx's view that a community can be formed, that man can be free, only to the extent that people can and do identify with, or share, various experiences, ends, and activities of other individuals. To the extent one can only identify with his own private needs or desires, a person is neither a member of a community nor free. To treat others as an essential part of oneself is to identify with the needs and desires of others; it is for others to be integrally a part of one's own self-development and self-determination. It is clear, then, that Marx expects a significantly different social consciousness under communism (cf. *MECW*, 6:504). How such a consciousness of oneself and others is to arise is not our present topic. It requires, to be sure, a revolution. Indeed, one of the ends of the revolution is to promote this new consciousness by ridding the antecedent consciousness people have of themselves and others of 'all the muck of [past] ages:'

> Both for the production on a mass scale of this communist consciousness, and for the success of the cause itself, the alteration of men on a mass scale is necessary, an alteration which can only take place in a practical movement, a *revolution*; the revolution is necessary, therefore, not only because the *ruling* class cannot be overthrown in any other way, but also because the class *overthrowing* it can only in a revolution succeed in ridding itself of all the muck of ages and become fitted to found society anew. (*MECW*, 5:52-3)

However, it does not follow that all members of a Marxian community must share the same intense experiences described above. Nor does it follow that they must always be in direct contact with others or that they cannot be allowed to go off by themselves either to work or for other reasons. Marx notes that 'when I am active *scientifically*, etc. − an activity which I can seldom perform in direct community with others − then my activity is [nevertheless] *social*, because I perform it as a *man*' (*MECW*, 3:298). Similarly, it does not follow that Marx's notion of community cannot allow for sub-communities and smaller groups of individuals in which members may experience their communal relations in more intense ways. Marx commended the views of the Paris Commune in which France was to consist of rural communes, of communes in even the smallest hamlet, of various 'united cooperation societies.'[33] Nor does it follow that the harmony or identification which exists amongst members of a community requires or implies the elimination of all differences in interests. Within a community people may still express themselves in different ways and have different interests. Marx's point is that these interests will be harmoniously related and united. They may be different as the notes of a musical chord, and yet still fit together to form a coherent, harmonious, meaningful whole. The unity or harmony of interests then will preserve the particularity of the individual parts: 'The unity of man with man . . . is based on the real differences between men' (*MECW*, 3:354).

Accordingly, it may be expected that in a community the different interests of individuals will harmonize in different ways. It may simply be that some want to do X whereas others want to do Y, where X and Y do not conflict and the doing of X and Y may be activities of mutual affirmation for those doing Y or X. In cases where there is potential conflict because not all who want can do X or Y, or doing X and doing Y may themselves conflict (but assuming that X and Y are compatible with other aspects of Marx's views on freedom), then various procedures might have to be followed depending on the nature and extent of the potential conflict: e.g. community-wide voting or mutually acceptable personal compromises. The extent to which Marx thought such difficulties would arise is unclear. Some might claim that given a harmony of desires and interests conflicts could never arise under communism. This is an optimistic and romantic view. Even brothers and lovers may quarrel. Further, Marx explicitly rejects the idea that a community is some purely loving, communing assemblage of people (*MECW*, 6:44-5). On the other hand, surely Marx intends that the nature of quarrels or conflicts under communism will be significantly different from those witnessed by pre-communist society. The fact that Marx allowed for democratic voting procedures and the reciprocal influence of individuals in their mutual determination of courses of action indicates that Marx clearly did not think that the harmony of people's interests simply takes place spontaneously in all cases. In some instances it does, in others it does not. Similarly, that democratic procedures have a place in the community confirms the claim that Marx did not hold that a harmony of interests entails an identity, an utter sameness, of all interests. Were people's interests all identical, and never in conflict, voting would be unnecessary — one could get the sense of the community by asking any random individual. Thus, it is not surprising that Marx allowed for various democratic procedures as well as positions of authority and leadership in his view of the community. The members of a community jointly participate in the control and direction of the affairs of their community. In so doing they further define and identify the course their interests will take. In addition, in so doing, each one essentially determines the concrete form his own self-objectification is to take. Individuals (and society as a whole) are not the puppets of independent social relations and powers, but jointly determine the nature and directions these relations and powers are to take. As such Marx's account of the community involves his account of democracy.

A communist community is not best compared, then (as some are wont to do), to a colony of ants in which each member spontaneously, but unreflectively and dumbly, does what is needed. Rather, it is a community of reflective, rational beings who perceive themselves not to be divided by their interests but united by those interests. If such claims seem exaggerated, they merely reveal the extent to which Marx believed that the source of social antagonism and disharmony amongst individuals' interests could be eliminated by social revolution.

VIII

Since individuals may have different interests, since they might disagree and even quarrel under communism, it is legitimate to ask which interests Marx identifies as the antagonistic interests which a social revolution will eliminate. To characterize these interests is to lend further content to Marx's notion of the community. It is also to move to a second level in the characterization of the community. First, and foremost, Marx's view of the community implies that the division of interests in production must be abolished. A harmony of interests in this fundamental area must be created. This implies, for Marx, the positive transcendence (the *Aufhebung*) of private property, competition, and the division of labor. It is important to use this dialectical formulation of Marx's views since Marx does *not* simply mean that all aspects of these various institutions will be completely abolished (cf. *MECW*, 6:498). Thus, it is to be expected that specialization in labor will remain, but the *forcing* of people into this or that area of labor, the coercion which makes them remain in a particular job, is to be eliminated. This is closely related to the argument in section III that it would not be impossible on Marx's views that a person might devote himself to some particular field of endeavor or activity. The point to be emphasized here, however, is that a community would continue to have people do different jobs – this could not be avoided. People would develop their interests in different areas. *As such*, people would have *different* interests. They supposedly would *not* have opposed, divided, or antagonistic interests because of the manner in which their labor was organized as well as the ends to which it was aimed.

Thus, regarding the manner in which such labor would be organized, the interchange of positions, voting on leadership in the workplace, joint determination of ends and manner of labor itself would be implications of the notion of community. Accordingly, it is false to suggest, as some have,[34] that in a community of free individuals no one could work under the control or direction of another. It is not the mere fact that the work of some is controlled or directed by others which implies a lack of freedom or absence of community. Rather, it is that such control or direction is not legitimate, that it is not founded upon or directed towards morally relevant ends and purposes. Such would be the case, for example, when a person has authority not because of his abilities and the approval of his fellow workers, but because of nepotism, financial influence, or outright physical domination. The ends to which labor would properly be directed would not be profit, but the fulfillment of social needs as well as the need of the worker himself for self-objectification and self-determination. Such matters would be the object of rational planning within the community, and part of the reason for viewing it as a rational order. The Marxian community, thus, constitutes a fundamentally different social order from civil or natural society. The moral standard which would characterize such a community of interests would be that the free development of each is the condition for the free development of all (*MECW*, 6:506). This standard, however, must be understood against the background of the preceding arguments. It is not to be understood as a Marxian version of Pareto optimality. It is not a criterion of justice or equality.[35] Rather, the free development of each is the condition for the free development of all since people are not separated or divided, but unified, by their interests.

Marx's views on the preceding, which he summarizes as his opposition to private property (*MECW*, 6:498), differ strikingly from the views of others on the relation of private property and freedom. Hegel, we have noted, held that individuals gained part of their self-objectification and realization through private property. To this extent, through private property they became free. To prohibit private property is then to violate the right of personality for Hegel. Since Marx adopted Hegel's notion of individuals' objectifying themselves through their (productive) activities, it is worth briefly noting the way in which Marx comes to such different conclusions from Hegel.

Hegel's account of private property is part of his account of civil society. Civil society, however, is the locus of conflicting interests and antagonistic needs. It is not a community. Hence, freedom in Hegel's views is achieved only by Spirit pushing on to other realms, e.g. religion and philosophy. Freedom comes with Spirit's absolute knowledge of itself. This Hegelian freedom, however, leaves civil society untouched. Marx, on the other hand, rejects such an idealistic 'resolution' of the conflicts of civil society. Freedom, if it is to be obtained at all, must be obtained by real, actual individuals in their joint and daily relations. Surely Marx is correct in this instance. Since the system of private property continues to expand, to dominate those within its world-wide grasp, since it reduces everything to levels of profit measured by the universal solvent money, Marx concludes that private property must go. It no longer fulfills the function which Hegel attributed to it. Nevertheless, as we have noted, Marx does not seek the total abolition of private property. Rather, he seeks the positive transcendence (*Aufhebung*) of private property. What this requires is the elimination of all private property which gives one person the control of the labor of other people simply on the basis of ownership. Accordingly, private property which did not have this nature might exist in communism.

Marx held that if there did not exist antagonistic interests at the basis of society, there would be a ripple effect on the rest of society. On the one hand, the personal relations amongst individuals would be changed. If one's labor does not set one off against others, make one feel threatened by others, then one's relations with others will be themselves more harmonious. There will be an overcoming of bourgeois society's predominant concern with self-interest, i.e. its concern with others only to the extent that they fulfill a person's own ends. In this sense, the harmony of basic interests not only itself constitutes but fosters a broader and deeper identification of one individual with others.

On the other hand, there are also structural implications Marx foresees for society. Among the more prominent are the following. Firstly, the elimination of different classes and of man's subordination to a class follows from the communalization of labor, inasmuch as the basis for class differences, according to Marx, rests on the division of interests within production. Secondly, the division and opposition between town and country is transcended: 'The abolition of the contradiction between town and country is one of the first conditions of a communal life, a condition which again depends on a mass of material premises and which cannot be fulfilled by the mere will' (*MECW*, 5:64). Accordingly, in the *Manifesto of the Communist Party*, Marx demands that one of the measures to institute a communist society is the 'gradual abolition of the distinction between town and country by a more equable distribution of the population over the country' (*MECW*, 6:505). Thirdly, the state itself becomes superfluous and is transcended. The state, too, in Marx's eyes, rests upon the division of interests characteristic of civil society (cf. *MECW*, 5:46). Its transcendence involves not merely the elimination of the oppressive mechanisms of the state, but also the end of the division of society into political and civil spheres, i.e. an end to the opposition between universal or common interests and private interests. 'The real, individual man reabsorbs in himself the abstract citizen.'

There may be some moral and empirical plausibility to these views, but Marx does little to establish either plausibility. Surely the transformation of private property and the division of labor along the lines Marx obscurely envisioned would have significant consequences for society. Some of these consequences, however, would be causal in nature; others would be logical or conceptual implications. Marx does little, however, to sort out these different implications. The purpose of the present remarks is, however, not to test the derivation of Marx's views so much as to portray their place in the context of his views on community and freedom. Marx was not simply opposed to the town/ country distinction, class society, and the state for aesthetic reasons, or even reasons related to justice. Instead, he opposed them because, like religion, they themselves denied man freedom, inasmuch as they rested upon a set of interests which were antagonistic. As such Marx would agree that 'the demands of freedom take us beyond the atomistic forms of liberalism where the individual and his goals are of ultimate importance and the task of society is to permit their fulfillment along with those of others.'[36] The important ends of life are not defined by private individuals pursuing private, exclusory ends. Rather, they are defined within communal relations to others. Social life with others, life of mutual self-determination or government based upon a harmony of interests, is not merely a servile or troublesome labor to be pursued only when one must and for ends external to it. It is itself essentially part of the free life.

IX

How is it that the preceding account of the community is an aspect of freedom? There are several responses Marx can make. Firstly, freedom is self-determination. It is the essential determination of a concrete totality of one's desires, capacities and talents. To live in a communal relation with others, we have seen, is to live such that the basic interests upon which a society is founded, those related to its productive life, are not antagonistic. If they are antagonistic, if private property, for example, characterizes life, then individuals (workers *and* capitalists) lose control of their social institutions and relations. In such a situation it is impossible for people to be essentially self-determining. Rather they are victims of a willful, uncontrolled fate. Marx's characterization of trade is to be understood in this context:

trade, which after all is nothing more than the exchange of products of various individuals and countries, rules the whole world through the relation of supply and demand — a relation which, as an English economist says, hovers over the earth like the fate of the ancients, and with invisible hand allots fortune and misfortune to men, sets up empires and wrecks empires, causes nations to rise and to disappear — whereas with the abolition of the basis, private property, with the communistic regulation of production (and, implicit in this, the abolition of the alien attitude [Fremdheit] of men to their own product), the power of the relation of supply and demand is dissolved into nothing, and men once more gain control of exchange, production and the way they behave to one another. (*MECW*, 5:48)

Traditional accounts of freedom narrow their vision to the individual and his particular relations to other individuals. They ask: are there obstacles to a person doing what he wants so long as he does not harm others? That the person may not want to live susceptible to the vicissitudes of economic crises and the like is not considered relevant since such crises are viewed, more or less, as natural. They are considered to be something over which there can be no control and which are independent of the antagonistic interests at the basis of society. Marx rejects this. Such crises can be controlled. The antagonistic interests which characterize private property, the division of labor, the town and the country, can be overcome in the community. To the extent that they are overcome, man is self-determining and, hence, free. The plausibility of these claims may well be disputed. The point here is to place them in their context within Marx's views on freedom.

Secondly, it is a bourgeois prejudice that freedom must separate people, establish barriers between them, rather than unite them. For Mill, one is absolutely free within one's private realm. Only if one steps out of that realm and would harm someone else does one rejoin society and at the same time experience a restriction of one's activities. Marx emphasizes the contrary view that through joining with other people, identifying with others, we may also gain freedom — a freedom of a higher and more significant kind. And surely there is something to be said for his view. The examples are many in which people who have sought freedom in independence from others eventually discover freedom in forming bonds with and commitments to other people. Freedom requires that identification between people which arises when they share harmonious and co-operative interests. Then one experiences others not as obstacles to, but integral parts of, one's own development and fulfillment. It is this aspect of freedom which Marx's notion of community captures. It is why the community, man's communal relations with others, is an important and plausible part of Marx's account of freedom.

Thirdly, Marx might point out that communal life, as described above, is an instance of freedom and also follows from the fact that man is a social being. 'The essence of man,' Marx says, 'is no abstraction inherent in each single individual [but] . . . the ensemble of social relations' (*MECW*, 5:4). By this Marx means, roughly, that individuals are defined

127

by and in their relations to others. There is no Aristotelian essence of rationality inherent in each person by which we can characterize man. If man had such a private essence, if each individual were uniquely characterizable without reference to others, then he could, theoretically, fulfill that essence by himself. Others would not be needed except incidentally to fulfill external, non-essential, characteristics and needs. Freedom, in such a case, would be realized by preventing others from encroaching upon one's private self.

However, Marx insists that man's essence has to be captured by an account of his relations. Further, if what is uniquely human about a person is captured in his relations to others, then only if those relations are positive and co-operative, i.e. communal, will people be free. Suppose, contrariwise, that man's relations were conflict-ridden and divisive. People had to protect and defend themselves at every turn. Other people or other classes were always prepared to attack or exploit them. Then man's essence would itself be conflict-ridden and divisive. Man would be divided against himself, subject to contrary pulls and tugs. What he would do would be opposed and limited by other aspects of himself. It is implausible to think that a being so characterized, one in effect at war with itself, could be called 'free.' Similarly, if human relations were characterized by indifference and non-intervention, man would experience himself indifferently as a divided and isolated being. With such a being, freedom might even be an irrelevant notion. Thus, if there is to be freedom, it seems that positive, co-operative, and harmonious relations with others are required. If one identifies with others, then others are no longer a threat to oneself. Their needs and demands are brought within the compass of oneself. They are not external, restraining forces, but internal expressions coincident with oneself. Though there may be disagreements, these exist within a common understanding and undertaking, one subject to rational resolution. Thus, Marx comments that 'as long as a cleavage exists between the particular and the common interests, as long, therefore, as activity is not voluntary, but naturally, divided, man's own deed becomes an alien power opposed to him, which enslaves him instead of being controlled by him' (*MECW*, 5:47). The community, however, is defined, in the various ways we have seen, by a harmony of interests. As such, in the community man comes into his own as a free being.

X

In conclusion, the preceding sections have developed the nature of Marx's notion of freedom. This complex notion, which clearly stands in the tradition of Western philosophy, lies at the center of Marx's ethics. That it has this central importance has been indicated by showing its relations to and connections with Marx's practical demands, as well as by the manifold citations from Marx himself. In succeeding chapters I will seek to establish further this central role of freedom in Marx's thought.

The aspects under which freedom has been characterized are clearly interrelated and connected. It is clear, however, that, for Marx, freedom is essentially self-determination. It is this basic characteristic which ties the various aspects of freedom together. That one objectify oneself in a concrete manner in his relations with other persons and with nature, as well as that one's objectification be communal in nature, are limiting conditions on the kind of self-determination which characterizes freedom.

Marx's ethics, as so characterized, is an ethics of virtue. It requires the development within individuals of certain character traits and dispositions. As such freedom is not only a moral but also an ontological notion. This does not mean that freedom is something innate in individuals. It must be prepared for, it must be taught, and it must be maintained by daily practice. It involves not simply thinking and feeling certain things, but acting in certain ways in certain situations.[37] It is a way of being. One might say that it constitutes a unity of theory and practice! Given that one has acquired this way of living or being, we can understand Marx's comments that under communism one can do as one pleases (e.g. *MECW*, 5:47). This is most clearly not the same as doing what one wants, which characterizes bourgeois freedom. One can also understand why Marx spends little time even attempting to detail how a person should decide this or that particular moral issue.

Inasmuch as freedom involves an ontological condition, a set of dispositions and traits, Marx does not have to fear the objection that he is simply imposing a moral principle, e.g. of self-realization, of Kantian duty, etc. on people. Rather, he claims to find in historical development (cf. Chapter 3) a development which leads to the creation in people of this very way of being. Thus his moral demands have a material or natural basis. Hence, his own ethical position does not conflict with his statement that:

> the communists do not preach morality at all. . . . They do not put
> to people the moral demand: love one another, do not be egoists,
> etc.; on the contrary, they are well aware that egoism, just as much
> as selflessness, *is* in definite circumstances, a necessary form of the
> self-assertion of individuals. (*MECW*, 5:247)

129

Surely such an ethics of freedom is related to self-realizationist accounts of Marx's views. One's self-development does play a role in Marx's views. But Marx's ethics of freedom is also, as we have seen, distinctly different from and superior to a self-realizationist ethics. Problems common to self-realizationist ethics are not problems for Marx. Marx is not committed to the realization of 'all' our capacities. The Marxian free person could never be taken to pose the problem which the artist poses for self-realizationist ethics, viz., that his fulfillment might be at the expense of others.[38] Marx does not postulate two selves, only one of which we are to realize, such as self-realizationist ethics commonly do. Finally, self-realizationist views are usually teleological. Thus, we are obliged to perform those actions which promote the end of self-realization. How such an end is to be measured is not the only problem of attributing this view to Marx. Another problem is his objection to imposing duties and obligations on people. Instead, Marx's view appears to be aretaic in the sense that freedom, this complex disposition to act in certain ways, is held to be morally good simply in itself. It is not good because it promotes some other end. It is simply good in and of itself.

The notion of freedom, as explicated in the preceding way, is the standard by which Marx measures the development, the progress, of man and society. A society is more or less developed, fulfills more or less the moral life, to the extent its members fulfill the above notion of freedom. What Marx appeals to in order to justify this notion of freedom was indicated in Chapter 3. In the following chapter we will further explore the nature of freedom by considering its relation to justice.

5 Capitalism and justice

he one hand the daily sustenance of
 a day's labor, while on the other hand,
can work during a whole day, that con-
. its use during one day creates, is double
)ays for that use, this circumstance is,
f good luck for the buyer, but by no means
ɔ the seller. (*Capital*, I:194)

.ticisms of capitalism has been that it gives rise
there are wide and unjust disparities in the
ıs, etc. of its members. One need simply recall
.tionary movements of the last two centuries
J important egalitarian measures into capitalist
the significance of this kind of criticism. The
ɩ, welfare measures, the opening of governmental
ction are all results of these movements.
g then that many have also seen in Marxism a criti-
ɔn behalf of justice. Any one of a number of com-
med that a passion for justice, an eye for the injustice
/stem, was basic to Marx's viewpoint.[1] Marx himself
this view. In one of his early analyses of capitalism

We ˎ ɾom an *actual* economic fact.
The w ɔecomes all the poorer the more wealth he produces, the
more his ˎ ɔduction increases in power and size. The worker
becomes aɪ. ever cheaper commodity the more commodities he
creates. The *devaluation* of the world of men is in direct proportion to the *increasing value* of the world of things. . . . It is true that
labor produces wonderful things for the rich — but for the worker it
produces privation. It produces palaces — but for the worker, hovels.
It produces beauty — but for the worker, deformity. (*MECW*, 3:271-3)

We must look, then, to Marx's views on justice. Does Marx's ethics include an appeal to justice which supplements his views on freedom? Does he criticize capitalism for injustice, or is this a mistaken interpretation as others have claimed? If he does criticize capitalism for its injustice, does he do this because it violates a principle of justice or justice conceived of as a virtue? In either case, is the standard involved one which he can apply not simply under communism, but also to capitalism and other social forms in the development of man? In short, what is the relation of freedom and justice in Marx's thought? In this chapter I shall discuss these questions and argue that Marx did *not* appeal to justice, either as a principle or a virtue, to criticize capitalism. Since those who attribute normative ethical views on justice to Marx do so in the form of a principle of justice, I will concentrate on the question whether Marx appealed to a principle of justice. My claim will be, once again, that Marx did not criticize capitalism for its injustice, but rather, as argued in the preceding chapter, for the lack of freedom which it provides to humans.

I

It is perhaps important to begin with a caveat, which is also a reminder of what has been said previously. It is not possible, as some seem to have thought, to establish what Marx's views are on any topic — but especially the present one — by simply stringing together a number of quotations in which Marx expresses himself in ways such that he seems to approve or disapprove of some particular point. Such quotations could at best, in the present instance, serve to establish an initial plausibility that Marx might have had a principle of justice on the basis of which he criticized capitalism. They cannot themselves establish this claim, since they can easily be counterbalanced by other quotations in which Marx is saying quite the opposite. Thus, on the one hand, Marx refers to the theft, embezzlement, robbery, fraud, etc., which are involved in the appropriation of surplus value. For example, Marx comments that the appropriation of surplus value is an act of embezzlement: 'the greater part of the yearly accruing surplus product, embezzled, because abstracted without return of an equivalent . . . is thus used as capital' (*Capital*: I:611). However, on the other hand, Marx also says in *Capital*, that

> If therefore, the magnitude of value advanced in wages is not merely found again in the product, but is found there augmented by a

surplus value, this is *not because the seller has been defrauded*, for he has really received the value of his commodity; it is due solely to the fact that this commodity has been used by the buyer. (*Capital*, I:585, my emphasis)

In the early writings, Marx also seems to indicate that he is not essentially concerned with the distributive share of income that the worker receives in wages: 'An *enforced increase of wages* . . . would therefore buy nothing but better payment for the slave, and would not win either for the worker or for labor their human status and dignity' (*MECW*, 3:280).[2]

Accordingly, one cannot establish Marx's position by simply showing that he says that capitalism is just or unjust in this or that place. We cannot exclude the possibility that Marx was sometimes inconsistent, that he tried to gain some tactical advantage through certain pronouncements, or even that he wrote informally at times, rather than strictly according to his theoretical commitments.[3] Thus, in approaching Marx's various comments on capitalism and justice, one must show how they best fit into his overall views. Unless these more inclusive views are taken seriously, and kept constantly in mind, his various comments will be misunderstood and misinterpreted.[4]

In following the preceding methodological point it is appropriate to begin by characterizing briefly, but more fully than we have so far, the nature of the relations of production which constitute capitalism and which would be the object of a critique on the basis of justice — if Marx so made one.

Capitalism is a system for the production and exchange of commodities. Thus, Marx begins *Capital* with a study of commodities. A commodity is a product which has been produced with the intention of selling it to other people. As such, it must have a *use-value* — that is, it must be able to satisfy some want that other people have or they would not bother to buy it. A commodity also has an *exchange value* which is the proportion in which various commodities are to be exchanged. Exchange value is not some intrinsic feature of a commodity as is its use-value. Rather, the exchange value is determined extrinsically on the basis of the amount of labor time which is required for the production of the commodities. This does not mean, however, as some have thought, that the more labor time it takes to produce the commodity the more value it has. Rather, the (exchange) value of a commodity depends upon the amount of socially necessary labor time which it requires on the average to produce that commodity. This is determined by the state of knowledge, technology, the geographical and environmental conditions of the production, as well as the historical stage of the society and its individuals.

Now the capitalist produces such commodities – or rather has them produced – not with the intention of fulfilling the wants or desires of various people in society. Rather, he produces such commodites with the sole – or at least primary – intention of producing a profit for himself. That he must produce commodities for others in order to do this simply happens to be the way, the only way, in which he can produce the end he really wants. Such commodities are simply means to this basic end. The basic problem, then, which Marx sets himself in the first volume of *Capital* is to explain the source of the capitalist's profit. From where does the capitalist derive the profit he seeks?

Marx argues that this profit does not come from the capitalist's purchase of various raw materials which go into the creation of the commodity. Neither does his profit come from the circulation itself of the commodities which have been produced. Marx assumes that each commodity is exchanged for its full value. This means that when the capitalist takes his particular commodity to the market he gets for it, either in the form of money or some other commodity, exactly the same value as the value of the commodity he brings to market – which is the amount of value (labor) which has been put into this commodity in its production. Obviously one does not create or acquire profit in this way.

Rather the profit which the capitalist seeks and acquires comes from the laborer in the production process itself. Just as the capitalist must buy various raw materials, or commodities which go into the production of a new commodity, so too he buys another commodity which the worker provides. This is the worker's labor-power. That is, the worker sells to the capitalist a very special commodity, his labor-power, which is the worker's ability to work, to labor, for a certain number of hours during a normal working day. Now this commodity, this labor-power, has an exchange value and a use-value just like any other commodity. In recognizing this fact Marx is able to indicate the source of the capitalist's profit.

The exchange value of the worker's labor-power is, like other commodities, equal to the amount of labor it takes to produce such labor-power. This involves providing the worker with sufficient food, clothing, shelter, both for himself and for his family. This amount of labor Marx calls 'necessary labor.' The use-value, however, of a worker's labor-power is not dependent on its exchange value. Rather, the use-value of a worker's labor-power is its ability to produce, to labor, for a normal working day. The point of crucial significance is that there is a difference between these two amounts. The number of hours which constitute the exchange value of the labor-power, i.e. the number of hours of necessary labor, is *less* than the number of hours during which such labor-power can produce. This difference is what the capitalist counts on when he purchases the labor-power of the worker. For since the worker produces for a longer period of time than it takes to produce his own labor-power, the worker produces *surplus labor*. And since it is labor which constitutes the value of products, the worker in working these extra hours has produced *surplus value* — which is in effect the capitalist's profit. Thus, by purchasing this singularly remarkable commodity — and recall that Marx assumes the capitalist pays the full value of each commodity he buys — the capitalist has been able to produce a profit for himself. It is this profit which is the whole point and purpose of this system.

With this brief description of the relations of production which characterize capitalism, we can now turn to Marx's views on the justice or injustice of this system. As it is needed, we shall further elaborate on the details of this set of productive relations. Before proceeding, however, there is a point of general agreement on Marx's views concerning capitalism and justice which might be noted.

This is the view that Marx can allow that various particular injustices do occur under capitalism to the extent that these injustices can be judged by the principle of justice which obtains under bourgeois society. For example, if a particular capitalist attempts to pay some workers less than the full value of their labor-power, these workers are treated unjustly. One way in which this occurs is when the capitalist tries to extend the working day beyond what it takes to reproduce the labor-power of these workers. He shortens lunch breaks, lengthens the number of hours they must be on the job, etc. In short, the capitalist tries to derive more work from them than a normal working day allows. This has the effect of shortening the lifetime labor-power which these workers can sell and hence of lowering the value which they can receive in return for their commodity — their labor-power — which they have to sell.

Such attempts can be said by Marx to be injustices which the worker suffers under capitalism (cf. *Capital*, I:233-4). Analogously, the capitalist can also be treated unjustly by the workers, when they withhold some of the labor-power which the capitalist has purchased.

This kind of injustice is not a problem in the interpretation of Marx's views since it is an injustice which can be measured by the principle of justice valid under capitalism. So far, all agree, Marx can surely go in seeing injustice in the capitalist system. But, clearly, to see such injustices is to say nothing about the essential justice or injustice of the capitalist system itself. Otherwise, it might be supposed that such injustices could all be eradicated and thence capitalism become a perfectly just system of productive relations.

It is at this point that the two main questions, which we shall discuss in this chapter, concerning the justice or injustice of capitalism arise. Firstly, it may be asked whether Marx held that capitalism is unjust even as measured by the principles which obtain under capitalism? Is it impossible, according to Marx, that such injustices as mentioned above could *theoretically* be eliminated from capitalism? Could it be that the capitalist system, with regard to its own principles of justice, must ever be said to be an injust system?

Secondly, independently of the answer to the first question, does Marx hold that capitalism is unjust on the basis of some communist principle which would apply not simply to communism but also to capitalism? That is, does Marx have a principle of justice which is trans-cultural and trans-historical? The answer to the first question could be positive or negative, capitalism could be said to be just or unjust on its own bases, and still the present question would remain an open question. It is these two general questions which will be discussed in the remainder of this chapter.

II

There are two reasons which might be given why capitalism could not, theoretically, be a just system, even on the basis of the principle(s) of justice which develop under capitalism. The first reason is this. Marx assumes, as we have explained, that the principle of justice which obtains under capitalism requires that each commodity be paid for at its full value. The full value of the worker's labor-power, we have also seen, is that labor-time which it would take in a normal working day to replace this labor-power:

> The value of labour-power is determined, as in the case of every
> other commodity, by the labour-time necessary for the production,
> and consequently also the reproduction, of this special article. . . .
> If the owner of labour-power works today, to-morrow he must again
> be able to repeat the same process in the same conditions as regards
> health and strength. His means of subsistence must therefore be suf-
> ficient to maintain him in his normal state as a labouring individual.
> (*Capital*, I:170-1)

However, capital is a restless search after surplus value (surplus labor) — it is ever devising ways to gain greater surplus value. By its very nature, capital ever seeks to derive more labor from the worker than a normal working day would justify. For capital, Marx claims,

the working-day contains the full 24 hours, with the deduction of the few hours of repose without which labour-power absolutely refuses its services again. Hence it is self-evident that the labourer is nothing else, his whole life through, than labour-power, that therefore all his disposable time is by nature and law labour-time, to be devoted to the self-expansion of capital. Time for education, for intellectual development, for the fulfilling of social functions and for social intercourse, for the free play of his bodily and mental activity, even the rest time of Sunday . . . — moonshine! But in its blind unrestrainable passion, its were-wolf hunger for surplus labour, capital oversteps not only the moral, but even the merely physical maximum bounds of the working-day. It usurps the time for growth, development, and healthy maintenance of the body. It steals the time required for the consumption of fresh air and sunlight. It higgles over a meal-time, incorporating it where possible with the process of production itself, so that food is given to the labourer as to a mere means of production, as coal is supplied to the boiler, grease and oil to the machinery. It reduces the sound sleep needed for the restoration, reparation, refreshment of the bodily powers to just so many hours of torpor as the revival of an organism, absolutely exhausted, renders essential. It is not the normal maintenance of the labour-power which is to determine the limits of the working-day; it is the greatest possible daily expenditure of labour-power, no matter how diseased, compulsory, and painful it may be, which is to determine the limits of the labourer's labour-power. (*Capital*. I:264-5)

Consequently, since capitalism ever seeks to transgress what the laborer has coming to him — according to its own principles of justice — capitalism is inherently an unjust system.

Now it might be thought that the self-interests of capital in preserving its workers would encourage it to curb its desire for surplus value (labor) (cf. *Capital*, I:265-9). And indeed in places Marx does say that the wages the worker usually receives suffice for the reproduction of his labor-power (*Capital*, I:581). Nevertheless, Marx also says that capital is always able to find enough workers available to it so that it does not have to care for the fate of the source of the surplus labor which it so greedily accumulates (*Capital*, I:269-70). That is, given the labor theory of value as indicated above, there does not seem to be any inherent necessity that that capitalist be concerned about whether the labor-power be produced and reproduced in this or that particular human being. The value of something is the amount of socially necessary labor-time which it takes to produce it. But any particular person is simply a vessel in which labor-power may be produced. If another vessel can be found in which the same amount of labor-power can be produced but for a lesser value, this should be the source of the labor-power the capitalist seeks.

Thus, it would seem that capitalist society could not even theoretically be a just society since the nature of the underlying force in capitalist society ever seeks to exceed the bounds of justice — that is, by its very nature capital tries to demand more from the laborer than the normal working day would allow.

Now even though the preceding characterization of capital is correct, the conclusion does not follow. To see this, one must understand that the normal working day — against which the full value of the worker's labor-power is measured — is a variable quantity. 'The working day is, therefore, determinable, but is *per se*, indeterminate' (*Capital*, I:232). As noted above, the length of the working day depends on a number of factors. To begin with, the very definition of the value of something was expressed in terms of the socially necessary labor where Marx indicates that this is dependent on various circumstances, 'among others, by the average amount of skill of the workmen, the state of science, and the degree of its practical application, the social organisation of production, the extent and capabilities of the means of production, and by physical conditions' (*Capital*, I:40; cf. 171, 559). However, ultimately, the extent of the working day is established by the class struggle between the capitalist and the working class: 'the determination of what is a working-day, presents itself as the result of a struggle, a struggle between collective capital, i.e., the class of the capitalists, and collective labor, i.e., the working-class' (*Capital*, I:235).

The implication of this is that when the working class is weak, the workers separated and divided from each other, the 'normal' working day will be a long, grinding period of labor. The quality of such labor will tend to be very low. Nevertheless, to the extent that the workers receive means of subsistence sufficient to sustain them at this low level they receive their just wage. This would even be the case in the extreme situation when they died in large numbers, but could be replaced by their children or laborers from other parts of the country or world. For even in this case, the fact that there is an excess of workers would also figure into the amount it costs to produce the labor-power of a worker.[5]

On the other hand, when the working class is strong, the quality of the labor-power renewed will be higher, since the working hours — the normal working day — will be shorter. But still, the worker will receive what is the full value of his labor-power.

Thus, it would seem that it is possible, not simply theoretically but also practically, that capitalist society could be just in spite of the nature of capital itself. Given the manner in which the normal working day is decided, the worker seems to receive what is just given the principle of justice in capitalist society. It must be admitted that this does not mean that the individual capitalist will not seek new and different ways in which to extract more surplus value. To do otherwise would be to act contrary to his nature. Still, given the manner of determination of the normal working day there would be pressures on such a capitalist to come back into line with the social norm. And it is the fulfillment of this social norm which is the measure of the justice in this instance.

Now one might complain that there is not a little cynicism in such a conclusion. Indeed, one might claim the only thing which has been shown is that such relations are *economically* just — not that they are *morally* just. Marx might well reply, however, that it is just his realism which sees how events really transpire under capitalism and consequently what things are not merely economically just but also morally just. If one wishes to complain about this state of affairs either one must show that another principle of justice actually obtains under capitalism or one must use some other principle of justice external to capitalism. We are assuming here that the principle of justice which is at issue is the one which obtains under capitalism. Whether Marx has or could have any other external moral principle of justice we have yet to discuss.

The second reason for which it has been claimed that capitalism cannot, even theoretically, be just has to do with the appearance and reality of wage labor. The appearance is that the worker is paid for the value of his labor — e.g. he is paid for the full twelve hours of his labor. 'On the surface of bourgeois society the wage of the labourer appears as the price of labour, a certain quantity of money that is paid for a certain quantity of labour' (*Capital*, I:535). This is supposedly demanded by the principle of justice that is used in capitalist society. However, the reality of wage labor is that the worker is paid only for part of his labor, though for the full value of his *labor-power*. Further, according to the principle of justice which is appropriate to capitalism, this is just. Thus, it is claimed: 'According to the principle that is used in capitalist society to appraise what apparently occurs, what really occurs is unjust; but it does not appear to be, because it does not appear. However, according to the principle that governs what really occurs, what really occurs is just.'[6] The argument continues,

> The practice of paying the laborer less than the 'value' of his labor conflicts with the principle which requires that he be paid a wage equivalent to the 'value' of his labor. Relative to that principle, the practice is unjust. Since it is that principle which the agents and apologists of capitalism use to appraise capitalist practice, capitalism is unjust by one of its own standards.[7]

There are two problems with this argument. Firstly, the principle that apologists, etc. of capitalism supposedly use is *inappropriate* to capitalism. 'A direct exchange of money, i.e., of realised labour, with living labour would either do away with the law of value which only begins to develop itself freely on the basis of capitalist production, or do away with capitalist production itself, which rests on wage-labour' (*Capital*, I:536). Hence, such a principle cannot really be used to appraise the justice or injustice of bourgeois practice. Perhaps an analogy might help here. If God really does not exist, then it makes little sense to say that a society is immoral because it does not follow God's wishes. People who still believed in God may believe such a society is immoral. But that no more shows that that society is immoral than the fact that some people believe in fairies proves that there are fairies or that we should do what they say. Similarly, the upshot of the above argument is simply to show that people in capitalist society use and believe in a principle of justice which is not applicable – it is not to show that capitalism is really unjust by this principle.

Secondly, and more importantly, the above argument claims that two different principles of justice are applied in capitalism – one on the level of appearance and one on the level of reality. However, one suspects that there are not really two different principles of justice involved, but one principle that receives two different applications. Thus, the bourgeois principle of justice might simply be specified as equivalents are to be exchanged for equivalents (cf. *Capital*, I:176). This, then, is misinterpreted and hence misapplied under capitalism to the extent that it is thought that what is exchanged is a wage for a certain number of hours of labor, instead of a wage for one's labor-power. There is, accordingly, no question of capitalism being unjust by its own standards. Rather under capitalism and its mystifications, people do not understand their own actions and appraisals. Specifically, the notion that one is paid for his labor instead of his labor-power is simply nonsense, according to Marx. Were one to be paid for his labor, i.e. the hours he works, then there would be no source of profit and capitalism would abruptly cease to exist.

But why should it be necessary to hide or conceal the real relations? Why are such mystifications necessary? Marx speaks of

> the decisive importance of the transformation of value and price of labour-power into the form of wages, or into the value and price of labour itself. This phenomenal form, which makes the actual relation invisible, and, indeed, shows the direct opposite of that relation, forms the basis of all the juridical notions of both labourer and capitalist, of all the mystifications of the capitalist mode of production, of all its illusions as to liberty, of all the apologetic shifts of the vulgar economists. (*Capital*, I:540)

Why is this self-delusion necessary? Suppose, indeed, that people were suddenly enlightened about the real economic bases of their capitalist society. They learn that they are not paid for the hours they labor, but instead are paid for the amount of labor required to produce their labor-power. They thought previously that the capitalist said to them, 'If you work for X hours, I will pay you for each hour worked.' Now they know that he actually says, 'If you will expend the energy which is your labor-power in laboring for me, I will pay you for what it took to produce that energy (labor-power).' They would realize, then, that as participants to this agreement they were bound to produce the full use-value of their labor-power, for which they are to be paid the full exchange value. But why should this be so dangerous to learn? Why should it be necessary or important that people believe that they are paid for each hour of labor rather than the amount of labor it took to produce their labor-power?

An answer may be given only if we proceed beyond the preceding statement of the situation to emphasize the fact that though the worker is paid the full exchange value of his labor-power, this amount is less than the amount of value which his labor produces. Certainly, this is just on the basis of the above account. But nevertheless one wants to know why this should be? Marx's answer, as we have seen, is that under capitalism this must be. The difference between these two values is the source of the capitalist's profit. Further, Marx holds that in *any* system there must be surplus labor – i.e. one must produce more than one receives back for the production of his labor-power.

> Surplus-labour in general, as labour performed over and above the given requirements, must always remain. In the capitalist as well as

in the slave system, etc., it merely assumes an antagonistic form and is supplemented by complete idleness of a stratum of society. . . . It is one of the civilising aspects of capital that it enforces this surplus-labour in a manner and under conditions which are more advantageous to the development of the productive forces, social relations and the creation of the elements, for a new and higher form than under the preceding forms of slavery, serfdom, etc. (*Capital*, III:819)

Thus, the necessity of the difference between what it takes to produce one's labor-power and that which one's labor-power can produce is not limited to capitalism. This feature of capitalism cannot be eliminated. Thus, it cannot be the source of an injustice under capitalism, unless Marx is to claim that all systems – even communism – are unjust!

Now if people under capitalism were to understand this too, they might still ask who it is that determines how much more – and on what basis – their labor is to produce than what it takes to produce their labor-power?[8] It has been indicated above that this is determined in the class struggle. But let us now consider the capitalist side of that class struggle. On what basis does the capitalist participate in this process? What legitimates his role in determining the amount one is to labor? A traditional answer is that his role is justified by the wealth of goods produced. But Marx rejects this answer. True, at times even a surfeit of goods is produced, still these do not reach the worker. As Marx comments, the more the worker produces the poorer he gets. No injustice is committed in this, however, since capitalism adheres to a procedural view of justice – not an end-state view of justice. A society is just, that is, not if it takes the form of some particular end-state – e.g. equal distribution of wealth. Rather, a society is just whatever end-state it realizes if the procedures by which it realizes this end-state are all of them just. And this is the case under capitalism, since each worker is paid the full value of his labor-power.

Another standard answer to the above question is that this system is justified because it protects individual freedom. Under capitalism one may – but need not – sell one's labor-power to this or that capitalist. One is free – one may do what one wants insofar as it does not harm others. But here is the rub. Here is to be found the reason why the mystifications of wage labor are necessary.

Let us consider the nature of the relations within which the bourgeois freedom is exercised. How did it come about that the capitalist plays a role in determining the amount one labors? To answer this question we must look at the nature of bourgeois relations of production in their historical setting. We might begin by noting that to understand the capitalist system of production on its own grounds, we must consider each individual act of exchange by itself. 'If, therefore, commodity production, or one of its associated processes, is to be judged according to its own economic laws, we must consider each act of exchange by itself, apart from any connexion with the act of exchange preceding it and that following it' (*Capital*, I:586). Thus, we can imagine two people bringing their products to market to sell. We assume that these products are the result of the labor of each of these people (cf. *Capital*, I:582). Now it should be noted here that the very fact that they have products for the market means that they do not need all the products they themselves have produced. Some are surplus which they can sell to others. Thus, already some of their labor was necessary and some surplus. Surplus labor here only means labor in addition to what is required to meet one's own needs.

Each of these products has a use-value — otherwise no one else would want it — and an exchange value — the amount of labor required to produce this product. When both products are exchanged for their full exchange value justice obtains. An equivalent has been exchanged for an equivalent. This kind of exchange is hardly capitalist. It has happened in earlier societies.

How, then, were these relations and this kind of exchange transformed into a capitalist system? 'In themselves money and commodities are no more capital than are the means of production and of subsistence. They want transforming into capital' (*Capital*, I:714). Marx's answer is that:

this transformation itself can only take place under certain circumstances that centre in this, viz., that two very different kinds of commodity-possessors must come face to face and into contact; on the one hand, the owners of money, means of production, means of subsistence, who are eager to increase the sum of values they possess, by buying other people's labour-power; on the other hand, free labourers, the sellers of their own labour-power, and therefore the sellers of labour. Free labourers, in the double sense that neither they themselves form part and parcel of the means of production, as in the case of slaves, bondsmen, etc., nor do the means of production belong to them, as in the case of peasant-proprietors; they are, therefore, free from, unencumbered by, any means of production of their own. With this polarisation of the market for commodities, the fundamental conditions of capitalist production are given. (*Capital*, I:714)

And what is the process whereby this situation is brought about?

> The process, therefore, that clears the way for the capitalist system, can be none other than the process which takes away from the labourer the possession of his means of production; a process that transforms, on the one hand, the social means of subsistence and of production into capital, on the other, the immediate producers into wage-labourers. The so-called primitive accumulation, therefore, is nothing else than the historical process of divorcing the producer from the means of production. It appears as primitive, because it forms the pre-historic stage of capital and of the mode of production corresponding with it. . . .
> The immediate producer, the labourer, could only dispose of his own person after he had ceased to be attached to the soil and ceased to be the slave, serf, or bondsman of another. To become a free seller of labour-power, who carries his commodity wherever he finds a market, he must further have escaped from the regime of the guilds, their rules and apprentices and journey-men, and the impediments of their labour regulations. Hence, the historical movement which changes the producers into wage-workers, appears, on the one hand, as their emancipation from serfdom and from the fetters of the guilds, and this side alone exists for our bourgeois historians. But, on the other hand, these new freedmen became sellers of themselves only after they had been robbed of all their own means of production, and of all the guarantees of existence afforded by the old feudal arrangements. And the history of this, their expropriation, is written in the annals of mankind in letters of blood and fire. (*Capital*, I:714-15)

The preceding lengthy quotations are justified in that they clearly show that Marx thought the whole system of bourgeois relations rested upon a previous history of force and coercion exercised on the producers so that they eventually had nothing left to sell but their labor-power. Marx's complaint is that the workers *must* sell their labor-power; they are *forced*, *coerced* into these relations. The producers do not have their own means of production. And yet they must work. Thus, in effect, the worker must pay the capitalist to use the latter's means of production to produce the necessities for his own existence. He pays his *tribute* to the capitalist (in the form of surplus labor) and acquires thereby with his work also the means of his own existence.

> Capitalist production, therefore, of itself reproduces the separation between labor-power and the means of labour. It thereby reproduces

and perpetuates the condition for exploiting the labourer. It incessantly forces him to sell his labour power in order to live, and enables the capitalist to purchase labour-power in order that he may enrich himself. It is no longer a mere accident, that capitalist and labourer confront each other in the market as buyer and seller. It is the process itself that incessantly hurls back the labourer on to the market as a vendor of his labour-power, and that incessantly converts his own product into a means by which another man can purchase him. In reality, the labourer belongs to capital before he has sold himself to capital. His economic bondage is brought about and concealed by the periodic sale of himself, by his change of masters and by the oscillations in the market-place of labour-power. (*Capital*, I:577-8)

Thus, the mystifications associated with wages are not needed in order to prevent workers from being aroused by unjust wage levels, or the like, so much as to prevent them from asking why it is that they are continually forced — as institutionalized in bourgeois production relations — to sell their labor-power in order to live. If I believe that I am paid for each hour and minute on the job, as determined by market conditions,[9] then though I may complain about the length of time and the conditions under which I work, still both my employer and I receive our due. However, if I come to learn that I am paid for my labor-power as determined by market conditions, that there is a difference between this value and the value I produce, that the size of this value differential and the ends towards which it is put is determined by relationships which rest upon the force and coercion which gave rise to them, as well as that the capitalist plays the role he does in determining the nature of this differential because our relations embody this constraint upon which capitalism was founded, then I may well raise my voice in protest, in outrage, at the unjustified structure of relations in my society, at the violence, force, and coercion which is done to me.[10] I may be paid what I have coming to me within the present set of relations, but I am forced to engage in these relations. I am told that a job is worth so much, but then I am coerced into taking that job. Justice has not been violated, but my freedom has been.

Now the freedom at stake here is not identical with bourgeois freedom — at least if bourgeois freedom is understood simply to require the absence of direct and immediate obstacles to human wants and actions. Accordingly, it cannot be objected, on bourgeois moral principles, that the coercion and force exercised upon the proletariat — and the consequent violation of their freedom — is itself an injustice. Bourgeois moral principles of justice as well as of freedom are fulfilled under capitalism. The danger here, then, is that if people come to understand the real basis on which they live and work, they will be pushed beyond the bourgeois view of freedom towards Marx's view of freedom, towards communism.

There is an important objection to this line of argument which I should like to consider before concluding this section. The objection is that Marx did speak of the surplus labor the worker yields to the capitalist as 'unpaid labor,' as labor of which the capitalist robs the worker. In short, for some of his labor the worker receives no equivalent (*Capital*, I:583). Do not such statements by Marx indicate that injustice was really part of Marx's attack on capitalism? There are (at least) three reasons why the answer is 'no.'

Firstly, it should be noted that Marx held that an exchange without equivalent occurred in many other forms and places under capitalism. That is, the capitalist does not pay for a number of the 'things' which he requires in order to survive. In addition to not paying (supposedly) for the worker's surplus labor, the capitalist does not pay for the benefits he derives from the division of labor (*Grund.*, 765), the scientific powers he uses (*Grund.*, 765; *Capital*, I:605), for the growth of the population he requires (*Grund.*, 765). Further, he does not pay for the extra force that comes from many workers working together (*Grund.*, 528; *Capital*, I:326, 333), or for the preservation of the value of the instruments of labor in the new product (*Capital*, I:206-7). Nevertheless, all of these are productive forces necessary to derive surplus value. Thus, we should not simply think that 'the exchange without equivalent' is unique to the case of the wage the worker receives in exchange for the labor-power he offers to the capitalist. Furthermore, since it is implausible to say that the capitalist is acting *unjustly* when he does not pay (to whom? how?) for the scientific powers he uses, for the benefits of the division of labor, or for the growth of the population itself, we should not hastily conclude that it is unjust in the case of the worker and his wage.

Secondly, the use of the phrase 'unpaid labor' is itself suspicious — and on grounds which Marx himself has given us. The 'value of labor,' the notion of buying, selling, or paying for labor is an irrational expression, a meaningless expression (*Capital*, I:537-9). 'The value of labor is only an irrational expression for the value of labor-power' (*Capital*, I:539). But the labor-power has been fully paid! So what can Marx mean by the phrase 'unpaid labor?' He must mean that the fully paid labor-power of the worker produces values which are in excess of the value which he was paid and which constituted a fair exchange. It is not that *some* of his labor is unpaid, since, in reality, he is paid for *none* of it! Nor is it that he is not fully paid for his labor-power. Rather it is that there is a difference between the value of his labor-power and the value of the products his labor-power can produce.

Now there is nothing strange in this, as we have noted before. It was because of this the capitalist purchased the labor-power in the first place.

> The value of labour-power, and the value which that labour-power creates in the labour-process, are two entirely different magnitudes; and this difference of the two values was what the capitalist had in view, when he was purchasing the labour-power. The useful qualities that labour-power possesses, and by virtue of which it makes yarn or boots, were to him nothing more than a *conditio sine qua non*; for in order to create value, labour must be expended in a useful manner. What really influenced him was the specific use-value which this commodity possesses of being *a source not only of value, but of more value than it has itself.* (*Capital*, I:193)

Further, in so using the laborer's labor-power the capitalist has *not* cheated the worker. Since he has paid the full exchange value, the full use-value (and its consequences) belong to the capitalist:

> The fact that this particular commodity, labour-power, possesses the peculiar use-value of supplying labour, and therefore of creating value, cannot affect the general law of commodity production. If, therefore, the magnitude of value advanced in wages is not merely found again in the product, but is found there augmented by a surplus value, this is not because the seller has been defrauded, for he has really received the value of his commodity; it is due solely to the fact that this commodity has been used up by the buyer. (*Capital*, I:585)

Thus, Marx's use of the phrase 'unpaid labor' is unhelpful and confusing; so too his use of 'gratis labor.' These are not literal descriptions of what occurs — Marx's own account shows that this is mistaken. Rather they are provocative phrases which should lead us to think — why would people work in such a way that they yield part of the values they create to another person to use as he sees fit? The answer Marx gives, as we have seen, is that they are forced to, they must give this tribute, in order to secure the work to create their own means of livelihood. The force may be hidden or open, the coercion may be explicit or implicit. But in any case, the objection that Marx holds against such a system of production is that its basis rests upon a ground of threats, force, coercion, and violence. In short, what Marx saw, and it underlay his objection to the 'exchange without equivalent,' was the violation of one's freedom.

Finally, what about Marx's comments that the appropriation of surplus value is robbery (*Capital*, I:582)? As we have already noted, Marx held that capitalism was historically based upon robbery as well as a series of other forceful acts: 'In actual history, it is notorious that conquest, enslavement, robbery, murder, briefly force, play the great part [in the primitive accumulation of capital and wealth]' (*Capital*, I:714). The objects of such violence and the manner of its employment were various:

> the spoliation of the church's property, the fraudulent alienation of the State domains, the robbery of the common lands, the usurpation of feudal and clan property, and its transformation into modern private property under circumstances of reckless terrorism, were just so many idyllic methods of primitive accumulation. (*Capital*, I:732-3)

Thus, the present relations within which people live and work in capitalism are the result, at least in part, of a period of robbery, fraud, etc. Now the sense of 'robbery' here is straightforward. Certain people took that which did not belong to them from other people. This was even recognizable as robbery under capitalist morality. However, capitalism holds to a statute of limitations; the sins of the fathers ought not to be visited upon the heads of its youth. Thus, we find J.S. Mill arguing that

> possession which has not been legally questioned within a moderate number of years, ought to be, as by the law of all nations it is, a complete title. Even when the acquisition was wrongful, the dispossession, after a generation has elapsed, of the probably *bona fide* possessors, by the revival of a claim which had been long dormant, would generally be a greater injustice, and almost always a greater private and public mischief, than leaving the original wrong without atonement.[11]

Thus, even if at the beginning of capitalism capitalist morality might be forced to admit that its origins involved robbery, and immorality, it protects itself from its origins, and proclaims the justice of its present relations.

Now Marx concurs with this assessment of capitalism — judged by its own standards its present relations are just. The individual relation of the worker and the capitalist involves no fraud or injustice. The present individual capitalist took no part in the early phase of capitalism; neither he nor his agents force this or that worker to sell his labor-power to him; further, he pays the full value of the labor-power. It is only when one shifts one's analysis from this individual level to the class level that Marx speaks of the robbery of surplus value:

> The means of production, with which the additional labour-power is incorporated as well as the necessaries with which the labourers are sustained, are nothing but component parts of the surplus-product, of the tribute annually extracted from the working class by the capitalist class. Though the latter with a portion of that tribute purchases an additional labour-power even at its full price, so that equivalent is exchanged for equivalent, yet the transaction is for all that only the old dodge of every conqueror who buys commodities from the conquered with the money he has robbed them of. (*Capital*, I:582)

Robbery, that is, if it occurs at all occurs on the class level, rather than on the level of the individual relations between this capitalist and that worker. However, to shift to this level, to speak of robbery which one class perpetrates on another class, is to apply standards external to capitalism:

> To be sure, the matter [of the wage a worker receives] looks quite different if we consider capitalist production in the uninterrupted flow of its renewal, and if, in place of the individual capitalist and the individual worker, we view them in their totality, the capitalist class and the working class confronting each other. But in so doing we should be applying standards entirely foreign to commodity production. (*Capital*, I:586)

Thus, if Marx's use of 'robbery' does reveal that he views capitalism as unjust, it does not do so on the grounds or standards of capitalism itself. Such a charge could be supported only on the basis of a principle which transcends capitalism.

We may, then, conclude this part of our consideration of Marx's views on justice. I have argued that the view that Marx criticizes capitalism for being unjust on its own grounds is unacceptable. Rather, if capitalism is to be faulted it must be for the violation of freedom which its productive relations institutionalize. However, such freedom is a non-capitalist freedom, a Marxist freedom, and hence requires that we appeal beyond the standards of bourgeois morality. Accordingly, I turn now to the broader topic of whether Marx had or could have had a principle of justice, which was trans-cultural and trans-historical, which held not only for communism, but which he could also use, as he used freedom, to criticize capitalism and other societies.

III

The main problem which confronts the claim that Marx uses a universal principle of justice to condemn capitalism derives from Marx's views on ideology. It is my contention that these views effectively prohibit an appeal to justice which is trans-cultural and trans-historical, even though they allow such an appeal in the case of freedom. We must, therefore, briefly refer to those aspects of Marx's views on ideology which seem to prohibit any such universal principle of justice.

The bases of all human society, Marx held, are to be found in the productive activities through which the needs and wants of people are fulfilled. These productive activities do not, however, merely satisfy the physical wants and needs of people (as well as create new needs and wants), they also determine the kind of consciousness people have of themselves, others, and their times. Now such consciousness takes various forms – religion, the state, law, morality, science, art, etc. – which reflect the modes of production out of which they arise and of which they are themselves in part constitutive. Accordingly, Marx contends, the moral principles of each society are a 'reflection' or an 'expression' of the underlying material conditions. They are also said to 'correspond' to these conditions. This is to say that such moral principles play a concrete role in the prevailing mode of production, that they function 'as an actual moment in the production process.'[12] They are, consequently, applicable only to, and valid for, those conditions or those societies. Thus, Marx's views on ideology seem to prohibit any universal principle of justice.

We can elaborate on this point and the matter of concern here by considering the (supposed) communist principle of justice, according to which capitalism is unjust. It is easy, too easy perhaps, to make a great deal of Marx's use of the phrase, 'From each according to his abilities, to each according to his needs' as constituting not simply Marx's views on justice under communism but a principle that would or should apply to all societies. The phrase is rarely used by Marx.[13] That is, Marx himself did not place a great deal of emphasis on it. However, it is not simply for this reason that it is mistaken for others to place great emphasis on it as characterizing Marx's views. The following points must also be considered.

Firstly, this principle of justice *cannot* be realized under capitalism: 'the realization of this [the communist] distributive principle of justice presupposes material abundance which results, on the one hand, from a high level of development of productive forces and, on the other hand, from a transformation of the nature and conditions of work and the attending change in the attitude toward work.'[14] Since this is the case, capitalism cannot be judged by this principle. Capitalism, and certainly previous societies, lack the material bases for such a principle of justice. To admit this point is to admit that it would be inappropriate to judge capitalism by this principle.

It has been replied that:

> the mere absence of the existential or institutional prerequisites for the realisation of norms does not in itself reduce these norms to insignificance. The Marxian norms of . . . equality, and justice are not reduced to insignificance merely because the institutional framework they require is absent under capitalism. Such norms serve a critical function in transforming the consciousness of the proletariat, in making it the power of the negative or making it the agency of revolutionary change.[15]

This reply, however, does not solve the problem. On the one hand, how is it that such norms could have such efficacy? If they could have such efficacy in the nineteenth century when (let us suppose) the existential prerequisites for such norms did not exist, then could they not have been similarly effective in the tenth century?! But clearly Marx holds this is nonsense. Various norms and ideals may indeed serve to transform the consciousness of the proletariat into a revolutionary force, but this can only occur given the appropriate material conditions. Otherwise, such a view is simply some form of idealism which believes in the dominance of ideas. On the other hand, to argue that the communist principle of justice, though not realizable by capitalism, can still be used to evaluate and condemn capitalism might be plausible if we could assume that capitalism operates upon ideological bases which are ultimately compatible with the communist principle, such that the conditions of existence under capitalism could, by degree, be brought increasingly into line with the communist principle of justice. This, however, is an unwarranted assumption. History is not the smooth continuous development of the ideological bases upon which some present or past society has rested. Marx sees difference and opposition in the ideological bases of present and past societies. Most moral philosophers have not understood this since they have implicitly assumed that the material conditions of existence are not morally relevant. Marx makes this assumption explicit and denies it. In denying it, he is also denying the assumption behind the above argument.

> Of course, the tendency towards equality belongs to our century. To say now that all former centuries, with entirely different needs, means of production, etc., worked providentially for the realisation of equality is, first of all, to substitute the means and the men of our century for the men and the means of earlier centuries and to mis-understand the historical movement by which the successive genera-tions transformed the results acquired by the generations that preceded them. (*MECW*, 6:173)

Accordingly, to speak of capitalism and capitalist justice is to speak of a set of conditions of justice which are incompatible with communism and which cannot be evaluated by a communist principle of justice.[16] Just as one does not and cannot evaluate moves in checkers by the rules of chess, so one does not and cannot evaluate capitalist distributive jus-tice by supposed non-capitalist principles of justice.

Secondly, it might be claimed that the communist principle of justice could be applied to capitalism since any society could be just — could fulfill the communist principle of justice — so long as it satisfied 'human needs within its own productive possibilities':

> Marx does not consider capitalism unjust because the technical base of its productive system does not generate the material abundance necessary for need satisfaction. Rather, he considers capitalism unjust because it does not satisfy human needs within its own productive possibilities and thus violates the principle of distribution according to need. He objects, not to the technical base, not to the productive forces, but to the social mode of their employment; that is, the social relations of production and particularly in the mode of appro-priating and distributing the annual produce.
>
> In order for a society to satisfy its needs, it must allocate the available labor time at the prevailing level of productivity to the pro-duction of the requisite goods and services. But capitalism has 'no conscious regulation of production.'[17]

Such a view, however, makes nonsense of Marx's views on the nature of social systems such as capitalism. The attempt consciously and rationally to allocate resources would spell the end of capitalism. But Marx cannot allow that the social relations constitutive of capitalism could be eliminated, at any time since their inception, so as to institute communist justice. On the contrary, capitalism is a necessary, and to this extent, legitimate stage in the development of communism. Only after capitalism has developed the forces of production such that communism can appear does he allow that capitalism can be overcome. The above argument separates in a non-Marxian way the forces of production and the relations of production. As the above argument has it, capitalism could institute quite different relations of production — consciously, rationally, allocating productive resources — and hence become just. Unless this were possible, capitalism could not fall under the scope of the communist principle of justice. But it is just this radical change of the relations of production rationally to allocate production goods that capitalism cannot do and remain capitalism. Consequently, it is mistaken to hold that capitalism can be evaluated by a communist principle of justice.

Thirdly, Marx comments in his *Critique of the Gotha Program*, shortly before he introduces the phrase 'From each according to his abilities, to each according to his needs,' that 'right by its very nature can consist only in the application of an equal standard.'[18] Under capitalism the equal standard is that of 'labor, human labor in the abstract.' When Marx then comments in the face of the inequalities that arise under a bourgeois principle of justice in the first phase of communism, that to avoid all these defects right, instead of being equal, would have to be unequal, he is in fact saying that it is impossible to come up with a principle of right or justice that will take into account the inequalities of individuals. 'Unequal individuals . . . are measurable only by an equal standard in so far as they are brought under an equal point of view, are taken from one *definite* side only, for instance, . . . are regarded *only as workers* and nothing more is seen in them, everything else being ignored.'[19] But this is to view people within 'a narrow horizon,' or under 'a bourgeois limitation.' Accordingly, principles of justice cannot, by their nature, treat people with regard to their individual complexities, capacities, and needs. They are, that is, by their nature incapable of treating people concretely. When Marx says then that only in communism can the narrow horizon of bourgeois right be crossed in its entirety, he means quite literally that principles of justice will be left behind. And if this be indeed correct, then Marx does not and cannot have a universal or absolute principle of justice that applies to all societies and by which he can criticize capitalist relations of production.

Finally, support for the above interpretation of Marx's statements and views can be adduced from various other comments of Marx on the nature of principles of distributive justice:

> Any distribution whatever of the means of consumption is only a consequence of the distribution of the conditions of production themselves. The latter distribution, however, is a feature of the mode of production itself. The capitalist mode of production, for example, rests on the fact that the material conditions of production are in the hands of non-workers in the form of property in capital and land, while the masses are only owners of the personal condition of production, of labor power. If the elements of production are so distributed, then the present day distribution of the means of consumption results automatically. If the material conditions of production are the cooperative property of the workers themselves, then there likewise results a distribution of the means of consumption different from the present one. Vulgar socialism . . . has taken over from the bourgeois economists the consideration and treatment of distribution as independent of the mode of production and hence the presentation of socialism as turning principally on distribution. After the real relation has long been made clear, why retrogress again?[20]

Now Marx is not simply saying that principles of justice have a certain genetic basis, a certain causal origin — but that this is a matter of indifference with regard to the validity of the systems to which they may be applied. Instead, he claims, principles of distributive justice are tied to particular modes of production. In fact there are two distributions to consider. The first, and most crucial, is that of 'the conditions of production themselves.' This distribution is logically tied to the mode of production: 'The distribution . . . is a feature of the mode of production itself' (*Grund.*, 151). The second distribution, that of the means of consumption, is a 'consequence' of the first distribution, but one that is said to result 'automatically.' The crucial principles of distributive justice, then, are those that relate to the distribution of the conditions of production. These are part and parcel of the mode of production itself. Hence, given the capitalist mode of production, one gets the system of bourgeois distributive justice.

Accordingly, the view that Marx has an absolute concept of justice can only be maintained by denying — or avoiding — Marx's views on ideology. Moral conceptions such as justice arise in certain epochs under particular modes of production, and are intelligible only within those conditions. Capitalist private property, relations of production, depend, for example, on the meaningfulness of distinguishing between various individual proceeds of labor. These individual proceeds of labor are appropriated by the capitalist. When this is done in such a way that the worker receives full payment for his labor-power, and the capitalist receives the full use-value of the worker's labor-power, then justice obtains under capitalism. But 'within the cooperative society [i.e. communism] based on common ownership of the means of production, the producers do not exchange their products. . . . The phrase "proceeds of labor" . . . loses all meaning.'[21] Thus, one of the bases of justice in the transactions of capitalism is undercut — and not in the sense that it is shown to be unjust, but in the more radical sense that it becomes meaningless. Once again, then, principles of justice appear to be relative to the particular modes of production.

I conclude, therefore, that Marx cannot have a universal, let alone absolute, principle of justice. To this extent, then, his condemnation of capitalism is not and cannot be a condemnation of it for its injustice — at least in so far as its holders follow the standards of bourgeois justice.

IV

If Marx's criticism of capitalism cannot be one of justice — its social relations fulfill the principles of bourgeois justice and there is no communist principle of justice which is applicable to capitalism — then why do not the preceding arguments also show that his critique cannot be one of freedom? How is it that Marx can appeal to freedom to criticize different societies, but not do so with justice?

Firstly, the likelihood that there is some sort of contrast in Marx's thought between justice and freedom should be noted. Whereas Marx rarely uses the word 'justice' in his discussions of capitalism and whereas when he does speak of capitalism using the word 'justice' he says, more often than not, that capitalism is not unjust (cf. *Capital*, I:194, 540, 585, 586), Marx is much more open and frequent in his discussion (and condemnations) of capitalism using the word 'freedom.' In a typical instance Marx says:

> This kind of individual liberty [under capitalism] is thus at the same time the most complete suppression of all individual liberty and total subjugation of individuality to social conditions which take the form of material forces — and even of all-powerful objects that are independent of the individuals relating to them. (*Grund.*, 131)

155

Marx never says — and given his views as explicated above it would be inconceivable — such things about capitalism, or bourgeois society, using the word 'justice.' He never claims that individuals under the bourgeois are subjected to a complete suppression of justice!

Secondly, the reason for this and why Marx can criticize capitalism for the deficient freedom it instantiates is that there are a number of underlying asymmetries between freedom and justice in Marx's views. They are similar, of course, in the following way. Principles of justice relate to the distribution of various goods, honors, conditions of production (e.g. property), etc. These (ideal) patterns of distribution vary from society to society and are themselves bound up with the modes of production in each society. Similarly, views of freedom also correspond to the modes of production. There is, accordingly, a particular view of freedom which is characteristic of bourgeois society. It is with this view of freedom in mind that Marx claims that the idea of freedom itself is only the product of a social condition based upon free competition (*MECW*, 6:464), and then goes on to say that 'By freedom is meant, under the present bourgeois conditions of production, free trade, free selling, and buying.' He continues,

> this talk of free selling and buying, and all the other 'brave words' of our bourgeoisie about freedom in general have a meaning, if any, only in contrast with restricted selling and buying, with the fettered traders of the Middle Ages but have no meaning when opposed to the communistic abolition of buying and selling, of the bourgeois conditions of production, and of the bourgeoisie itself. (*MECW*, 6:499-500)

An initial significant difference between justice and freedom has to do with the difference in their relation to the mode of production. In the case of justice (as noted above), a particular mode of production gives rise to, involves, a particular (principle of) distribution. The two are tied, more or less, closely together. In the case of freedom, there is an intervening factor, viz., the effect of the mode of production on the individuals and society in which it is found. The issue here, as we have argued in Chapters 3 and 4, relates to Marx's views on praxis. Specifically, the way in which people fulfill their needs and wants (i.e. by their mode of production) creates not simply the means and distribution of their livelihood, but also the people themselves. Marx was explicit:

> The way in which men produce their means of subsistence depends first of all on the nature of the actual means of subsistence they find

in existence and have to reproduce. This mode of production must not be considered simply as being the reproduction of the physical existence of the individuals. Rather it is a definite form of activity of these individuals, a definite form of expressing their life, a definite *mode of life* on their part. As individuals express their life, so they are. (*MECW*, 5:31)

Accordingly, the development of the modes of production through various historical epochs is itself the development of the potential and actual powers of individuals and society. Further, it is this development of man, his capacities and abilities, through his productive forces and relations towards a conscious mastery and control over these forces and relations (particularly those of his own creation) which constitutes freedom. That is, freedom is linked to the development of the productive forces and relations through the mediation of the development of the powers and abilities of individuals. It is this, we have seen, that serves as the basis of Marx's critique of capitalism on behalf of freedom. Capitalism restricts such freedom to individuals.

Now there is no comparable basis for justice. Justice concerns either the pattern of distribution of goods or some set of rules for distributing goods regardless of the resulting pattern.[22] In either case, justice concerns the ordering imposed on social goods (etc.), not the state of development of those goods. Further, this ordering is 'only a consequence of the distribution of the conditions of production themselves. . . [This distribution is in turn] a feature of the mode of production itself.'[23] But, again, a society is not more just simply because it possesses a more highly developed mode of production. There is, then, given Marx's views on ideology, no basis for trans-cultural appraisals of justice. Freedom, however, is different. There is a basis for appraisals of freedom, as opposed to appraisals of justice, in the ontological dimension which attaches to freedom. Freedom too, like justice, is not autonomous, some ideal which Marx imposes on society. But as opposed to justice, freedom is not simply an outgrowth of, but to be appraised in terms of, the development of the forces and relations of production upon which all societies are based. The basis of freedom, that is, is the self-development of man and society through the development of the productive forces of society. No similar basis, to repeat, exists for justice.

Two objections to this view should be considered. Our discussion of these objections will elicit further asymmetries in Marx's view between justice and freedom. Firstly, it might be claimed that, though justice does indeed concern the distribution of (social) goods, freedom is itself a social good. What is wrong with capitalism, then, is that it constitutes an unjust distribution of freedom. The capitalist makes the decisions, the worker executes them. The capitalist enjoys freedoms denied to the worker. Thus, capitalism, in giving the worker less freedom than the capitalist, violates the worker's freedom, does him an injustice.[24] The answer to this objection is relatively uncomplicated. On the one hand, this objection mistakenly portrays the nature of Marxist freedom. Such freedom is not simply another 'social good' which must be distributed. Rather, it is the human good, the way in which all people ought to live. Though one society may more fully realize such freedom than another society on a different historical level, Marxist freedom is not something which can be unjustly distributed as can income, wealth, and the like. Marxist freedom is a characterization of the nature of the relations within which people live, rather than of the distribution of particular goods — be they income or bourgeois freedoms — which individuals receive under those relatons. Hence, it is mistaken to treat freedom as one among many social goods which require distribution. On the other hand, the objection above is correct in that surely the capitalist can do things (i.e. has freedoms) the worker cannot. But this is not the point of Marx's critique. Marx's ethics of freedom says that the capitalist himself also lacks freedom in the significant Marxian sense developed in Chapter 4. Furthermore, the freedoms (in the bourgeois sense) that the capitalist does enjoy were granted to him by the free and voluntary (also in the bourgeois sense) decision which the worker made in selling him his labor-power. Thus, if one appeals to the bourgeois sense of freedom, there is no basis for bourgeois or proletarian to complain of a lack of freedom which the other has. On the other hand, if one appeals to the Marxist sense of freedom, neither bourgeois nor proletarian are free. Hence, again there can be no legitimate complaint of one being less free than the other. Thus, the first objection seems groundless.[25]

Secondly, it might be objected that, independently of who has more or less freedom, the interference with one's freedom is itself an injustice. One of the classical sources of such a view is to be found in Kant. According to Kant, 'anything that is unjust is a hindrance to freedom according to universal laws.'[26] Or again, as a commentator has put it, 'according to the Universal Law of Justice it is juridically wrong, or unjust, for anyone to interfere with the lawful freedom (or freedom according to universal law) of anyone else.'[27] Now the basis for this claim is the view that individuals have a moral right to the exercise of their freedom. The interference with one's freedom is, then, the violation of one's moral right. And since the violation of one's rights is an injustice, the interference with one's freedom is an injustice. Accordingly, since capitalism constitutes an interference with the freedom of human beings (both capitalist and proletarian) it stands condemned as unjust.

This objection too is unfounded. To begin with, the general relation between capitalism and communism (Marxist freedom) is not that the former restricts the latter, but that the former is a necessary stage in the development of the latter. Capitalism develops the necessary productive forces without which communism would be an idle hope. Only when capitalism is fairly advanced does Marx speak of its productive relations acting as fetters, restraints, or limitations on the growth of the productive forces. Capitalist productive relations then hinder the further development of its productive forces as well as the transition to communist productive relations. Now, inasmuch as freedom has been linked with the development of the productive forces of individuals and society, such restrictions can be said to constitute interference with freedom (in the Marxist sense). Can this fact then serve as the basis of claiming an injustice done to people living under capitalism? It could if one simply identified justice and morality. Then it would have to be conceded that the violation of one's freedom is an injustice. However, this would be to 'solve' the present problem by conceptual legislation. Such a 'solution' I take to carry little weight, since it seems more plausible to hold that not every action or situation which is morally justified involves justice, or, conversely, not every unjustified situation, condition, or action is or constitutes an injustice. Granted that some philosophers, such as Plato and Kant, have tended to identify the whole of morality with justice, nevertheless such an identification is unjustified. There are actions, e.g. cowardice, incest, etc., which though morally wrong are not questions of injustice. Aristotle was clear on this:

> That there is such a thing [as justice which is only a *part* of virtue or morality] is indicated by the fact that while the man who exhibits in action the other forms of wickedness acts wrongly indeed, but not graspingly (e.g. the man who throws away his shield through cowardice or speaks harshly through bad temper or fails to help a friend with money through meanness), when a man acts graspingly he often exhibits none of these vices — no, nor all together, but certainly wickedness of some kind (for we blame him) and injustice. There is, then, another kind of injustice which is a part of injustice in the wide sense, and a use of the word 'unjust' which answers to a part of what is unjust in the wide sense 'contrary to the law.'[28]

We must distinguish, then, between the whole of morality in which some actions and character traits are justified and some are not, and that part of morality in which some justified or unjustified actions and character traits are just or unjust. The question is, then, does the interference of capitalist productive relations (and their defense by the capitalist class) with the advent of communism, Marxist freedom, constitute an injustice (in this sense) on Marx's view?

Whether or not it constitutes an injustice would seem to depend on whether Marx holds that people under capitalism have a moral right to Marxist freedom. The answer to this question might seem positive for the following reason. To have a moral right to something is, according to Kant as well as many other philosophers, to have the authorization to coerce others to behave in certain ways. Now Marx believes, as we shall discuss in Chapter 6, that the proletariat is justified in using coercion and force to bring about communism. To this extent he would seem committed to holding that people have a right to freedom and that, hence, any violation of that right is an injustice. However, the picture is more complicated.

The notion of a right is an individualistic notion based on a law conception of morality.[29] Marx seeks to break away both from an individualistic morality in which people have rights (and may exercise coercion over others) and from a law conception of morality. His concept of freedom is not, as we have seen in Chapter 4, explicated in terms of rights that people have, but rather in terms of a certain kind of life which people ought to live. The question here, however, is whether he is committed to holding that people have a moral right to such freedom, however freedom itself is to be explicated.

The reason to think that Marx did not believe himself to be so committed is that Marx will have nothing to do with rights in his ethics of freedom. Thus, Marx speaks of 'the faith of individuals in the conception of right, which they ought to get out of their heads' (*MECW*, 5:362). The realm of rights is a realm of individuals divided and separated from one another — a realm in which rights authorize coercive and forceful crossings into the private territories of others. Thus, Marx maintains 'right . . . arise[s] from the material relations of people and the resulting antagonism of people against one another' (*MECW*, 5:318). But communism transcends such antagonisms. The moral life is not one in which we defend ourselves from each other by various rights. The moral life is not, as Kant viewed it, an eternal struggle of the conflicting desires of oneself and others, on the one hand, and the universal law, on the other hand. Accordingly, Marx rejects Stirner's view that 'in communist society there can be a question of "duties" and interests [since these are] . . . two complementary aspects of an antithesis which exists only in bourgeois society' (*MECW*, 5:213). The moral life, if such there be, is one in which, having eliminated the sources of conflict, we experience an harmony of interests. Hence, notions such as right and justice, inasmuch as they are bound up with the notions of coercion and antagonism, are themselves overcome in communism. Accordingly, it seems misdirected, wrongheaded, to claim that Marx's ethics of freedom rests upon a right to freedom which, being violated, interfered with by capitalism, leads him to condemn capitalism as unjust. This is not to say that Marx held that there was no place or role for appeals to rights. He says that 'the proletarians arrive at this unity [a unity which enables them 'to put a summary end to the entire hitherto existing world order'] only through a long process of development in which the appeal to their right also plays a part.' But, he immediately adds, 'Incidentally, this appeal to their right is only a means of making them take shape as "they", as a revolutionary, united mass' (*MECW*, 5:323). That is, appeals to right are or may be made *before* the occurrence of communism. They play a tactical, instrumental role in uniting the proletariat. This is intelligible since during this time capitalism still reigns, with its concepts of right and justice, with its underlying class antagonisms. However, these concepts are used to transcend not only capitalism but the concepts themselves. In medieval times the political expression of the medieval mode of production was privileges; in modern times the political expression of the modern mode of production has been rights (*MECW*, 5:327). With communism, rights will disappear just as with capitalism privileges disappeared as the basis of the system. But then so too any basis upon which capitalism could be said to be unjust will disappear.

In conclusion, it is fitting to comment more generally on the nature of the dispute in this chapter. There is not much point, obviously, in simply twisting words so that this or that thesis can be maintained. At issue should remain substantive problems. In this light, the preceding discussion might be summarized. What I have attempted to show is that Marx condemns capitalism and does so on the basis of his views on freedom. Now if capitalism's lack of fulfillment of this Marxist freedom is, in some broad sense, an injustice, then so be it. This might be maintained, I indicated, if one identifies justice and morality. However, I believe this to be unjustified. In any case, what should be noted is that such an injustice does not constitute a separate principle of justice, but is simply the lack of fulfillment of Marxist freedom. One could just as well say that it is wrong, mistaken, unjustified not to fulfill such freedom, as to say that an injustice occurs when it is not fulfilled. My concern throughout has been with the question whether there is an independent and separate principle of justice which must be appended to Marx's views on freedom. To admit the preceding is not to admit that there is any such independent, separate principle of justice.

In addition, the position defended above seeks to show that Marx's critique of capitalism is not a critique based on the maldistribution of goods under capitalism. Thus, the answer to the question, 'Isn't Marx really concerned with justice since he is talking about the distribution of the means of production?', is 'no.' He is talking about the nature of these conditions. It is not that private property is morally acceptable, but we have to distribute it differently. It is that the institution itself has to be eliminated and be replaced by social property. This calls for a qualitatively different institution. 'Redistribution' suggests rearranging what is already there. Marx seeks to change radically what is there and bring about a new order. If private property were simply theft, then one might try to take it back from the capitalist and give such (private) property to the proletariat. That would be redistribution in an intelligible sense. But Marx does not consider doing this.

Now it might be contended that I — or Marx — have built justice into the notion of freedom. Freedom, as explicated in Chapter 4, involves harmonious relations with others. This is, it might be claimed, implicitly to embed a principle of justice in freedom. The answer to this objection is that the harmonious relations Marx foresees under communism are based on a growth of the productive forces as well as a change in the nature and consciousness of people which will eliminate the conditions which have been traditionally required for a principle of justice. Thus, on the one hand, the productive forces will be so developed under communism that competition will become superfluous (*MECW*, 5:329-30). But if competition is superfluous, then, it is doubtful that a principle of justice is required. Hume comments that justice is required only where there is a scarcity of goods, where people must compete for goods. If this condition does not obtain then justice is not required. On the other hand, the consciousness of people will be so changed that again justice does not seem required. Again, Hume commented that, even if there were scarcity, if people related to others in non-competitive ways, etc. then justice would also be superfluous.[30] But the harmonious relations Marx projects would seem to constitute such a situation. Thus, it does not seem correct to say that Marx embeds a principle of justice in his account of freedom; rather he seems to exclude the conditions which call for such a principle. *A fortiori* he could not have a principle of justice whereby he condemned capitalism for being unjust.

What, then, does Marx say of the interference of capitalism with freedom? What is the moral situation of the proletariat under such fetters as capitalism has come to constitute? Marx would and does maintain that the proletariat is historically (and morally) justified in overthrowing capitalism. The justification is based on the notion of the life which the transcendence of capitalism will bring about. That is, it is justified by the establishment of the realm of freedom. Justice — or rather the injustice of capitalism — does not play a role in this condemnation of capitalism. Accordingly, when Marx speaks of the exploitation of the worker he cannot be using 'exploit' to connote an instance of injustice. What, then, does this word connote? The answer to this question has already been given. In so far as the word 'exploitation' carries a negative moral connotation, it relates to the lack of freedom the worker experiences. He is forced to work in situations and in various ways which are not of his choosing and which do not promote his development. He is not free, in the Marxist sense. Thus, it has been correctly noted that 'Marx endeavored to show that the mechanism of exploitation is based not on malversation and cheating of workers but on the fact that labor is treated as a commodity, exchangeable for an equivalent commodity.'[31]

6 Revolutionary morals, violence, and communism

To revenge the misdeeds of the ruling class, there existed in the Middle Ages, in Germany, a secret tribunal, called the '*Vehmgericht*'. If a red cross was seen marked on a house, people knew that its owner was doomed by the '*Vehm*'. All the houses of Europe are now marked with the mysterious red cross. History is the judge – its executioner, the proletarian.[1]

In this chapter I wish to trace the implications of Marx's ethics in two different directions. Firstly, I wish to consider the implications of his ethics for those living in pre-communist society. By 'pre-communist society' I understand not simply those living under capitalist society, but also those living in a society which has thrown off capitalism but which has not yet achieved communism. Such a transition society is often designated, by Marx, the first stage of communism. It appears only after the communist revolution and is characterized by the dictatorship of the proletariat. It is communist society 'just as it *emerges* from capitalist society.'[2] Since the problem of primary concern to Marx was the bringing about of communism, the problem which is foremost in importance to consider here is the implications of Marx's ethics for the bringing about of the full communist society. What are people to do, how are they to act, to achieve this end? Of central concern in this part will be Marx's views on the use of violence, force, coercion – and hence, revolution – by communists in order to achieve communism.

The second part of this chapter is to trace the implications of Marx's ethics for those living under communist society, 'as it has *developed* on its own foundations.'[3] Such a society is designated by Marx as the second, fully developed stage of communism. Since the first part of the chapter has concentrated on the issue of the use of violence and coercion, the second part of the chapter will also make this issue of central concern. Can any kind of force, violence, or coercion legitimately be used against those living under communism? In particular, we will consider what Marx has to say about the punishment of individuals under communism. Since the central element of Marx's ethics is the notion of freedom, and since such freedom entails the removal of force, violence, and coercion from the lives of humans, it is a legitimate question how Marx could justify the use of punishment under communism. Such questions lead us once again to the basic assumptions and fundamental views upon which communism is constructed.

I

In his speech at Marx's graveside, Engels said the following of Marx:

> For Marx was before all else a revolutionist. His real mission in life was to contribute, in one way or another, to the overthrow of capitalist society and of the state institutions which it had brought into being, to contribute to the liberation of the modern proletariat, which *he* was the first to make conscious of its own position and its needs, conscious of the conditions of its emancipation. Fighting was his element. And he fought with a passion, a tenacity and a success such as few could rival.[4]

It is important in discussing Marx's ethics neither to forget nor to underplay the extent to which Marx was, or at least saw himself to be, a revolutionist. However, it is just as important to be clear as to what this means and not to overplay this fact for sensationalist purposes. One should, perhaps, recall that in a very clear and intelligible sense Rousseau, as well as Gandhi, Lenin, and Martin Luther King were revolutionists. Thus we must see what it meant for Marx to be a revolutionist. What kinds of means can be used or must be used in order to bring about communism? In short, what are the implications of Marx's ethics of freedom for revolutionary morals?

One of the obvious characteristics which distinguish Marx's views on revolution from some who have effected revolutions is that Marx clearly thought that force, violence, and coercion may be needed and justified in order to effect the revolution he had in mind. For example, Marx claims that 'the weapon of criticism cannot, of course, replace criticism by weapons, material force must be overthrown by material force' (*MECW*, 3:182). In the *Manifesto of the Communist Party* Marx and Engels maintain that 'Communists openly declare that their ends can be attained only by the forcible overthrow of all existing social conditions' (*MECW*, 5:519). Even more emphatically, Marx claims, in the early 1850s, that 'impending bloody conflicts' faced the German proletariat:

Above all things, the workers must counteract, as much as is at all possible, during the conflict and immediately after the struggle, the bourgeois endeavors to allay the storm, and must compel the democrats to carry out their present terrorist phrases. Their actions must be so aimed as to prevent the direct revolutionary excitement from being suppressed again immediately after victory. On the contrary, they must keep it alive as long as possible. Far from opposing so-called excesses, instances of popular revenge against hated individuals or public buildings that are associated only with hateful recollections, such instances must not only be tolerated but the leadership of them taken in hand.[5]

Thus, Marx's view that violence, force, even acts of terror may be necessary to establish communism would seem clear enough. Further, he claims, that 'in most countries on the Continent, it is force [*Gewalt*] that must be the lever of our revolutions; it is to force that it will be necessary to appeal for a time in order to establish the reign of labor.'[6]

But though Marx may have thought that violence would be needed to establish communism, it is important to note that he does *not* claim that such violence will be necessary on *every* occasion. He clearly says that on other occasions radical change can be effected by peaceful measures. Thus, he claims that 'we are aware of the importance that must be accorded to the institutions, customs and traditions of different countries; and we do not deny that there are countries like America, England (and, if I knew your institutions better, I would add Holland) where the workers can achieve their aims by peaceful means.'[7] Correspondingly, Marx condemns those who claim that violence is an essential element of all revolution:

It is self-evident that these *conspirateurs* do not limit themselves to the mere task of organising the proletariat; not at all. Their business lies precisely in trying to pre-empt the developing revolutionary process, drive it artificially to crisis, to create a revolution *ex nihilo*, to make a revolution without the conditions of a revolution. For them, the only necessary conditon for a revolution is an adequate organisation of their conspiracy. They are the alchemists of the revolution, and they share all the woolly-mindedness, follies and *idées fixes* of the former alchemists. They throw themselves on discoveries which should work revolutionary wonders: incendiary bombs, hell-machines of magical impact, *emeutes* which ought to be the more wonder-making and sudden the less they have any rational ground. Always busy and preoccupied with such absurd planning and conniving, they see no other end than the next toppling-over of the existing government. Hence their deepest disdain for the more theoretical enlightenment of the workers about their class-interests. Hence, their not proletarian, but rather plebian, anger at those gentlemen in black coats (*habits nois*), the more or less educated people, who represent this side of the movement, and from whom they never manage to free themselves wholly as the official representatives of the party.[8]

Two conclusions follow from the preceding. Firstly, if we may assume that the use of peaceful means may involve a gradual process, one requiring a certain amount of time, then Marx allows that the transition to communism need not be sudden or abrupt. It is often maintained, however, that because of Marx's views on dialectics, the change to communism must be abrupt.[9] This change is the sudden qualitative change which occurs upon the foundation of the accumulated quantitative changes in capitalism. A prolonged peaceful transition would not constitute a revolution, but would simply be an evolutionary change, a reformation. Such views, however, are refuted by Marx's comments on the possibility of a peaceful transition to communism. Further, there is no reason to think that significant historical changes must occur abruptly on Marx's views. Certainly, he never gives this impression with regard to the transitions from the ancient world to the feudal world, or from the feudal world to the modern bourgeois world (cf. *MECW*, 5:372-3). Nevertheless, clearly Marx thought that the development of the bourgeoisie was a revolutionary development. Further, one need not put 'revolution' in quotes when one speaks of the Industrial Revolution. And yet, once again, the changes which constituted this revolution were *not* abrupt. What is crucial in such changes is that what comes after is significantly different from what comes before. If this occurs, then we may correctly say the change was revolutionary.

The reason why many claim that the communist revolution must be abrupt is that they wish, correctly, to distinguish the Marxist view of history from the bourgeois view. The latter is the view that history is or constitutes 'a smooth line of evolution.'[10] Thus, to admit that communism might come about by means of a prolonged peaceful transition would seem to adopt the bourgeois view of history. But this is mistaken. Marx may hold that historical development is not a smooth continuous evolution, and still maintain that communism comes about by means of a prolonged peaceful transition. All that he has to maintain is that communism is not simply the extension of the assumptions, values, and structures of capitalism, but constitutes radically different assumptions, values and structures for human life. Whether the transition from one set of assumptions, etc., to the other set is abrupt or prolonged is not important, for in either case history is discontinuous in a way in which it is not on the bourgeois view. Thus, whether communism comes about by a prolonged and peaceful means or by forceful, violent, and abrupt means, Marx can continue to speak of the communist revolution.[11]

Secondly, it also follows from the comments above that Marx's view as to whether or not violence is required is context-dependent. 'What should be done at any definite, given moment of the future, and done *immediately*, depends of course entirely on the given historical conditions in which one has to act.'[12] Marx has no one solution — violence or peaceful means — which he applies blindly to all situations. In his later writings he emphasizes this point when he claims that his views were constructed primarily with Western Europe in mind and that they do not therefore necessarily hold for Russia, or for other parts of the world.[13] In this way, Marx was obviously more reasonable than many others who have declared themselves revolutionaries and advocated violence regardless of the situation. Analogously, I would add, he was more reasonable than those who declare that violence is never justified or permitted. For Marx, violence was purely a means; it was never an end. That communism can come about peacefully indicates that Marx's ethical views are not directly linked to violence, force, or coercion; they do not, in and of themselves, require violence. Other factors make such violence necessary.

But how did Marx differentiate between situations? On what basis was violence justified in one situation but not in another? What purposes was violence to serve, which could not be achieved peacefully? Before turning to these questions, it is important to recall, in this context, the general view which Marx held of the society which was to be transformed by a communist revolution.

At the beginning of the *Manifesto of the Communist Party*, Marx and Engels made this general view clear: 'the history of all hitherto existing society is the history of class struggles' (*MECW*, 6:482). At the heart of capitalist society, as all other societies, has been the struggle, the war, between classes. This point they emphasized in a circular letter in 1879 to the leaders of the German Social Democratic Party: 'For almost forty years we have stressed the class struggle as the immediate driving power of history and in particular the class struggle between bourgeoisie and proletariat as the great lever of the modern social revolution.'[14]

Now though this class struggle has at times been carried on by peaceful means, it is unintelligible unless one recognizes that at basis it rests upon relations involving force, violence, and coercion. This is true in at least three distinct senses. Firstly, there are the overt, direct acts of violence and coercion which have characterized the class struggle. The very foundation of capitalism in Great Britain was laid, Marx argues, by the forceful expropriation of the peasants from their land (*Capital*, I:713-41).[15] Furthermore, not only in capitalism but also in earlier forms of society, the state is essentially a coercive power, a power by which the *status quo* defends itself: the state is 'merely the organised power of one class for oppressing another' (*MECW*, 6:505). The police, the army, the courts, etc., stand ready to compel dissidents to abandon their efforts to change the *status quo*. Consequently, the advances that the working class has gained in various countries have been due to the veiled as well as the open threats of violence and force, which the working class might use. The communist party has only been as successful as it has been, Marx claims, because it has not renounced the use of force and violence:

> But what is the secret of the Red bogey if not the bourgeoisie's dread of the inevitable life-and-death struggle between it and the proletariat? Dread of the inevitable outcome of the modern class struggle? Do away with the class struggle and the bourgeoisie and 'all independent people' will 'not be afraid to go hand in hand with the proletarians'! And the ones to be cheated would be precisely the proletarians.[16]

This violent character of the class struggle is simply, Marx holds, a basic fact which one must recognize and confront. The historical development of society is an affair in which violence, coercion, and force have played a significant role. It is in this sense that Marx claims that 'force is the midwife of every old society pregnant with a new one' (*Capital*, I:751). One who does not or cannot recognize these facts is not a materialist.

It is not by chance, then, that Darwin's *The Origin of Species*, with its discussions of struggle and conflict in the plant and animal world, was of considerable interest to Marx. What Darwin described as characteristic of the plant and animal world, Marx held was also characteristic of human history. In fact, Darwin had simply seen in the non-human world what has hitherto characterized the human world.

> It is remarkable how Darwin recognises among the beasts and plants his English society with its division of labour, competition, opening up of new markets, 'inventions', and the Malthusian 'struggle for

existence'. It is Hobbes' *bellum omnium contra omnes*, and one is reminded of Hegel's *Phaenomenologie* where civil society is described as a 'spiritual animal kingdom', while in Darwin the animal kingdom figures as civil society.[17]

Where Darwin was wrong was not in seeing struggle, violence, and conflict, but in believing or suggesting that all life, including human life, must *always* operate on these principles. This was the conclusion that Spencer and the political economists of his time drew. Contrariwise, Marx held it possible for man to overcome such violence and conflict. The first step is that we must recognize their historical nature. That they could be overcome, though not without further struggle and violence, was a basic premise of Marx's thought.

There is, however, a second, more subtle sense of violence which Marx also saw underlying personal and class relations in pre-communist society. This is the sense suggested when Marx speaks of the force, the violence and coercion which workers experience in their everyday work and life, but refers not to the direct, but the indirect, effects of other people or classes on the workers. These are the cases in which people labor or live under conditions which harm and dehumanize them but which the ruling class, though it could change them, does not.[18] The fact that the ruling class, or its various members, lifts not a finger to alter these conditions is another way in which violence is directed against the working class. Thus, for example, Marx reports that 'in one scutching mill, at Kildinan, near Cork, there occurred between 1852 and 1856, six fatal accidents and sixty mutilations; every one of which might have been prevented by the simplest appliances, at the cost of a few shillings' (*Capital*, I:481). Such inactivity to relieve significant harm which occurs under capitalism and which could be relieved within the presently existing social relations is just as much an instance of violence by the ruling class as the first kind of violence distinguished above.

Finally, there is one last kind of violence to which the worker (as well as the capitalist) is subjected under capitalism. This is the violence or the coercion one experiences because of the very nature of the relations characterizing capitalism. The business of life is the life of business under capitalism and both are abandoned to the law of supply and demand which is taken to be a natural, unalterable law which rules human life.

> Trade, . . . the exchange of products of various individuals and countries, rules the whole world through the relation of supply and demand — a relation which, as an English economist says, hovers

over the earth like the fate of the ancients, and with an invisible hand allots fortune and misfortune to men. (*MECW*, 5:48)

And though under these conditions people seem freer than before, in reality, Marx claims, 'they are less free, because they are more subjected to the violence of things.'[19] However, people are forced to act in ways which injure them not simply by the law of supply and demand. In general, both capitalist and worker are subjected to the 'external coercive laws' of the capitalist system (*Capital*, I:592). Since these laws and the conditions in which they are valid are not eternal or unalterable — even though the capitalist may think this is the case — the injury and harm people suffer in these conditions constitute acts of violence and coercion which people inflict upon themselves.

In the third sense, then, violence is institutionalized. It is part of the daily course of affairs. It is not a particular, exceptional action, or the inaction of anyone or any institution. Rather it characterizes the structure of present relations. What distinguishes the second and third senses of violence is that the relations within which inaction occurs in the second sense need not themselves be of a violent or coercive nature. Further, in the second sense the person or institution could theoretically be brought to grant the possibility of eliminating the force, violence, or coercion involved; while in the third case, given the nature of bourgeois society, this is not possible. To grant the coercive or violent nature of bourgeois relations would be to give up one's theoretical framework.

Thus, in capitalism people live within a social system which is not only on occasion explicitly and directly violent, but at all times implicitly, or covertly, violent and coercive. As we have seen, Marx characterizes various aspects and elements of this system — e.g. laws, actions, things, people, nature, and institutions — as violent or coercive. In these various cases, it is clear that Marx uses the notions of coercion, compulsion, force and violence in rather broad and overlapping senses. Each of them is used to characterize the three different senses of violence noted in the preceding paragraphs. What unites these various concepts or senses of violence is that in each instance something is done or happens to some or all people, be it with greater or lesser force, which works to their harm, injury, or degradation (whether or not it is so intended) but which is alterable by man (even if the individuals involved may not so believe). Now it might be objected that such a broad view itself does 'violence' to our ordinary notions. There would be some merit to this objection. However, Marx might respond that this objection merely reflects the limited, subjectivist, and ideological interpretation which is ordinarily given to these terms. The ordinary understanding of violence, which tends to see violence only in overt actions intended to harm someone, is functional within capitalism in that it protects the system from serious questioning and demands for change. Contrariwise, once one recognizes the broadly violent character of capitalist life, as Marx describes it,[20] one can no longer acquiesce in the continued existence of such a system. How, one wants to know, may capitalism be transcended? Must additional violence be used? Or may a (relatively) peaceful transformation be expected? As we have noted, Marx held that the answer depends on the particular society in question. Nevertheless, though Marx must decide in each particular situation whether or not communists should use overt force and violence, his general view is, then, that in *all* situations communists, as well as all other people, are the object of force and violence, whether explicit or implicit. Accordingly, whenever he claims that force must be used it is always an instance of meeting force with force, violence with violence!

This situation is not one that Marx moralizes about. He does not see it simply as an evil which could be expunged from present society. Such a separation of good and evil is not possible. In this, as well as in other instances, good and evil are inextricably bound up together. The possibility of change for the better rests (at least in some situations) on a further use of violence and force effectively and radically to change society. But how, then, did Marx differentiate between societies and situations? On what basis was violence justified in one situation but not in another?

Marx's analysis of the conditions justifying a violent revolution changed in his own development. It is possible here to distinguish between his earlier and later views. Even so, in both his early and later writings, the conditions for a justified violent revolution are for Marx linked with the conditions for a successful violent revolution − i.e. a revolution which actually changes society toward communism. A revolution, or rebellion, which did not succeed in creating the first stage of communism would not have been a justified communist revolution. Theory and praxis, justification and realization, are *not*, as we have seen in Chapter 3, separated by Marx.

In his early views, up until 1845, which were primarily concerned with a revolution in Germany, Marx argued that the following conditions suffice to justify a revolution:

Firstly, there must be a need for a radical change. Marx's analysis of man and society reveals that human life, under capitalism, is defined by relations 'in which man is a debased, enslaved, forsaken, despicable being, relations which cannot be better described than by the exclamation of a Frenchman when it was planned to introduce a tax on dogs: Poor dogs! They want to treat you like human beings!' (*MECW*, 3:182). This view derives both from Marx's view 'that man is the highest being for man' (*MECW*, 3:183, emphases omitted), as well as his study of German society:

> it is a case of describing the dull reciprocal pressure of all social spheres on one another, a general inactive ill humour, a limitedness which recognises itself as much as it misjudges itself, within the frame of a governmental system which, living on the preservation of all wretchedness, is itself nothing but wretchedness in office. (*MECW*, 3:177)

Life in these conditions is not simply a violation of, but an affront to, freedom; not merely the lack of, but the active denial of, freedom. Life in these conditions demands illusions. Hence, 'the demand to give up illusions about the existing state of affairs is the *demand to give up a state of affairs which needs illusions*' (*MECW*, 3:176). It is a state of affairs which requires a radical change.

Secondly, the situation must be such that it cannot be remedied by partial, merely political revolutions. 'Germany . . . will not be able to throw down the specific German limitations without throwing down the general limitation of the political present' (*MECW*, 3:184). There are various reasons for this view. A central reason is that the realm of the political in capitalist society is separated from, and opposed to, civil society. It is itself a reflection of 'the division of the human being into a *public man* and a *private man*' (*MECW*, 3:155):

> Where the political state has attained its true development, man — not only in thought, in consciousness, but in *reality*, in *life* — leads a twofold life, a heavenly and an earthly life: life in the *political community*, in which he considers himself a *communal being*, and life in *civil society*, in which he acts as *private individual*, regards other men as a means, degrades himself into a means, and becomes the plaything of alien powers. The relation of the political state to civil society is just as spiritual as the relation of heaven to earth. The political state stands in the same opposition to civil society, and it prevails over the latter in the same way as religion prevails over the narrowness of the secular world, i.e., by likewise having always to acknowledge it, to restore it, and allow itself to be dominated by it. In his *most immediate* reality, in civil society, man is a secular being. Here where he regards himself as a real individual, and is so regarded

by others, he is a *fictitious* phenomenon. In the state, on the other hand, where man is regarded as a species-being, he is the imaginary member of an illusory sovereignty, is deprived of his real individual life and endowed with an unreal universality. (*MECW*, 3:154)

Thus, the attempt to eliminate the conditions which constitute the need for radical change *within* the sphere of the political does not and cannot call into question one of the very sources of the problem. In addition, the backwardness and the egoism of the classes in Germany provides no hope even for a political revolution, a 'revolution which leave the pillars of the house standing.'

> On what is a partial, a merely political revolution based? On the fact that *part of civil society* emancipates itself and attains *general* domination; on the fact that a definite class, proceeding from its *particular situation*, undertakes the general emancipation of society. This class emancipates the whole of society but only provided the whole of society is in the same situation as this class, e.g., possesses money and education or can acquire them at will. (*MECW*, 3:184)

But no class in Germany has the courage or the ruthlessness which would allow it to play this role. Accordingly, there is hope neither for a partial remedy of the above situation nor, by means of political change in any sense, for a complete remedy.

Thirdly, Marx maintains that in these conditions, a complete change is required — a revolution which will undercut the pillars of the bourgeois house. But because of these conditions, because of the backwardness and anachronism of German classes, government, and the German kind, a new element must be forged in German society which could effect such a change. This is the proletariat — a class which is not a class of civil society and which knows the universal sufferings which are the material basis for a revolution. In addition, despite its sufferings and degradation, the German proletariat is particularly fitted for its revolutionary role since it is possessed of excellent capabilities for education and for being the theoretician of the European proletariat (*MECW*, 3:201-2). Thus, Marx asks and answers his own question:

> Where, then, is the *positive* possibility of a German emancipation? *Answer*: In the formation of a class with *radical chains*, a class of civil society which is not a class of civil society, an estate which is the dissolution of all estates, a sphere which has a universal character by its universal suffering and claims no *particular right* because no

particular wrong but *wrong generally* is perpetuated against it; which can no longer invoke a historical but only a *human* title; which does not stand in any one-sided antithesis to the consequences but in an all-round antithesis to the premises of the German state; a sphere, finally, which cannot emancipate itself without emancipating itself from all other spheres of society and thereby emancipating all other spheres of society, which, in a word, is the *complete loss* of man and hence can win itself only through the *complete rewinning of man*. This dissolution of society as a particular estate is the *proletariat*. (*MECW*, 3:186)

Consequently, because the conditions in Germany are as described above, Marx concluded that any revolution in Germany will be and must be a violent revolution: 'The weapon of criticism cannot, of course, replace criticism by weapons, material force must be overthrown by a material force' (*MECW*, 3:182). A violent revolution is both needed and justified in Germany. At such times, 'the most heroic devotion . . . is therefore imperatively called for' (*MECW*, 3:164). His argument, in short, is simply that no other way is possible given the degrading, morally corrupt, and backward economic, social and political conditions in Germany. With France the situation is different. In France the economic, political and social conditions are in advance of Germany. Thus, 'in France it is the reality of a gradual liberation . . . that must give birth to complete freedom.' In France,

the role of *emancipator* therefore passes in dramatic motion to the various classes of the French nation one after the other until it finally comes to the class which implements social freedom no longer on the basis of certain conditions lying outside man and yet created by human society, but rather organises all conditions of human existence on the presupposition of social freedom. (*MECW*, 3:186)

But in Germany, again, the practical life does not allow for such a gradual solution. Instead, only when they are *forced* by their situation, by their chains, will the Germans demand the dissolution of their present society (*MECW*, 3:186).

Will such a revolution in fact occur? Will the proletariat do that which it is called to do, that which the present situation morally justifies? Marx certainly thought it would:

As philosophy finds its *material* weapons in the proletariat, so the proletariat finds its *spiritual* weapons in philosophy. And once the lightning of thoughts has squarely struck this ingenuous soil of the people the emancipation of the *Germans* into *human beings* will take place. (*MECW*, 3:187)

Thus, a violent revolution against bourgeois German society is justified. And given the success of the critical activities of philosophy, as well as the suffering and degraded conditions in which the proletariat exists, such a revolution will occur. Then will the proletariat rise, weapons in hand, and strike its enemy.

A number of features of this early account should be noted. Firstly, Marx's ethics of freedom plays an essential role. A necessary condition for the justification of violent, revolutionary acts is that people within a society are dehumanized, they do not achieve freedom in the full sense. Marx is quite clear, as early as 1843, that it is the social conditions of life which must be altered in revolution — not simply or primarily the political conditions — in order to achieve freedom. Indeed, because the proletariat has hitherto thought in terms of the framework of politics, it has seen 'the curse of all evils in the *will*, and all means of remedy in *violence* and in the *overthrow* of a *particular* form of state.' In this it has been wrong. Consequently, it has 'squander[ed] its forces in senseless, useless revolts, which [have been] drowned in blood' (*MECW*, 3:204). Accordingly, given that man is denied freedom, that freedom (as defined in Chapter 4) — and not simply the overthrow of the present form of the state — is the object of proletarian efforts, and that non-violent means cannot essentially change society, a violent revolution is justified. Secondly, Marx does not, however, rest his argument for violent revolution simply on the preceding three factors. Theory alone (not to mention theory in the situation of Germany) is impotent. '*Ideas* can never lead beyond an old world order but only beyond the ideas of the old world order. Ideas *cannot carry out anything* at all. In order to carry out ideas men are needed who can exert practical force' (*MECW*, 4:119). Marx's ethics, however, is not impotent not simply because Marxists use it to clarify and enlighten others as to the reality of their situation, but also because reality itself strives towards such theory (*MECW*, 3:183). There is a need, a real interest, within society for such a radical change. This need is experienced in the degradation and misery people suffer. It is the aim of Marx's theoretical works, as well as the practical activity of communist groups and parties, to awaken the vast number of people to their degradation and misery, to this need. Once they self-consciously and knowingly experience this need for radical change, it is expressed in their indignation and denunciation. Thus, Marx's argument has a double basis: once the real situation of people is made clear to them *and* they experience their need for revolution, a justified revolution (and in Germany a violent revolution) will occur:

> Since man has lost himself in the proletariat, yet at the same time has not only gained theoretical consciousness of that loss, but through urgent, no longer removable, no longer disguisable, absolutely imperative *need* – the practical expression of *necessity* – is driven directly to revolt against this inhumanity, it follows that the proletariat can and must emancipate itself. (*MECW*, 4:37)

Thirdly, the suffering which the proletariat experiences is twofold. On the one hand, it suffers from not having enough to consume, to wear, a healthy place to live, etc. But, on the other hand, it also suffers from the conditions under which it produces – these conditions limit and restrict its development, exhaust its members, etc. That is, the proletariat suffers both as consumer and producer. It has been claimed that it is the second side of human suffering which is crucial in the conditions of a communist revolution: 'It is man as frustrated producer rather than man as dissatisfied consumer who makes a revolution, and the need of man as producer is to freely develop and express his manifold powers of productive activity, his creative potentialities in material life.'[21] Though there certainly is this 'rebelliousness of man as producer against his life conditions,'[22] it is doubtful, I think, that it is on this basis alone that Marx foresees a revolution. Too often he emphasizes the revolutionary, the subversive side of poverty. The reason such 'rebelliousness of man as a producer' is emphasized is because it is rightly seen that Marx's views are not utilitarian, not hedonistic, and are not based on justice – his ethics is not one which simply seeks to eliminate suffering or attain an equal amount of consumer goods. The end in terms of which a revolution is to be justified – i.e. communism – is not essentially connected with suffering *per se* so much as it is with a way of life which people as people should live – the life of freedom. This is not, however, a reason why Marx may not appeal to such suffering as a material condition for a successful and justified revolution. Indeed, to the extent a person experiences *either* kind of suffering such a person is not free according to Marx.

Finally, the conflict between the forces and relations of production, which plays such a significant role in his later views, plays little or no role in his early views. Likewise, though Marx's early account of the mode of production includes the relations of classes, the role of classes is relatively undeveloped in this account. Indeed, it is partly the case that a revolution is needed in Germany just because the productive conditions, as well as the classes, are so backward. In fact, because of its universal interests, the proletariat is counted as a non-class. Nevertheless, the mode of production does play an important role in Marx's early account. He recognizes that 'the proletariat is coming into being in Germany only as a result of the rising *industrial* development' (*MECW*, 3:186). In addition, since the proletariat is produced by private property, he claims that 'private property drives itself in its economic movement towards its own dissolution' (*MECW*, 4:36, cf. p. 282). Still, the role the mode of production plays omits various essential features which characterize his later views. Indeed, it is because of the modifications, in his later views, of the role the mode of production plays in revolutions that some have maintained that violence is no longer essential for a revolution.[23] It is to these later views I now turn.

Marx's later theory of revolution and violence is distinguished from his earlier views in various ways. On the one hand, some aspects of his early views are changed; on the other hand, new elements are added to these early views. Remaining constant is his appeal to the ethics of freedom, his insistence that violence is justified only if other means are not available, his view that theory plays an important role in revealing to people what their real situation is, as well as his claim that reality itself must strive towards theory in the sense that a need for radical change must develop in, and be experienced by, the proletariat.

One of the new elements in Marx's account is the conflict between the forces and relations of production. In each social formation hitherto, the social relations of production have set limits to the development of the forces of production. When the latter presses on the former then and only then can a revolution occur. Now if the forces of production are not sufficiently developed, then any revolutionary acts will either fail to change the system or should they change the system they will not result in a further step towards communism but, perhaps, in some reactionary form of government. As we have seen, Marx is rather vague and indeed open about how advanced such forces of production must be. Clearly, he does not think that a totally automatized industrial system of production must first be in place before revolutionary acts would have any chance of succeeding and hence possibly be justifiable. On the contrary, Marx seems to have held that the development of the productive forces in the advanced nineteenth-century Western societies was a sufficient basis for communism. In addition, since Marx was not a fatalist, it would not be inconsistent for Marx also to hold that various revolutionary acts might not be directed simply at changing the relations of production, but also at the forces of production themselves.

Marx's thought is wholly misunderstood if one believes that one must simply sit and wait until all the pieces, all the forces of production, are in place before one may dare to act. A Marxian revolutionary could justifiably act to 'push' the productive forces along as well. There are, however, clearly limits to how much and far such actions could advance the productive forces. The point is, however, that Marx's views do not exclude the possibility of revolutionary action in this sphere as well.

Secondly, as in the early views, revolutionary violence is only justified if, given the fullness and maturity of the forces of production, there is no other possibility to change the relations of production. Speaking of Germany in 1848 Marx claims that 'there is but one means for shortening, simplifying, concentrating the murderous death pangs of the old society and the bloody labor pains of the new, *only one means: revolutionary terrorism.*'[24] Revolutionary acts, violent acts, however, must have the real possibility of changing the system. Isolated acts of terrorism, or even crime against the *status quo*, are not, therefore, condoned or justified by Marx. They are simply foolish acts.

Now it has been claimed that Marx in fact holds that when the material conditions are ripe, are ready for a revolution, no force or violence will be needed. 'Recourse to terror is, according to Marx, an ultimate proof that the aims the revolution wishes to achieve cannot be achieved at present. Terror is less a means towards the realisation of a revolutionary aim than a mark of failure.'[25] Thus, it is maintained that Marx 'consistently opposes all radical attempts at armed insurrection.'[26] Violence, terror, force are only part of 'a subjectivist fallacy, abstracted from the real economic and social circumstances.'[27] When the social and economic circumstances are ripe, the revolution may be accomplished without force.

Such an interpretation of Marx's views on violence and revolution, as the preceding discussion should have shown, is untenable. It is correct that Marx actively opposed many groups who sought to throw themselves into battle against bourgeois society before he believed the time was ripe for revolution. But it does not follow from this that when the conditions are right for a revolution violence and force may not still be needed. Violence is a part of life, in Marx's views, before communism. He sees no reason why it should not also be used, when needed, by the proletariat in the creation of a life beyond violence.

Thirdly, classes play an essential role in Marx's later views. The proletariat is no longer deemed a non-class, but a class in the full and legitimate sense of the term. Indeed, a revolution is only possible to the extent that the proletariat unifies and constitutes itself as a class. This signifies Marx's changed perception that, in order to create communism, the proletariat must first capture political power and exercise that power even after the revolution. Thus Marx comments that

> the proletariat will use its political supremacy to wrest, by degrees, all capital from the bourgeoisie, to centralise all instruments of production in the hands of the State, i.e. of the proletariat organised as the ruling class; and to increase the total of productive forces as rapidly as possible. Of course, in the beginning, this cannot be effected except by means of despotic inroads on the right of property. (*MECW*, 6:504)

Such political power will be exercised by the dictatorship of the proletariat. It is not the aim of the present section to discuss this feature of Marx's later views on revolution. Suffice it to say, however, that Marx understood the concept of dictatorship in a manner rather different from that common today. To begin with, the dictatorship of the proletariat is the dictatorship of a class — which consists of the vast majority — over another class. Accordingly, Marx spoke of the proletariat winning the battle of democracy. Furthermore, by the 'dictatorship' of the proletariat Marx refers to its rule which uses force, coercion, and violence against the capitalist class. As such the significance of the dictatorship of the proletariat has been greatly overplayed. The bourgeois class has likewise used force, coercion, and violence against other classes. Accordingly, Marx also speaks of the dictatorship of the bourgeoisie (cf. *MECW*, 10:122, 125, 131). However, whereas great concern usually greets the phrase 'dictatorship of the proletariat,' relatively little attention is paid to the phrase 'the dictatorship of the bourgeoisie.' Consistency would seem to require a similar concern with the force and violence used by both dictatorships. Marx expresses his concern in so far as he justifies the violence, oppression, etc. of proletarian dictatorship as merely instrumental to communism — i.e. to the elimination of the use of such social means of control. The notion of the dictatorship of the proletariat is, then, Marx's recognition that the proletariat must capture political power and use it — which by definition is oppressive and more than likely involves the use of force and violence. Only in this manner could society hope to progress beyond violence.[28]

Finally, there is one further point which plays an important role in Marx's later deliberations on the justification of violence in revolution. This is the effect of the revoluton on the participants in the revolution. Marx held that such a revolution in some way purifies or cleanses the participants. Thus he claims:

> Both for the production on a mass scale of this communist con-
> sciousness, and for the success of the cause itself, the alteration of
> men on a mass scale is necessary, an alteration which can only take
> place in a practical movement, a *revolution*; the revolution is neces-
> sary, therefore, not only because the *ruling* class cannot be over-
> thrown in any other way, but also because the class *over-throwing* it
> can only in a revolution succeed in ridding itself of all the muck of
> ages and become fitted to found society anew. (*MECW*, 5:52-3)

It is far, then, from Marx's view that the use of revolution and the
violent acts which may attend it might contaminate the people who
would build a new society. The views of Gandhi, Martin Luther King,
and the like are quite remote from Marx's views. One ought not engage
in passive disobedience, à la Thoreau, so as to prepare oneself for a
society in which there will be no violence, in which coercion is ended.
Rather, the use of violence is fully compatible with the end Marx demands and indeed helps to foster it, rather than infect it, as others have
claimed.

Now it might be asked how Marx could hold such a view. If, as he
contends, individuals are significantly shaped by their environment, as
well as by the activities in which they engage, why would revolution
and violence not corrupt people, infect them rather than cleanse them
for life in communist society? I think there are two answers. On the
one hand, we must recall that contemporary bourgeois society is itself a
violent society. Violence and force characterize everyday life. Accordingly, the fact that the proletariat uses violence in the communist revolution does not mean that they are suddenly acting in ways which are
wholly unfamiliar and strange. Thus, the question really is: How is it
possible for violent, pre-communist society to be transferred into an
harmonious communist society? The answer to this question is Marx's
view that the multiple sources of violence — private property, competition, division of labor, wage labor, classes, etc. — will be eliminated by
the revolution. These institutions are also part of 'the muck' of past
ages of which the proletariat will rid society.

The second answer Marx may give refers us to his views on dialectics
as well as on the dynamics of social formation. Marx held that in the
course of human development social conditions undergo various qualitative changes. I think we see an illustration of this in the case of
violence (as well as egoism, suffering, need, etc.[29]) which occurs *before*
communism but which, given the change to communism, is effectively
excluded from society. The views of Gandhi, King, and the like are
distinctly non-dialectical in these regards. What one does for them to

bring about a new society will continue to affect those living in the new society. Moses, too, was not allowed to cross over into the Promised Land. But on Marx's dialectical views, there occurs a qualitative change in human relations and in humans themselves which protects life under communism from the effects of the violence that was used in bringing it about. Whether this is plausible or not depends, of course, on the conditions which Marx describes as obtaining under communism and the conditions under which he holds that people resort to violence.

It should be remembered, however, that the qualitative change which occurs in communism may be prepared for through a more or less long period during the first stage of communism. Indeed, given the vile nature of the first stage of communism it might seem that the period of time required would not be short. The following is Marx's rather graphic description of this first stage:

in its first form . . . the dominion of *material* property bulks so large that it wants to destroy *everything* which is not capable of being possessed by all as *private property*. It wants to disregard talent, etc., in an *arbitrary* manner. . . . Finally, this movement . . . finds expression in the brutish form of opposing *marriage* (certainly a *form of exclusive private property*) the *community of women*, in which a woman becomes a piece of *communal* and *common* property. It may be said that this idea of the *community of women gives away the secret* of this as yet completely crude and thoughtless communism. . . . This type of communism — since it negates the *personality* of man in every sphere — is but the logical expression of private property, which is this negation. (*MECW*, 3:294-5)

Accordingly, the change which people undergo, and must undergo, in the creation of communism need not be, and most probably could not be, a sudden one. As if to emphasize this point, Marx comments that 'the revolution . . . is no short-lived revolution. The present generation is like the Jews whom Moses led through the wilderness. It has not only a new world to conquer, it must go under in order to make room for men who are able to cope with a new world' (*MECW*, 10:117). Thus, the realization of communism may wait upon a new generation — perhaps even two (Moses wandered for forty years). It is, however, fruitless to speculate how long it might take to establish communsim. The point to be made here is that the time frame need not be a short one and that during this time the effects of the use of violence and coercion which have characterized previous societies and individuals might be overcome by eliminating their sources. *Will* these effects be overcome? Again, that will depend upon whether Marx correctly identified the sources of violence as well as the dialectical process by which men and society change.

There is a moral objection here, however, which has often been brought against Marx's views. Throughout the preceding discussion the instrumental nature of violence has been noted. It is the end of communism, complete human freedom, which ultimately justifies the use of violence in revolutionary situations. This view, which is taken to be but a salient instance of the view that the end justifies the means, is frequently received with shock and dismay. Can Marx, or anyone for that matter, really hold such a view? Doesn't such a view permit, if not promote, the use of extreme and unacceptable means to achieve one's ends? Marx condoned, as we have seen, acts of revenge during a revolution against 'hated individuals or public buildings that are associated only with hateful recollections.' With such a view, it would seem that there are few limits to the violence which might be exercised in a revolution. One supposes that Marx did not think that such 'hated individuals' would include neighbors amongst the proletariat who have a running personal dispute. Violence and terror should be limited to those who are members of the opposing, bourgeois class. But even this is problematic since Marx held that as individuals they too were trapped in their roles. The capitalist too is alienated. The makings for tragedy are abundant here.

Marx's answer to the first question above is, quite simply, 'Of course the end justifies the means — if the end does not justify them, what else does?' This is a view that not only Marx, but also many other philosophers have held as well. The problem with the above objection is that it interprets this answer to mean that the end then justifies any means — even though Marx's reply need not be interpreted in this way. To establish that Marx is not committed to objectionable means some have cited Marx's comment that 'the end which requires bad means is not a good end.'[30] This, however, is of doubtful help since it comes from Marx's earliest views, from a time before he had developed any of his views on historical materialism, ideology, or class struggle. Indeed, it stems from a time during which Marx spoke little if at all about revolution.

On the contrary, I suggest, Marx thought that vile ends would have to be used in bringing about communism. As I indicated above, Marx held, in general, that the development from capitalism to communism must go through a brutish, violent, terrible stage. But then did Marx place any limits on the means which communists might use to bring about communism? Are violence, terror, deceit, double-dealing, etc. all justified whenever the proletariat desires to use them? The answer, we have seen, is 'no.' Such means are only justified when the following conjoint conditions are satisfied: (a) they would be efficacious in bringing about communism; (b) other peaceful, open, and/or honest means are unavailable or prohibited to the proletariat. When communist parties are not banned, hounded, or repressed, they seek to proclaim openly their aims (*MECW*, 6:481). They do not simply for the love of intrigue form secret societies. Nor do they make hypocritical compromises and alliances simply out of a spiteful spirit: 'For such is the law and usage of struggle, and only from the *struggle* of parties can the future welfare arise — not from seemingly clever compromises or from a hypocritical alliance brought about despite conflicting views, interests and aims' (*MECW*, 7:27). Rather, means which traditionally have been condemned are used only when other means fail.

It must be remembered that this answer is given to a question raised in the context of capitalist society, which is itself characterized by the very means which the bourgeois world would seek to deny to communists. The proletariat, we have seen, is daily and hourly subjected to violence and coercion. *Capital* seeks to document the number and ways in which workers are deformed, maimed, and killed by such violence. And when they are not directly killed by the violence, they kill themselves — they commit suicide (cf. *MECW*, 4:597-612). If communists give up even the threat of violence they will be the losers. It is silly, then, to demand that communists be saints in the hell of capitalism. Indeed, there is a significant moral difference, Marx can claim, between the use by communists as opposed to capitalists of violence, terror, and deceit. Communist actions are consciously directed towards bringing about a morally superior society, a society free from such means. Capitalist actions, the violence and means used in bourgeois society, though unconsciously, unwittingly, and indirectly promoting communism are consciously, overtly, and directly opposed to such a society. Indeed, they are directed towards maintaining a violent society. Thus, if violence and other unsavory means are to be used, surely the means of the communist are less to be condemned, are more plausibly justifiable, than the capitalist means. Those who protest against such violence are simply those who have closed their eyes to capitalist violence. Thus, the implication of Marx's views on freedom for those living in capitalist society is the struggle to create the conditions upon which a successful revolution — whether peaceful or violent — can be had.

Obviously, it is a difficult question to answer, on the above account, whether a particular violent act is justified in a specific situation. However, such practical questions are fraught with difficulty on *any* theory of violence and revolution. There are no simple, easy answers to such questions. What Marx does do is to indicate some general and objective guidelines to consider in deciding these questions.

In conclusion, Marx's ethical views clearly permit — and even require — the use of violence (at least on occasion) in the establishment of communism. Whether the communist revolution requires the concerted action of a class or a non-class, whether a dictatorship of the proletariat is required or not, what positive as well as negative functions violence might be said to have are all particular issues which receive different answers in Marx's early or mature works. What does *not* change are his views that violence will most likely need to be used, that violence is justified by the end it is to promote, that such violence is simply a response in kind to bourgeois society, and that the individual under communism will not be negatively affected by the means which are used to bring about communism. In an important sense, violence is one of the central themes of Marx's meditations on bourgeois society. In Marx's eyes violence was a Protean notion; one of the failures of bourgeois society was its inability to see the different forms and shapes of violence as well as the integral role of violence in bourgeois society. The use of violence to transcend a society based on violence, in order to establish a free society, typifies Marx's revolutionary morals.

II

Supposing that a communist revolution — peaceful or violent — is successful, and (further) that the initial socialist stage is transcended, then a fully-fledged communist society will exist. People will have achieved freedom. The illegitimate power, violence, and coercion which may be exercised by, as well as over, people, classes, institutions and relations will have been eliminated. People will exercise effective control over their own lives — over their relations to others and to nature. They will live in 'an association, in which the free development of each is the condition for the free development of all' (*MECW*, 6:506).

The nature of Marxist freedom has already been discussed. However, the discussion in the preceding section suggests a different and interesting viewpoint from which to further illuminate the moral life *qua* free life under communism. In bourgeois society morality permits and sanctions the use of coercion and violence against various individuals as well as classes. Sometimes this takes the form of punishment; sometimes it does not. What role might violence, coercion, and punishment play in communism? May they be used legitimately against those living under communism, who have violated, in some way, the moral standards of communism? What is to happen to those who harm others? Will they be punished? How will moral discipline be effected? What role will authority play in such a society? To discuss these questions provides us with another opportunity to reflect on the nature of freedom and communism.

It might be doubted at the outset that there is anything to be discussed along the suggested lines. Under communism, as it is frequently portrayed, people will not injure, coerce, or impose themselves on others. People will uniformly act as they ought to act. Since man's relations will be fully in his control, they too will not coerce him. There will be no struggle or conflict. People will go about their daily activities in perfect freedom and peace. After all, Marx did claim that communism is 'the *genuine* resolution of the conflict between man and nature and between man and man — the true resolution of the strife between existence and essence, between objectification and self-confirmation, between freedom and necessity, between the individual and the species' (*MECW*, 3:296). Thus, it is claimed that there will be no question of harm, no use of violence, coercion or punishment under communism.[31] This is part and parcel of what Marx meant when he referred to the new kind of person to be realized under communism and the new consciousness which that person will have. Revolution will clear away the muck of preceding ages. A humanity liberated from violence, coercion and punishment will flourish afterwards.

Such a conclusion, however, is a hasty one. Though Marx may have thought that communism would be constituted by such a life at times, he does not seem committed to such a utopian ideal at all times or even fundamentally. Indeed, the above intepretation presupposes a kind of perfectibility in humans that seems rather implausible. I prefer then to interpret Marx's views as calling for a new human being, but one who is not omnipotent, omniscient, who does have (on occasion) failings. At least it is in this way we can formulate the most plausible and sympathetic reconstruction of Marx's views on communism. If these views then are found lacking, so much the worse for them — at least they have been given every possible opportunity. Accordingly, I suggest that Marx did indeed hold that, under communism, the institutions, social conflicts, and class antagonisms which occasion the injury and violence people do each other — and require subsequent punishment — are eliminated. In this sense communism is the resolution of the conflict between man and man. But it does not follow from this that, on occasion, a person might not, for individual reasons, harm or transgress against others. This is suggested by Marx's comment that

the bourgeois mode of production is the last antagonistic form of
the social process of production — antagonistic not in the sense of
individual antagonism but of an antagonism that emanates from the
individuals' social conditions of existence — but the productive
forces developing within bourgeois society create also the material
conditions for a solution of this antagonism.[32]

Though individual antagonism and injury will be greatly lessened by
communism, it would be rather utopian to believe that it could be
totally eliminated from any human society.[33] One can harm others out
of altruistic motives as well as egoistic motives, out of (temporary)
insensitivity as well as (long-standing) malicious insensitivity, out of
the lack of knowledge of another's interests as well as out of the knowledge that another's interests are vulnerable. Impulsiveness, anger, lack
of reflection may occasion the harm of individuals just as the oppression, exploitation, and slavery which one class imposes on another class
may harm the individuals in the latter class. How Marx thought the
prior kinds of causes of harm in individual relations were to be handled,
whether punishment can or should be used, suggests an important way
to further reveal his views on communism.

In striking contrast to his views on the necessity and legitimacy of
violence against various people in order to bring communism about,
Marx holds that, under communism, violence against people is out of
place. '*Punishment, coercion*,' Marx claims, 'is contrary to *human* conduct' (*MECW*, 4:179). Does it follow that there is to be no violence or
constraint then? Are those who harm others or who violate the moral
standards of communist society not to be punished? Yes, they are, but
only in the sense that they punish themselves for their misdeeds:

Under *human* conditions punishment will *really* be nothing but the
sentence passed by the culprit on himself. No one will want to con-
vince him that *violence* from *without*, done to him by others, is
violence which he had done to himself. On the contrary, he will see
in *other* men his natural saviours from the punishment which he has
imposed on himself. (*MECW*, 4:179)

Under communism, then, there will be punishment, but it will all be
self-punishment. Any violence which people might legitimately use will
be that violence they do to themselves.

Now however peculiar and implausible such a view might initially
sound as a theory of punishment, there is certainly nothing self-
contradictory about this suggestion. We do speak of a person punishing

187

himself for having done this or that. He blames himself for his misdeed. Usually this involves feelings of responsibility for something done, as well as feelings of remorse, regret, or guilt for having done it. However, self-punishment need not be simply a question of feelings. A person might also punish himself by denying himself certain things he likes or favors, or by forcing himself to do certain things or undergo various experiences which he dislikes. Indeed, such self-punishment can be as severe or more severe than publicly administered punishment. At least some instances of suicide exemplify the extremity to which self-punishment may go.

It is also important to point out here that to allow that there is self-punishment under communism is to allow that there are certain ways of acting which may be justified or unjustified, and that, consequently, people may or may not act as they should. In short, it implies that there are moral standards which even though generally followed are not always followed. This corroborates my suggestion above that the most appropriate way to interpret Marx's views on communism is to allow for human failings. I take it, then, that it is mistaken to claim, as it often is, that 'in the perfect post-revolutionary society moral efforts would no longer be necessary, since the existence and behavior of every individual would coincide with the expectations and desires of all.'[34] This view of communism in which no one does or can do any wrong is, I suggest, a caricaturization of communism. It is important, admittedly, not to underestimate how radically different communist society will be. On the other hand, it is also important to try to view it as a society of human beings, not of angels. Hence, it is also dangerous to view communism as involving such a radical change that it slips away into a mere utopian phantasy. Punishment connotes sanctions brought against a person for something wrong he has done. Thus, unless people can act wrongly it would be senseless to say that they can be punished or punish themselves.

Finally, it might be noted that Marx's view of punishment draws on Hegel's theory of punishment. Indeed, punishment under communism, as portrayed by Marx, might be said to be an *Aufhebung* of punishment, as portrayed by Hegel, under capitalism. It was Hegel's view that those who committed crimes should be punished by the state for their crimes. Punishment negates or annuls the crime which was itself a negation of someone else's right. However, such punishment is pointless unless the criminal sees in his punishment his own self-judgment: 'The injury [the penalty] which falls on the criminal is ... *eo ipso* his implicit will, an embodiment of his freedom, his right ... it is also a right established within the criminal himself, i.e. his objectively embodied will, in his action.'[35] As in so many other cases, Marx saw a kernel of truth in Hegel's claim which he sought to preserve in communism. To begin with, Marx does not accept or draw on Hegel's view that punishment annuls or negates the crime. This in itself is significant. If punishment is the negation of a crime which negates a person's right, then punishment is the reaffirmation of that right.[36] However, I have argued in Chapter 5 that Marx does not formulate his theory of the moral life in terms of rights. Accordingly, it should be no surprise, and is an important confirmation of the argument in Chapter 5, that Marx does not adopt the annulment view of punishment Hegel proposes. Instead, Marx fastens on Hegel's notion that a person's punishment must be the result of his own self-judgment. Though Marx does not say that punishment is an embodiment of one's right, he would say (with Hegel) it is an embodiment of one's freedom. Hegel erred not only in retaining the violence which the state brought to bear against individuals, but also in retaining the state and the civil society upon which it rested. Accordingly, Marx claims, the kernel of truth in Hegel's views, the self-judgment of the criminal, 'remains a mere "idea", a mere speculative interpretation of the *current empirical punishments* for criminals' (*MECW*, 4:179). In his rejection of Hegel's transcendental sanction of the rules of existing society (*MECW*, 11:496-7), Marx adopts merely Hegel's notion of self-judgment and transforms it into his view on the self-punishment of individuals under communism. Thus, though what Marx advocates comes as close to the complete elimination of punishment as one might imagine, still one cannot say that Marx totally eliminates punishment.

Now under what circumstances might Marx's view of punishment as self-punishment be plausible? My answer will be developed in three steps. The first step is to note the different kinds of causes which Marx believes lie behind crime and the need of punishment in capitalism. His proposals to eliminate these causes constitute an important part of the reason why he finds self-punishment plausible. In general, Marx holds that crime is due to social or environmental conditions. Thus, he claims that if people are criminal or, more generally, immoral, 'the crime must not be punished in the individual but the anti-social sources of crime must be destroyed' (*MECW*, 4:131).

Under this general view Marx points to at least two different environmental situations, which are the occasion of crime under capitalism. Firstly, crime may be due to conflicts which exist between the egoistic interests of individuals and the dominant social relations. On this view crime is 'the struggle of the isolated individual against the predominant relations. . . . [It] is not the result of pure arbitrariness. On the contrary,

189

it depends on the same conditions as that domination' (*MECW*, 5:330). Now the dominant relations depend on the material life of individuals, their mode of production and form of intercourse, which mutually determine each other (*MECW*, 5:329). But what is it about this material life that crime depends on? Marx answers that 'it is precisely because individuals who are independent of one another assert themselves and their own will, and because on this basis their attitude to one another is bound to be egoistical, that self-denial is made necessary in law and right' (*MECW*, 5:329). That is, crime arises when one does not deny oneself, but egoistically asserts one's own interests — there is a clash of interests between the individual and the dominant interests. Thus, the individual capitalist against his 'contract and the law of exchanges' greedily attempts to derive more surplus labor from the worker than he is entitled to (*Capital*, I:234, 242). Similarly, greed and egoistical calculation may lead others to steal or harm people. Crucial to this view of crime, then, is the independence and separation of individuals from each other, and their consequent egoistical assertion of their wills. In short, crime on this view is a consequence of the type of individual which is especially characteristic of capitalism. Since not all such individuals will restrain their individual, egoistic wills, crimes are committed.

Secondly, and more specifically, crime arises out of the social and economic consequences of the relations which define bourgeois society. Such consequences are the increasing pauperism, economic distress, and alienation of the proletariat. For example, Marx claims that between 1841 and 1848 the amount of pauperism increased as well as the number of criminals (*MECW*, 11:359). Regarding this period, Marx comments 'to the same extent, however, that pauperism increases, *crime* increases and the life source of the nation itself, the *youth* is demoralised' (*MECW*, 7:334). Additionally, Marx notes that, in the development of the proletariat, working people

> direct their attacks not against the bourgeois conditions of production, but against the instruments of production themselves: they destroy imported wares that compete with their labor, they smash to pieces machinery, they set factories ablaze, they seek to restore by force the vanished status of the workman of the Middle Ages. (*MECW*, 6:492)

That is, because the workman of capitalism is merely an instrument of the machine, because his work is degraded, alienated work, he is led to commit crimes — smash machinery, commit arson, steal to preserve his life. Accordingly, the causes of crime in capitalist society are various: the individualistic, egoistic self-assertion of individuals against the dominant relations, poverty, economic distress, as well as alienation. Marx even suggests in one aside that some crime might be due 'partly from inclinations' (*Capital*, I:734).

In general, however, Marx held that each of the preceding causes or occasions of crime was social or environmental in nature. As we have seen, man is shaped by his environment, and he can be shaped by it both for good as well as for evil. Further, each of the above causes is taken by Marx to be amenable to correction by social action, by modification of the social environment, through the institution of a system of social relations which would eliminate poverty, reflect the harmonious relations of social individuals, and allow for full human development. In order to accomplish such a radical change it must be recognized that the causes of crime do not relate so much to the particular political institutions in any country as to the underlying conditions of modern society itself: 'It is not so much the particular political institutions of a country as the fundamental conditions of modern *bourgeois* society, which produce an average amount of crime in a given national fraction of society' (*MECW*, 11:497). Because the basic conditions of bourgeois society give rise to crime with 'the regularity of physical phenomena,' Marx argues that there is 'a necessity for deeply reflecting upon an alteration of the system that breeds these crimes, instead of glorifying the hangman who executes a lot of criminals to make room only for the supply of new ones' (*MECW*, 11:497-8). Accordingly, Marx proposes (as we have seen) that under communism private property, exchange, money, the division of labor, classes, the division of town and country will all (among others) be abolished. The elimination of these basic social conditions and relations will eliminate the cause of crime and hence the necessity of punishing, inflicting violence on, other people.

The question is, however, how do these views affect the plausibility of self-punishment? Marx's answer is that if the preponderant causes of crime are social, and if these social conditions can be remedied, we need grant only two further conditions in order to establish the plausibility of self-punishment. On the one hand, we must hold that there is nothing inherently evil in human beings, that given the chance, i.e. given communist living conditions, they can be and would be good. This is but another way to say that man is basically good. As Marx says,

> there is no need for any great penetration to see from the teaching of materialism on the original goodness and equal intellectual endowment of men, the omnipotence of experience, habit and

education, and the influence of environment on man, the great significance of industry, the justification of enjoyment, etc. how necessarily materialism is connected with communism and socialism. (*MECW*, 4:130)

The second point that must be granted is that if people are basically good and are given an environment in which there are no environmental forces or conditions which would lead or force them to commit crimes, to breach society's rules, then, if a person did do something against others, he would understand and feel that he himself was responsible. He could not blame his misdeed on others or on the environment. If, then, one were to take such responsibility for one's acts, one would blame and condemn oneself, not others, for what one did. In so acting, one would be punishing oneself.

However, would a person take such responsibility? What reason is there to believe that a person would or could impose such self-discipline upon himself if that is the sole kind of discipline to which a person must accord? Indeed, how is he to know what he should be doing? To answer these questions, we must turn to the second step of the argument.

One of the consequences of the radical change (e.g. abolition of private property) Marx envisions is that the state together with its court system will be also abolished. In this manner, one of the significant means by which violence and punishment is inflicted on people will also be transcended. Likewise, one of the significant sources of enforcing social discipline will be eliminated. However, one must remember that for Marx the state is defined as an institution for the oppression of subordinate classes. Consequently, Marx is not committed by his claim regarding the abolition of the state to the further claim that relations of authority, of legitimate power, over people are to be abolished. Instead, he is merely committed to the weaker claim that what will disappear will be illegitimate instances of the power of one person over another. Legitimate cases of power over individuals, instances of authority, may remain. In this sense Marx is fully in the moral and political tradition of Western philosophy regarding the legitimation of the power of some people over others. Marx notes explicitly in *Capital* that

all combined labor on a large scale requires, more or less, a directing authority, in order to secure the harmonious working of the individual activities, and to perform the general functions that have their origin in the action of the combined organism, as distinguished from the action of its separate organs. A single violin player is his own conductor; an orchestra requires a separate one. (*Capital*, I:330-1)

Even in that well-known bucolic passage in *The German Ideology*, in which Marx speaks of a person hunting in the morning, fishing in the afternoon, rearing cattle in the evening, etc. 'just as I have a mind,' Marx is still at pains to note that this requires that society regulate the general production (cf. *MECW*, 5:47).

Furthermore, Marx had maintained earlier that the authority in the workshop and in society stood in an inverse ratio (*MECW*, 6:185). Thus, in capitalism there was a great deal of authority in the workshop but little in the rest of society. Marx further suggests in *The German Ideology* that with regard to work, under communism, one will have a great deal of choice. The implication would seem to be that in communism which sought to loosen the authority in the workshop there would be much more authority in society.

One might ask, then, what role such authority will have in communist society? What powers will it have? Marx does not, however, speculate on such matters. For example, he comments that

the question then arises: what transformation will the state undergo in communist society? In other words, what social functions will remain in existence there that are analogous to present functions of the state? This question can only be answered scientifically, and one does not get a flea-hop nearer to the problem by a thousandfold combination of the word people with the word state.[37]

Nevertheless, for our purposes we do not need the details to questions that Marx never answered. We can more generally note that there will be authorities and that they will have the powers, as noted above, of 'securing the harmonious working of all individual activities.' But what does this mean or involve? Since it is a non-political authority, it is an authority which is non-coercive. Suppose, however, that one or more people do not agree with the authority's assessment of the situation and refuse to go along with the proposed activities? Can they be censored? Can sanctions be brought against them? And if so, how is this different from punishment?

Marx has, I think, two answers here. Firstly, there is no reason to suppose that before general plans and social agreements have been formulated everyone must mindlessly agree to what others suggest. Marx can allow that disagreement and dispute take place over what the best general decisions would be to fulfill the social needs of a group of people. The preceding questions are misleading if they suggest that this is not possible or plausible under communism. Secondly, however, *after* general plans and decisions have been agreed upon, Marx apparently did not think that problems of social discipline would arise. He drew upon two different kinds of evidence. The first was the experience gained by the various co-operative movements in the early nineteenth century:

> The value of these great social experiments cannot be over-rated. By deed, instead of by argument, they have shown that production on a large scale, and in accord with the behests of modern science, may be carried on without the existence of a class of masters employing a class of hands; that to bear fruit, the means of labour need not be monopolised as a means of dominion over, and of extortion against, the labouring man himself; and that, like slave labour, like serf labour, hired labour is but a transitory and inferior form, destined to disappear before associated labour plying its toil with a willing hand, a ready mind, and a joyous heart.[38]

These 'great social experiments' were significant not only for the preceding reasons but also because they were instances of authority, of supervision, which were not antagonistic: 'In a cooperative factory the antagonistic nature of the labour of supervision disappears, because the manager is paid by the labourers instead of representing capital counterposed to them' (*Capital*, III:387). These experiments gave Marx reason to believe that under communism people might co-operatively, harmoniously, live and work together.

The second kind of evidence he drew from the experiences of contemporary revolutionary actions and groups. For example, Marx took the Paris Commune to be at least a partial confirmation of his views. Admittedly, the Commune could not be said to have achieved a communist society. Still Marx was eager to note the decrease in crime, the safety with which people could go about the streets: 'Wonderful, indeed, was the change the commune had wrought in Paris! ... No more corpses at the morgue, no nocturnal burglaries, scarcely any robberies; in fact for the first time since the days of February, 1848, the streets of Paris were safe, and that without police of any kind.'[39]

Accordingly, in answer to the questions raised above (pp. 192-3), self-discipline will be buttressed by the discipline which is required by authorities in society. Such authorities are themselves necessary to the functioning of modern communist society. Nevertheless, such social discipline is non-coercive, and non-violent. It does not involve or use punishment. The point, however, is that self-discipline is not left simply to itself. It is, at the least, informed as to its responsibilities by social authorities. But how is it, then, that a person comes to take upon himself those responsibilities such that failure to fulfil them results in self-punishment? Doesn't this remain a significant problem? The third part of Marx's view provides the answer.

Apparently Marx thought that such a problem would not arise since the consciousness and very self-identity of those living under communism would be effectively changed: 'The individuals' consciousness of their mutual relations will, of course, be completely changed, and, therefore, will no more be the "principle of love" or *dévoûment* than it will be egoism' (*MECW*, 5:439). Here we come to Marx's notion of the self, and its relations to others and to the communist community. This is the ultimate basis upon which Marx's thought rests. It is the essence of his ethics of freedom.

As we have seen, Marx holds that 'as individuals express their lives, so they are' (*MECW*, 5:31). Now how they express their lives is a function of the conditions of labor, etc. Under communism individuals are allowed the many-sided development of themselves. With this there is a development of the universality of the individual: 'In the case of an individual, for example, whose life embraces a wide circle of varied activities and practical relations to the world, and who, therefore, lives a many-sided life, thought has the same character of universality as every other manifestation of his life' (*MECW*, 5:263). With communism, that is, a universalization of individuals takes place. One is no longer the one-sided, limited, atomistic being which characterizes bourgeois society, but has become a universal being. What this means in terms of the harmony of interests that prevails between individuals and amongst the members of the communist community has already been discussed in Chapter 4.

It is, however, this universalization of the individual which lends plausibility, in the end, to the notion of self-discipline and self-punishment. One must remember that if the narrow, one-sided, egoistic bourgeois self is the consequence of bourgeois society, then a very different self is to be the consequence of communist society. The self which punishes itself is not a self fundamentally at odds with others or society. It is not a self which 'speculates on creating a *new* need in another, so as to drive him to fresh sacrifice, to place him in a new dependence and to seduce him into a new mode of *enjoyment* and therefore economic ruin. [It does not try] ... to establish over the other an *alien* power, so as thereby to find satisfaction of [its] own selfish need' (*MECW*, 3:306). In short, it is not a self which defines itself in opposition to others. Rather, it is a self which positively takes its identity from its mutually supporting and co-operative relations with others. Marx illustrates the most thoroughgoing instance of such an identity by singling out the relationship of man to woman:

> the relation of man to woman is the *most natural* relation of human being to human being. It therefore reveals the extent to which man's *natural* behavior has become *human*, or the extent to which the *human* essence in him has become a *natural* essence — the extent to which his *human nature* has come to be *natural* to him. This relationship also reveals the extent to which man's *need* has become a *human* need; the extent to which, therefore, the *other* person as a person has become for him a need — the extent to which he in his individual existence is at the same time a social being. (*MECW*, 3:296)

To the extent that a person identifies with others, finds his identity in his relations with others, one needs others as persons. One is directly and significantly affected by the consequences one's actions have on the needs and interests of others. In such a situation, we — all of us — 'realise each other in [an] intense, pathetic, and important way.'[40]

Accordingly, it is mistaken to characterize as a 'doubtful assumption,'[41] Marx's view that self-punishment connotes self-discipline without social discipline. As we have seen (in the preceding step), in communist society there will be authorities and social discipline, albeit non-coercive and non-violent. But more importantly, one must also recognize that under communism since people are closely bound up and identified with each other, it is incorrect to think that they view each other distantly — that the 'business' of each is simply his own 'business.' People are interrelated — not only in their interests and problems, but also in their formulation of the general plans and decisions by which society is to be run. Thus, though others have something to say in evaluation and criticism of one's actions, such considerations do not constitute acts of coercion, constraint or violence. Public criticism and public exposure of one's misdeeds — which one would meet with self-criticism and self-punishment — might play an important role in such a system. Whether such criticism by others constitutes an infringement of one's freedom will depend on how restricted or enlarged a view of one-self one has. If one's self is viewed as limited, confined to one's own body and private experiences, everything else will be an encroachment. On the other hand, if one's self is universalized under communism, if one identifies with others, with their needs and interests as well, then no more would one's neighbor's or friend's demands on one be felt as an unjustified impingement, than would be the demands of one's stomach. Just as self-rule is not achieved at the expense of others, so my self-punishment is not something I engage in to the exclusion of others.

By way of concluding, we may consider two objections to the above account which are often made. Firstly, it is objected that such a theory might be plausible for small homogeneous groups. In such groups the immediate presence of people with whom one is closely bound up might be the basis for such self-control and self-punishment. However, in a large, culturally diverse, and mobile society such a theory loses even this plausibility. Such cultural diversities attenuate the immediacy one person feels for another and hence also the restrictions one is likely to impose on his conduct.[42] Because people are more mobile, because they have 'more changing and varied beliefs about right and wrong conduct' in such a modern society, people are less sensitive to others, less moved by fear of public disgrace and shame. Hence they are also less responsible.[43]

This criticism underestimates how radically Marx envisions the change in society to be. Indeed, it presupposes the continued existence of a pluralistic liberal society. On the contrary, Marx envisioned a communist society as literally a world society without many of the national, cultural, and social barriers and diversities that presently exist. 'The working men have no country' (*MECW*, 6:502), says Marx. 'National differences and antagonisms between peoples are daily more and more vanishing. . . . The supremacy of the proletariat will cause them to vanish still faster' (*MECW*, 6:503). Instead of various cultural and national literatures there will be a world literature (*MECW*, 6:488). Racial differences too will not be recognized and accepted but also abolished: 'Even naturally evolved differences within the species, such as racial differences, etc. . . . can and must be abolished in the course of historical development' (*MECW*, 5:425). In effect, Marx's suggestion is that we must turn the world into a global community, or (as some have referred to it today, in non-Marxist contexts) a global village. The motivation and justification for Marx's efforts in this direction were his belief that 'for the people to be able truly to unite, they must have common interests' (*MECW*, 6:388). He pursued these efforts to the elimination of those cultural, social, and natural diversities upon which the above objection rests.

Secondly, it is objected that the kind of world or global community Marx envisioned in which self-punishment would (let it be granted) be plausible would constitute a deadeningly uniform society. Once cultural, national, racial differences are transcended, and all individuals are able to identify with others because of similar interests, one has a world of bland sameness. In response, Marx might point out that this objection, made by those in capitalism, is interesting since, by their own categories, it does not rest on moral grounds so much as aesthetic grounds. Yet their own theories give morality precedence over aesthetics. Accordingly, the bourgeois could not raise this objection as a fundamental objection. Further, if it is diversity the bourgeois seek then surely capitalism itself must be condemned, for obviously capitalism has reduced the diversity which has heretofore existed in the world:

> The bourgeoisie, by the rapid improvement of all instruments of production, by the immensely facilitated means of communication, draws all, even the most barbarian, nations into civilisation. The cheap prices of its commodities are the heavy artillery with which it batters down all Chinese walls, with which it forces the barbarians' intensely obstinate hatred of foreigners to capitulate. It compels all nations, on pain of extinction, to adopt the bourgeois mode of production; it compels them to introduce what it calls civilisation into their midst, i.e. to become bourgeois themselves. In one word, it creates a world after its own image. (*MECW*, 6:488)

Given the sameness of the world which capitalism is creating, the point is not whether or not there will be such uniformity in the world, but how it will be organized and to what ends? Surely a world such as is being created anyway which is organized on the basis of freedom is superior to one organized for the production of surplus value. Finally, though the world of communism will be uniform in a way which is unprecedented, Marx might still object that it will not be a deadening uniformity. It would be deadening only if people, their thoughts and actions, were censored, restricted, and confined. But communism is the attempt to expand the real freedom people experience. Only if we believed that people will stop being creative, imaginative, and innovative might we expect this uniformity to be deadening. But there is no reason to believe that this will occur.

In conclusion, then, Marx's view of punishment under communism provides us with but another way to see the fundamental role and nature of freedom in Marx's thought. His view was a grand one — one at the end of a long line of Western thought. Granted his views on the nature of crime, authority, and individual identity, one may understand the possibility he held out for self-discipline and self-punishment under communism. Granted his views on freedom, alienation, and violence, one may understand his condemnation of capitalism. Granted his views on historical materialism, ideology, and justification, one may accept his claim that his condemnation of capitalism was not based on just another external ideal applied to Western man. In each of these instances

I have suggested that his views are part and parcel of Western philosophy. And thus, Marx might say, if many react against his views, that it may be that they perceive, however darkly, the negative implications and weaknesses of their own views in his work. It is not inappropriate to remember his words: *'De te fabula narratur'* — this story is about you.

Part three
An evaluation of
Marx's ethics

7 Moral implications and ethical conclusions

> There is no royal road to science, only those who do not dread the fatiguing climb of its steep paths have a chance of gaining its luminous summits. (*Capital*, I:21)

Marx's ethics is an ethics of freedom. His criticism of capitalism rests upon no other foundation. Unless one understands Marx's notion of freedom one cannot understand Marx's other views. Marxist freedom, I have argued, is the all-encompassing notion of individual self-determination within concrete and harmonious relations to nature and to other persons. It is both an inspiring and a troublesome notion. The universal community of man defines, in part, such freedom. Nevertheless, its realization presupposes class-struggle, violence, and revolution. Individual self-development is central to Marxian freedom. But the individual self seems to be transcended in its development. Marx's notion of freedom stands in the tradition of German philosophy since Luther. The problems of this tradition were also his, though his solutions were uniquely his own. Indeed, Marxian freedom is an extension and development of the notion of freedom which has played a central, if not the central, role in Western moral and political thought for almost a millennium. And to the extent that his ethics is an ethics of virtue, the roots of his thought go back two millennia to Greek philosophical thought.

Understanding of Marx's views, however, should also give rise to evaluation and appraisal. It is easy, I suppose it might be granted, to find faults and problems in Marx's thought. Certainly not all the difficulties which have been discovered – or claimed to be discovered – in Marx are really there. Thus previous simplistic interpretations of historical materialism and his views on ethics must be seen as either misinterpretations or willful attempts to condemn his thought.

There are, however, real difficulties in Marx. He simply does not go into the details that are both necessary and desirable for a plausible, fully-fledged account of historical materialism. The ethics underlying

203

his thought is only implicit and fragmentary. He does not critically develop or defend his views on freedom, egoism, justice, etc. in the manner which they require. That he might have spoken more directly about communist society is a fault noted by many.

Still, though the finding of such faults and problems is part of the evaluation of a thinker, certainly it cannot constitute the entire evaluation. It is not terribly difficult to find difficulties in the work of Descartes, Kant, Hume, or Mill. If they were to be evaluated simply on the basis of the errors and problems in their work, it is to be doubted that we would ever speak of their work today or hear their names mentioned. Clearly, they cannot be measured by the sum of their errors. Neither can Marx. Accordingly, we must also look to that which is positive, interesting, and insightful in a thinker. And this too we must do in this concluding chapter.

The preceding text has been divided into two parts: Marx's methodological, or meta-ethical, views and his normative moral views. In this chapter I will keep roughly to this division as well. Obviously I cannot discuss the merits and faults of all the points touched on in the preceding chapters. Nor is it my intention to discuss and evaluate Marx's various particular views on the transcendence of private property or the division of labor, not to mention the different predictions, both historical and economic, which have been attributed to him. Rather I will restrict my discussion to Marx's basic ethical and moral ideas which lend the demands he does make the intelligibility they may possess. Marx's views have much that is interesting and potentially fruitful in them. They are also disturbing in many ways. This chapter seeks to bring out both these aspects of Marx's ethics of freedom.

I

One's approach to moral problems determines a great deal of the results with which one ends. For Marx, one's philosophic and/or scientific methodology must be, to be significant at all, systematic, material, and historical. It must seek to grasp the real, material embodiment of the objects it investigates, rather than simply the current conceptualization of those objects. Further, the object of criticism, the phenomenon, must be studied and understood not as something which is static and isolated, but as that which is dynamic and interrelated with other phenomena. In this way, Marx assumes, one's methodological approach reflects and captures what is real or true as opposed to what is apparent or ideological.

Since the free life is Marx's ultimate concern, we must study man as he actually is, and not simply as he conceives of himself in his ideas and theories. We find, Marx contends, that human life is divided into various roles, power relations, and hierarchies of activities, the dynamics of which are ultimately founded upon those basic relations which are created to fulfill the needs and wants of individuals. We also find a historical and moral development in these relations, their underlying productive forces, and the social forms of life associated with them. Some of this is manifest, some lies beneath the surface of mystification. However, it is only through the investigation of these fundamental productive realities within which humans live that we can grasp the nature and conditions of freedom. Such an investigation − such an ethics − is singularly comprehensive in its grasp; it may also be said to have a materialistic or naturalistic aspect to it.

In this approach, Marx stands in stark contrast to contemporary Anglo-American ethics. Whereas Marx takes man in his basic social relations to be the direct object of investigation, contemporary ethics has taken the moral judgment and the language used to express it as the direct object of investigation. Marx studies man in his historical, social, economic and psychological contexts. In general, contemporary ethics studies moral language and judgments independently of such contexts. For Marx, the central question of ethics concerned the discovery and further realization of the values presupposed in man's historical development. Whereas for contemporary ethics the central issue concerns the question 'What ought I to do?'[1] for Marx, it was the social contexts and historical settings which were essential to an understanding and revolution of man and society. For contemporary ethics a non-historical understanding of the principles of ethics is generally the (unrecognized) goal; change, it is assumed, will follow if all men of goodwill will reason together. Marx maintains a broad, inclusive view of morality; contemporary ethics insists on a narrow, more restrictive, view of morality. In these various contrasts, we may see the strengths and weaknesses not only of Marx's view but also those of contemporary ethics. There are two central groups of issues arising out of these contrasts that I would like to discuss.

Firstly, it is one of the strengths of Marx's ethics that the social and historical contexts of morality play a prominent role. There are several reasons for this view. Because Marx concentrates on the social and historical dimensions of morality, he questions various assumptions unwittingly made by contemporary ethics − e.g. the independence of morality from class interests, the atomistic characterization of individuality, and the non-historical nature of human values and moralities.

Because Marx's method leads him to question such assumptions his ethics is much less likely to be simply an unreflective defense of the *status quo*. There is, consequently, a potential openness and flexibility to his ethics. Further, because his discussion of ethics and morality themselves are to be understood in the context of the historical development of human productive activities, the results of his ethics are inherently practically oriented; they are designed to show where, in these contexts, moral change can come and must come; they are designed to have an effect rather than simply to moralize about the evil in society. In short, Marx's approach is interesting and fruitful not only because it opens up questions contemporary ethics tends to leave closed, but also because it defines itself in the thick of battle; that is, it conceives itself to be giving not simply another moral interpretation but rather concrete answers to practical questions drawn from a study of the complex phenomenon itself.

Each of these reasons, I suggest, reflects corresponding weaknesses in contemporary ethics. Two examples may serve to illustrate the point. On Marx's view people may be mistaken, systematically mistaken, in their ideas and values — i.e. they may possess an ideological or false consciousness. Contrariwise, contemporary ethics has quite commonly held that an individual's choices, if made by one who is 'free, impartial, willing to universalise, conceptually clear, and informed about all possibly relevant facts,'[2] are justified. This is, however, not to raise important questions about the nature, the source, and the role which the basic attitudes of such individuals play. Though contemporary ethics allows that individuals may have mistaken beliefs and values, that there may be a systematic nature to these mistakes and that the source of such false consciousness may lie in the structure of society are possibilities which it has rarely considered. This is not to say that there are not significant problems in Marx's analysis of this issue. What criteria can be used for distinguishing false from true consciousness? What role does an individual's consent play in the determination of his true wants or needs? When is a need or want a 'real' want or need? These questions, as well as others, Marx would ideally have considered much more closely. But in an age of mass advertising, mass communication, and rampant other-direction, it is important that questions about false consciousness, the course and nature of one's basic attitudes, wants, and needs be asked. And it is this to which Marx's ethics is committed.

Similarly, since Anglo-American ethics has concerned itself with moral judgments and language independently of its social and historical interrelations, it has scarcely considered the prejudices and value assumptions which might be built into such judgments and language.

The possibility, for example, of sexist elements in language is simply not a problem given the approach of contemporary ethics. What is the effect, what are the moral implications, of using 'he' for male as well as female? How does this affect the value picture of male and female? What power relationships does language reflect? To what extent is the medium the message? These questions cannot be answered here. It is enough to indicate that contemporary ethics tends to block out such questions in order to contrast it with Marx's approach which, to its advantage, embraces such questions. Thus, it is a question for Marx whether or not and to what extent our language carries implicit values and assumptions upon which we should not construct a morality. It may be that we cannot simply accept our present moral language as the ultimate touchstone of an ethics. Indeed, Marx claims at one point that our language is so alienated that were we to speak now in a non-alienated language, we would hardly understand each other:

> The only intelligible language in which we converse with one another consists of our objects in their relation to each other. We would not understand a human language and it would remain without effect. By one side it would be recognised and felt as being a request, an entreaty, and therefore a *humiliation*, and consequently uttered with a feeling of shame, of degradation. By the other side it would be regarded as *impudence* or *lunacy* and rejected as such. We are to such an extent estranged from man's essential nature that the direct language of this essential nature seems to us a *violation of human dignity*, whereas the estranged language of material values seems to be the one well-justified assertion of human dignity that is self-confident and conscious of itself. (*MECW*, 3:227)

Surely there are good reasons and historically explicable grounds for the preceding differences between Marx's ethics and contemporary ethics. Indeed, a great deal of contemporary ethics would claim that the preceding questions are not properly philosophical questions at all, but rather empirical questions whose determination may involve philosophical questions and carry significance for normative conclusions. And if philosophy is defined as an *a priori* endeavor, separate and distinct from other fields of study, there is something to this view. Only Marx, and a good many others, will have nothing to do with such a view. Factual and conceptual questions are bound up together for Marx. It is a mistaken, as well as an alienated exercise, to try to discuss them separately. Accordingly, philosophy or criticism cannot simply be an *a priori* enterprise. It encompasses a much broader reach. Ethics, epistemology, aesthetics, etc. must reach out beyond their conceptual hedges to the empirical world and seek to measure the influence and significance of that world for their own endeavors. The basic premise of each must be that without detailed information about human relations, moral and mental processes, institutional settings and forces, the understanding they can achieve and the answers they can give are impoverished.[3] Correspondingly, the grasp and responsibility of philosophy as a whole enlarge. Philosophy becomes a rational account, beginning with 'the unique forms of existing reality'[4] and ending with practical implications, of the various interrelated parts and aspects of the human totality.

Now I do not think one has wholly to accept Marx's views on the nature of philosophy and ethics to allow that a broader view of philosophy than that which has characterized Anglo-American philosophy is desirable. The view of the philosopher as a subordinate, *a priori* piece-worker may keep the philosopher's feet on the ground and his head out of the clouds. But it may also result in his head being buried in the ground between his feet. Better to attempt a broader, more inclusive view of oneself and one's society, than to discover both have passed one by. Marx's view of philosophy is a vital reminder of this point. Contemporary ethics, if it wishes to shake off the sterility of which it has been accused, cannot simply concentrate on the study of moral judgments and language apart from the historical, social, and psychological — i.e. their material — context. To this extent, then, ethics must again become systematic. It ostensibly swore off system-building because of the excesses to which such system-building led. But it has not thereby avoided its own, unconscious, subordination to the dominant social philosophical system within which it exists.

It should not be thought, however, that the preceding strengths of Marx's method do not conceal other, related weaknesses in Marx's method. Because it has concerned itself with the larger, historical picture, as well as the virtues constituting the free life, it has tended to neglect not only particular moral questions which individuals ask but also formal or logical questions about the nature of morality and moral judgments. Marx seems to assume that if general questions about the material and historical bases of ethics are answered, the particular questions about individual actions as well as the formal questions about morality would take care of themselves. This is not, however, true. Three consequences are worth noting.

Firstly, Marx's ethics has required supplementation so as to answer the particular questions that individuals raise. This has been especially required for individuals who are not members of a communist society[5] and yet cannot morally accept bourgeois society. However, even supposing that communism existed and, hence, individuals under it were free, particular moral questions would remain for which Marx provides little help. For example, what is the free person to do when important interests of two persons conflict because of his own limited time or resources? How is he to decide between them? What is he to say about abortion, the needs of future generations, and the interests of distant people *vis-à-vis* those closer to him? Marx was not led by his methodology to raise or try to answer such questions. It is a glaring omission in Marx's ethics. Thus, we have the attempts by existentialists, phenomenologists, and even analytic philosophers to read into or append to Marxism some means to answer the particular questions individuals raise. The attempt to read Kant into Marx at the turn of this century was also one of these moves. Secondly, since Marx said so little on this score, the latitude of interpretation has been wide. Accordingly, this side of Marx's views lent itself to vulgarization, to despotic, tyrannical interpretations, to the inventing of easy and unfortunate answers to complex questions. Marx is himself, in part, to blame for this since he gave insufficient attention to these matters.

Thirdly, Marx did not pay attention to various logical subtleties and intricacies concerning individual moral questions and phenomena which might greatly have aided and clarified his case. Both Hegel and Marx reacted against the purely formal character of Kant's ethics. Marx seems to assume that the historical development of man and society into communism will materially embody the formal requirement of universality which Kant emphasized so much. Thus, Marx investigates man's historical and material development. However important such investigations may be, they are no substitute for the formal analyses of morality and moral judgments which an ethics should also give us. We require analyses of the sense(s) in which what is morally good or virtuous holds for all people, of the kinds of determination which are incompatible with morality, and the kinds of appeals people may make to excuse as well as to justify their actions. Little of this Marx explicitly gives us. In addition, more particular analyses by Marx of his most basic concepts, such as freedom, needs, exploitation, harmony, classes, co-operation, rationality, etc. would have, or at least could have, gone a long way towards clarifying Marx's own views and protecting them from the corruption they have so often suffered. Had Marx offered such analyses it may well have been that he would not have felt constrained to say, late in life, 'I am not a Marxist.'[6]

II

There is a second general way in which Marx's approach contrasts sharply with contemporary ethics. It is Marx's contention that the standards by which man can and should be measured must come from the study of man himself. They must be in some sense, inherent, not extrinsic to man. In this way Marx continues the concern with human autonomy which had so troubled Kant. Marx differs from Kant in that he holds that moral standards are derived not *a priori* from the nature of reason, so much as from the nature and experience of a historically developing man-in-society. Whereas Kant eschews such anthropology in the construction of his ethics, Marx's ethics rests upon a philosophical and historical anthropology.

But such a naturalistic or humanistic approach to ethics runs up against, as we have seen, the infamous problem of the division of facts and values, of 'is' and 'ought,' which has haunted ethics for the past two centuries. It is clear that Marx was aware of this problem. It is also clear that he thought he had either circumvented it or resolved it. With Hegel, Marx took philosophy or science to be (at least in part) characterized by overcoming oppositions, antagonisms, and conflicts. The dichotomy of 'is' and 'ought' was one of those oppositions they believed they had overcome.

Marx's solution had various aspects. Marx claims that our categories of thought, observation, and language are themselves theory and value laden. There is no 'neutral' theoretical characterization of reality which is separate from human needs and values. That which we know as reality is known only through the social forms of life within which we live. Thus there is no sharp is/ought distinction. Rather that which man ought to be is discovered in the historical development which mankind effects. It is in this sense that Marx claims that theoretical problems (such as the is/ought problem) can only be solved in practice, and that in communism we see the solution of these problems. Marx's contention is that a correct characterization of man and his course of development shows that freedom, as Marx defines it, is the object of man. This Marx takes to mean that morality and the basic values of humans have an historical and material basis which is not simply a condition for their realization but also the basis for their validation. Thus, his characterization of man's history and development *is* his justification of his ethics.

This manner of justifying ethical claims and overcoming the is/ought problem will doubtlessly not satisfy many ethicists today. Facts, they will say, can be separated from values; descriptive statements and prescriptive statements are logically distinct. Marx simply confuses the two. He camouflages prescriptive statements as descriptive ones. And, of course, given *their* framework, appeals to the historical development of society are not directly relevant. Rather to resolve the is/ought problem on their view one may do one of two things. On the one hand, one may resort to various logical tricks, which do not, however, provide a satisfactory resolution of the problem. On the other hand, one may argue that the justification of ethical claims rests on reasons or measures 'capable of determining the intellect.'[7] Thus, the justification of ethics is placed on an individual and intellectual level — Marx would say a subjectivist and idealist level.

Now if Marx were right in his ethical framework and in his characterization of man, then the preceding objections would seem mistaken. Marx's ethics would be justified. An analogy might help. If the proper characterization of the nature of a cherry tree is as it exists in an orchard then the conclusion that it ought to be treated in certain ways — e.g. cared for so that it produces ripe cherries — would seem to follow. So too if we see human history as a continuous series of class struggles and modifications in the mode of production, which are interrelated and progressive in their development of man according to the categories Marx picks out, then the conclusion that man is a being which ought to be treated in certain ways — e.g. allowed to live and act freely — would seem to follow. It might be objected, as noted in Chapter 3, that even though this is how humankind has developed, still perhaps it ought to develop and be treated in different ways. This objection cannot be excluded. Still, *if* one does accept Marx's view of history, such an objection is surely but empty words. That is, if we could determine that certain values were presupposed in the development of man, that present society embodies one form in the development of these values and finds itself drawn to develop them further in another radically new society, that these values exclude excesses such as racism, genocide, and universal mistrust, while including values such as universal fraternity and self-determination, then though one might object that mankind ought to go in another direction and be judged by other standards, that objection would have but a whimsical air to it.

The issue then between Marx and contemporary ethicists turns on which framework for viewing moral questions we ought to adopt. Surely there is a good deal about the Marxian framework which recommends itself. Its insistence that we view moral questions as essentially interrelated with other aspects of society, that those aspects of society centered on productive activity play a pervasive and ultimately significant role in the character of society, that we must view moral questions in an historical context are all reasons which recommend it. They are also areas within which contemporary ethics reveals itself to be weak and superficial. Still, surely there are serious problems and questions raised by Marx's account of history and society. To begin with, there are a number of particular aspects of Marx's account which subsequent history has rendered dubitable: e.g. the imminence of a proletarian revolution, the ability of the working class to resist pacification, or perhaps, embourgeoisement, the inflexibility of capitalist systems. The historical development of contemporary society raises significant problems for each of these aspects of Marx's views. It follows that a contemporary who would be a Marxist must not only reject certain views standardly linked with Marx's name, but also must surely revise and modify the grounds upon which Marx arrived at these views.

In addition, however, there is a more basic problem regarding Marx's account of history, society, and ethics. Initially, Marx stated his views on man's historical development in an all-encompassing fashion. Later he restricted it increasingly to Europe and then to Western Europe. Yet if his ethics is to have the universal validity he claims for it, it must be possible to show that the historical development of man in other parts of the world as well also supports his ethics. That is, because Marx holds that what each society (or the ruling class) professes is moral, unless he also holds that there is an interconnected series of societies in human development, he cannot say that there are higher, universal moral judgments that can be made. A theory of the universal, historical development of man seems to be needed for his ethics. Nevertheless, Marx does not provide convincing evidence for such an account, and it is doubtful that he could. Indeed, on this point, his realism increasingly seemed to be at war with the foundations of his ethics. Further, even within the Western world it is far from clear that Marx's account is plausible in its particulars. Marx assumed more readily (in good nineteenth-century fashion) than seems possible today the perfectability of man and the progressive development of society. An example from Marx's life, if contrasted with a current event, might highlight this point. Supposedly, Marx once noticed, with great excitement, an electric locomotive on exhibition and exclaimed that the political revolution must surely follow upon the creation of such a productive force.[8] One may legitimately wonder if, today, he would similarly respond to the demonstration of the latest nuclear reactor. The complexities and uncertainties in the relations of technology, human values, and social and political systems, which characterize life today, challenge the optimism of the nineteenth century. In Marx's age the underdeveloped forces of production and technology promised to aid in the reconstruction of society. In our age, the forces of production and technology threaten to destroy any reconstruction of society. And even if this contrast be too simplistically drawn, it is, at least, no longer clear that simply more and greater technology is crucial to the resolution of society's basic problems. Nor is it clear that we live within an historical movement which is progressive.

Accordingly, Marx's views on the nature of historical development and its relation to ethics requires rethinking.[9] The direction this might most plausibly take would be to construct the justification of a Marxist ethics on the basis of an account of human interests, understood to include the fulfillment of human abilities, capacities and talents. Rejecting any religious or authority basis for ethics, it would take as its basic premise the view that 'man is the highest being for man' (*MECW*, 3:182). The grounds for such a premise might be sought in man's purposiveness and his creation of values. If mankind cannot be conceived of without these categories, then that man realizes the ends and goals set by himself and in so doing develops himself might justifiedly be taken as a non-arbitrary objective basis for ethics. Such a view could allow for and would seek to discover changes in our concept of the self. It would also be sensitive to accounts of historical developments in human relations, as well as to psychological and genetic determinants of moral behavior. Thus it need not simply exchange the objectivist grounding Marx sought for a subjectivist basis. Obviously much more would be required to fill out such an ethics. It is not possible here to make this attempt. Rather the present point is to indicate the directions in which a Marxist ethics might go which viewed the historical sanction Marx provided for his views as excess Hegelian baggage. To traditional Marxists, this might well be heretical, but moral views such as Marx expresses do carry an impact and might be grounded even without the historical analyses he gave. Such a modified view could still speak of class struggle; it could attribute special significance to the mode of production in a society; it might still see a progressive development of freedom in European society from feudal to modern times; hence such a view could plausibly still be called Marxist. But it would not make the same universal historical claims for all mankind that Marx at times made. Surely this significantly changes Marxism, and specifically Marx's historical materialism. But it might leave important elements of Marx's ethics in place. Further, it would have the advantage that people do not misunderstand Marx to be saying that some change in human affairs is inevitable — even without their efforts. The responsibility for change could be placed squarely on their shoulders — not the shoulders of history — while still recognizing the limitations which their historical situation places on them. Finally, it would avoid the tendency of Marx to cast history into periods of development of which the last one is communism. The whole idea of a last period of historical development raises inevitable and obvious problems that a Marxist ethics would better avoid.

In sum, any proof or demonstration must begin at some point, with certain basic premises. This has been a commonplace since Plato and Aristotle. Marx recognized it as evidenced by his comment on 'non-arbitrary premises.' The question is, then, which approach — Marx's or that of contemporary ethics — is likely to carry us further, shed more light on our moral life, and the life of freedom? Perhaps this question, so bluntly put, cannot be answered. But surely Marx's approach recommends itself. It forces us to see the systematic nature of moral values, i.e. that moral values are not simply individual but social matters. Similarly, it forces us to see the interconnections of good and evil in a society — that evil conditions cannot simply be removed without often affecting the very structure of a society. Finally, it forces us to see that moral change is not simply a matter of will, but a matter of social, material and historical forces. In these regards Marx's ethics has much to recommend it. Still, given the deficiencies of Marx's ethics, it seems obvious that substantial rethinking and revision of the methodological side of Marx's ethics is in order.

III

What about Marx's view of freedom? It is difficult to compare Marx's view with the contemporary view of freedom, since there is no clear single contemporary view of freedom. There are many views. What might be done, however, is to discuss the view of freedom Marx holds in light of various common problems, criticisms, and characteristics which generally typify contemporary views. How does Marx's view look in these lights?

To begin with, a number of points might be noted upon which recent discussion has achieved some agreement and with which Marx agrees. For example, it is generally agreed now that that which limits freedom need not be deliberate. J.S. Mill and Isaiah Berlin appear uncertain on this point.[10] Marx, however, is not. He was quite clear, as are most contemporary accounts, that one's freedom may be impeded or restricted by the unintentional as well as the intentional actions and effects of other people. This is significant for it allows that class relations, institutions, and the like which are the unintended consequence of human activity and/or which have various unintended consequences may be said to constitute interferences with one's freedom. Secondly, also in agreement with most contemporary accounts, Marx did not hold that any and every incapacity constituted a lack of freedom. As it was argued in Chapter 4, there is no reason to believe that Marx had to hold that the failure or inability to fulfill any wish a person might have, as well as, more generally, the failure to fulfill each and every capacity a person might have, necessarily constituted grounds for saying that that person was not free. Finally, if freedom is defined as the ability to do what one wants, as traditional liberal and Millian accounts of freedom maintain, it may be objected that one might accordingly increase one's freedom by diminishing one's wants. Thus, one who wanted nothing, or but to sit and stare at a blank wall, would be free, perhaps even most free. The slave in chains would be free, so long as he wanted to have his life determined by others and loved his chains. But all this sounds counter-intuitive. It is a view which has been often attributed to the ascetic, the stoic, and the Buddhist. It is a view, however, which both Marx and contemporary accounts of freedom reject. Freedom is not to be achieved by withdrawing into a cave and disclaiming any desires one might have, but by fulfilling and even developing one's desires. On this and the preceding issues Marx and contemporary accounts appear to be in agreement. However, let us now look to some of those issues on which Marx and contemporary accounts seem to differ.

There are three different issues important in current discussions against which Marx's views on freedom might be weighed. These are: (a) the distinction between positive and negative freedom, (b) the breadth or narrowness of an account of freedom, and (c) the relation of the individual self to others which is assumed in accounts of freedom. I will discuss each of these in the remainder of this chapter.

The distinction between positive and negative freedom, brought to recent prominence by Berlin, is a problem which has exercised contemporary discussions of freedom a great deal. Negative freedom is that kind of freedom 'involved in the answer to the question "What is the area within which the subject — a person or group of persons — is or should be left to do or be what he is able to do or be, without interference by other persons?"'[11] In brief, negative freedom is freedom from coercion, from the interference by other people and human institutions. Positive freedom, however, is that freedom 'involved in the answer to the question "What, or who, is the source of control or interference that can determine someone to do, or be, this rather than that?"'[12] To be free in a positive sense is to have self-mastery, self-control, to be self-directed, to participate in the process by which my life is to be controlled.[13]

There are two reasons why Berlin's distinction is important to consider here. Firstly, there is the significance of the distinction itself in helping us to understand accounts of freedom. According to Berlin, Marx's views were representative of positive freedom rather than negative freedom. Secondly, the positive view of freedom is supposedly a dangerous view, given to promoting bullying, despotism, and tyranny. The reason is that the notion of positive freedom as self-mastery suggests a distinction between the real self of a person and his empirical self. The real self has as its goal a rational self-control, which may or may not characterize the empirical self. But since this goal is what each person's real self aims at, proponents of positive freedom have felt justified in imposing on everyday empirical selves the ends they perceive to be fulfillments of people's real selves. More than this, they declare that people are actually aiming at what they make them do, though in their benighted state they consciously resist it. Their real self, of which their empirical self may have little knowledge, is the only self that deserves to have its ends taken into account. Those who resist the imposition of these ends are those who are mistaken, deluded about the nature of their real goals, about rational self-determination, and hence are justifiedly constrained. Once a person takes this view, Berlin concludes, he is 'in a position to ignore the actual wishes of men or societies, to bully, oppress, torture them in the name, and on behalf, of their "real" selves, in the secure knowledge that whatever is the true goal of man . . . must be identical with his freedom — the free choice of his "true" albeit often submerged and inarticulate, self.'[14]

Now at first glance Berlin may seem to have been correct that Marx's views exemplify positive freedom. For example, Marx clearly thought that force may have to be used against some members of society to overcome their opposition to communism. In this sense, he held that people may have to be forced to be free. Secondly, the notions of self-determination and ideology — both notions central to Marx's view of freedom — are of a kind that seemingly fit Berlin's characterization of positive freedom. For example, because of their ideological or false consciousness people may resist the attempt to achieve a society which permits their own rational self-determination. Finally, Marx himself distinguished between political emancipation and human emancipation. The former was identified with various political freedoms and rights — e.g. freedom of speech, assembly, private property, and religion. Such freedoms constitute the area within which individuals are to be protected from interference with their activities by others and the state. However, Marx criticizes such freedoms as characteristic of bourgeois or

216

civil society with its egoistic individuals. In contrast to such freedoms Marx defends human emancipation, which proclaims the freedom of individuals to do certain things, or more generally to be, to live, a certain kind of life. Do we not have here Marx's own distinction between positive and negative freedom and his subscription to the former notion?!

It should be clear, however, from the discussions in Part two of this book, that Marx's views do not merely not fit Berlin's characterization of positive freedom, they also place in question the plausibility of his distinction. On the one hand, though Marx indeed is concerned about the rational self-mastery or self-determination of individuals, this view is discussed in the context of freeing individuals from their oppression at the hands of the bourgeoisie, from their class relations, from nature uncontrolled by man or the community, from money, from the division of labor, from the division of city and country, and from private property. It would require no small Procrustean effort to try to force Marx simply into the category of positive freedom. In terms of Berlin's distinction, Marx is clearly concerned about *both* positive and negative freedom, both are part of his concept of freedom. On the other hand, though Marx does think that some people are deluded about their present relations as well as about how they ought to live, that some may have to be forced to give up their capitalist ways, he does *not* distinguish between people's real selves and their empirical selves and attempt to impose the former on the latter.[15] That is, Marx does not think that the notion of freedom, or of self-mastery or self-determination, leads to a bifurcation of the self in which the rational part of each person is actually striving towards a state of affairs resisted by the person's empirical part. Thus, this initial dangerous step, according to Berlin, of positive freedom is not taken by Marx. Rather, Marx measures capitalism and communism by the extent to which they allow individuals to be free. There is no claim on Marx's part that what he is urging is what the people's real selves really want, but from which they are obstructed by their empirical selves. Marx says, more honestly, that some people may really want their capitalist ways of life, but they are wrong, given his ethics of freedom. Such a move is fully compatible with the tradition of Western ethics and social and political philosophy. In this tradition, which has largely been objectivist in nature, people can simply be mistaken or wrong about their moral values and the lives they lead. Accordingly, the enforcement of objective moral standards upon recalcitrant individuals may be justified. Further, it would not be wholly unusual within this tradition to say that, since what is imposed upon such individuals is objective and rational, were they more rational this is what they really would want. The important difference is that in this tradition it has not usually been claimed that there is a more real part of people's selves which actually and presently wants what they are forced to do. Marx, I suggest, is part of this tradition, not part of some sleight of hand tradition in which people do not do that which they really want to do.

Thus, Marx does not fit nicely into that tradition which Berlin describes as the tradition of positive freedom. What Marx referred to as human emancipation in fact includes one's freedom from the various obstacles and restrictions characteristic of bourgeois society. Nor is Berlin's claim that 'this monstrous impersonation, which consists in equating what X would choose if he were something he is not, or at least not yet, with what X actually seeks and chooses, is at the heart of all political theories of self-realisation' true of Marx's account.[16] Marx may have believed that he knew what was best for capitalists, but he did not claim that they really wanted what he believed to be for their best. Thus, for this reason, Berlin must be said to be mistaken on the dangerous nature of Marx's views. Furthermore, the distinction between positive and negative freedom seems of little value in helping us to understand and place Marx's views on freedom. It is far better to see Marx to be holding a unitary view of freedom on this particular issue. What Berlin characterizes as positive and negative freedom is simply two different sides, two different aspects, of Marx's concept of freedom. Berlin's initial mistake was to conclude that because the two questions he used to characterize positive and negative freedom were logically distinct, the answers to these questions must refer to two different things or concepts.[17] However, this does not follow. The question, 'What is the largest statue in New York Harbor?' is logically distinct from the question 'What famous gift did the French nation give to the US in 1886?' But both questions refer to the same thing and have the same answer. Similarly, Berlin's two logically distinct questions need not be taken to be referring to two different concepts of freedom. Once we recognize the preceding point and consider Marx's view that many of the reasons, e.g. ignorance, private property, division of labor, why people cannot achieve what Berlin calls positive freedom are actually due to the deliberate as well as non-deliberate action or inaction of others, Berlin's claim that there are two distinct concepts of liberty becomes much less plausible. In effect, then, there is no reason why Marx's view of freedom cannot be said to fit the triadic relation model of freedom that MacCallum has suggested. This is the view that freedom is 'always *of* something (an agent or agents), *from* something, *to* do, not do, become, not become something.'[18] Accordingly, on

Marx's view, freedom may be said to be a matter of individuals (and/or the community) being free from a variety of things — private property, division of labor, money, coercive laws, etc. — so that they may be self-determining, concretely objectify themselves and live in harmonious relation with others. There would seem to be no problem of fitting the Marxian view into this triadic account. As such Berlin's distinction is not needed. Consequently, in the current discussion of the issue of positive and negative freedom, Marx would seem to be on the side of those who find this distinction unhelpful.

IV

When it comes to questions concerning the breadth or narrowness of freedom, Marx's view differs substantially not only from those who identify different concepts of freedom but also from those who maintain that the concept of freedom is unitary. As we have seen, Marx's view of freedom is unusually inclusive. Various characteristics such as the development of one's abilities and talents, self-mastery, and concrete self-objectification are part and parcel of the realization of one's freedom on Marx's views. However, most contemporary accounts would reject such an inclusive view of freedom. Freedom, it is said, is one value amongst many. An acceptable account of freedom must allow that it would rub shoulders or conflict with other values such as justice, fraternity, solidarity, etc.

Two specific objections will lend some content to the objection that Marx's view of freedom is unacceptably broad. For example, it has been argued that accounts of freedom which include the development of human abilities are mistaken since the deprivation of one's ability to perform an act is not a curtailment of one's liberty. In defense of this view it is contended, for example, that if a person is shot in the back, though he is deprived of the ability to walk, he is not thereby rendered socially unfree to walk.[19] Thus, it is claimed 'the terms "deliberate deprivation of ability" and "interference with freedom" have different designata' and a proper account of freedom would not refer to abilities.[20]

Similarly, it is maintained that the self-determination or self-mastery which Marx identifies with freedom does not reflect what we ordinarily mean by liberty. Consider, it is said, the situation of an addict who is driven to steal in order to support his habit. 'The addict exhibits little or no rational self-mastery, yet he still has the social freedom to engage in illegal activities; indeed this is precisely the problem confronting law enforcement officials, who must attempt to render him at least temporarily unfree to do so.'[21] Thus, the loss of rational self-mastery may well lead to, but is not constitutive of, unfreedom as we ordinarily conceive of it. In either case, then, freedom must be seen as a more modest, a less inclusive notion, than Marx took it to be.

There are three different kinds of responses which Marx might appropriately give to these objections. Firstly, it is not absolutely crucial that one adhere to the dictates of ordinary speech in giving a theory of freedom. The dictates of ordinary speech may be diverse as well as, Marx would say, alienated. A theory of freedom should take us beyond the level of the views embodied in ordinary language. Accordingly, even if ordinary language suggested a narrow concept of freedom, we need not strictly adhere to such a concept.

Second, consider each of the two objections above. Now, in one sense, it is correct that the issue whether abilities are or are not part of the account of freedom may not be important since if they are recognized as a necessary condition for the enjoyment of freedom, even though not a necessary characteristic of freedom itself, we will still want to ensure that people have those abilities.[22] Still, surely there is reason to include abilities in an account of freedom. If freedom is not artificially conceptualized (and hence narrowed) as negative freedom, but understood as the triadic relation *of* an agent, *from* something, *to* do or be something, then the abilities one exercises in that which one does or attempts to be are part of the notion of freedom. They are not merely conditions of freedom. To be free implies having certain abilities and exercising them. Even Mill, whose definition of freedom is traditionally looked to as epitomizing a narrow, 'negative' view of freedom, held, when it came to elaboration on his view of freedom, that the development of one's abilities, and more generally, one's individuality, was crucial to, if not the centerpiece of, his views. Accordingly, one might sketch the example given in the above objection in a slightly different way. Suppose, rather, that I had been bound in chains but now someone comes, releases me from my chains, and tells me that I am free to walk away — but as I leave he shoots me in the back, such that I can no longer walk. Has that person merely deprived me of my ability to walk — or has he also deprived me of my freedom to walk, to leave? Surely he has done both. In depriving me of my ability to walk, he has deprived me of my freedom. To be free, in this case, would be to be able to walk away. Similarly, a person crippled from a gunshot wound might say to a non-crippled person, 'You're free to come and go as you please! I'm confined to this wheelchair.' Whether it follows from such views that the deprivation of any ability is an interference with one's freedom is less clear and need not be argued here. What is clear, however, is that the view that to be free involves having and exercising certain abilities is not as implausible as some would have us believe.

The second objection above also seems to be incorrect. It views freedom as wholly external to the individuals said to be free. Freedom is something which others or the state 'gives' to a person. Since this external, social situation still allows the person to do something — which is assumed to be the same as saying he has freedom — it is assumed that the person himself is free, even though he does not have self-mastery or self-determination. Yet it would seem, contrariwise, that a person who is an addict and is, as such, compelled or coerced to act in certain ways is not free. Just because he is free in other regards does not mean that in the instance of his addiction he is also free, or that self-mastery in that instance is not part of freedom. Indeed, according to the present objection one would also have to say that a person paralyzed by anxieties, fears, and suspicions is free since he has social or political freedoms. Now of course such an individual may have certain social freedoms, but this merely shows that to have such freedoms is not a sufficient ground to say that the person is free in other respects; indeed, it suggests that social freedoms, i.e. political freedoms, are not sufficient to a person being free! In short, it does not seem implausible that abilities and self-mastery have a legitimate role to play in an acceptable account of human freedom.

Finally, we may turn to the third kind of response and note what is truly distinctive in Marx's view of freedom. In so doing, we may identify what ultimately underlies his arguments against the preceding two objections. What hangs on the issue whether freedom is a broad or a narrow notion? Why are contemporary philosophers insistent on interpreting freedom in a narrow sense? One reason, we have seen, is the penchant of many for negative freedom. Another reason is the fear that if freedom is allowed to expand it will subsume other values and a value monism will result. Yet another reason is conceptual clarity. For example, Berlin comments that 'Everything is what it is: liberty is liberty, not equality or fairness or justice or culture, or human happiness or a quiet conscience.'[23] A related point concerns the meaningfulness of the notion of freedom: 'For freedom is not the mere absence of frustration of whatever kind; this would inflate the meaning of the word until it meant too much or too little.'[24] However, as we have seen, it may be that conceptual clarity and meaningfulness demand linking freedom with other notions. Further, Berlin's distinction between positive and negative freedom seems unjustifiable. Both these responses support a broad view of freedom. But there is a more general reason why Marx held that a broad concept of freedom is required.

221

Each of the preceding objections assumes, it should be noted, that freedom consists of certain social or political rights to engage in various private activities. As such, freedom is taken to be a political notion. Consequently, the abilities, capacities, and self-mastery of the individual do not receive primary focus. Instead, the political view of freedom focuses on which barriers should be erected between individuals themselves and between individuals and the state. It is assumed, more or less, that if the political domain is structured properly, if the appropriate barriers and fences are erected, the private domain, as well as society as a whole, will flourish. It is but a political version of Adam Smith's economic invisible hand. But Marx disputes this. To begin with, the division between the political domain and the civil or private domain is an instance of alienation. Thus, one cannot ask about Marx's *political* concept of freedom or liberty. This is to look for something which he rejected. This explains, in part, the differences which exist between Marx's concept of freedom and most contemporary non-Marxian accounts. The latter assume a division between the political domain and the civil domain of private individuals. On this view, the crucial questions are: Which actions are free? Which interferences by the state and other people must be blocked so that one may do as one wishes? On Marx's view the crucial questions are: What constitutes the free life? What is it to be free? Given Marx's answer to these questions both the notion of distributive justice and the concept of political freedom become inoperative. Instead, Marx concerns himself with a way of life which he views as the free life. It would be better then if Marx had distinguished clearly between liberty — which would be taken to be a political notion and one he rejected — and freedom, which would be taken to be the broader notion.

Accordingly, one of the central characteristics of Marx's ethics of freedom requiring comment is his opposition to the political/civil dichotomy in society and his demand that it be transcended. One of Marx's main reasons for attacking the division between the political and the civil, or private, is that what was expelled from the former as a limitation on freedom, still finds a home in the latter. Religion, private property qualifications, wealth, birth, rank, etc. are excluded from the perfect political or human state as irrelevant distinctions (*MECW*, 3:153), but still exist and dominate people's private lives. Marx argues that if such distinctions and institutions must be excluded from the former as restrictions on one's freedom, they must also be excluded from the latter. A life genuinely free would not permit such features to continue to characterize it and would not allow such a division of itself wherein they could continue to play an active role. The free life is whole, not an isolated part of one's life. It demands a coherence in our personal and public existence.

Now there is something appealing in this demand for a moral coherence to our lives, for a society in which one would not appeal to universal interests, brotherhood and co-operation on one level but practice egoism, provincialism, and hostility on another level. It would be desirable if society could be so constructed that egoism, greed, fetishism, alienation were not simply officially condemned but practically eliminated. The demand for such a society is a demand for moral honesty as well as moral coherence. And surely Marx was right that the characteristics of civil or pre-communist society can not be eliminated simply by moralistic preaching, but by significant changes in the structure of society. Indeed, it has increasingly been accepted, in this century, that the granting of political liberties may merely mock the real condition of people unable to take advantage of those political liberties. Thus, people have sought to supplement political freedom with economic and personal freedoms. Different kinds of freedom have been introduced as stop-gap measures. Marx, however, would insist that these measures leave the basic structure of society intact, and hence treat the symptoms rather than the causes. They continue to presuppose the dichotomy between the political and the civil in society. Instead, Marx demands a unitary view of freedom. Freedom is one and whole. One does not seek to stop the deficiencies of political freedom by the use of economic freedom. Rather one changes both by changing the basic conditions of society. Then such patchwork activity is not needed.

There are two troublesome features to this view. Firstly, there is the legitimate worry that, in the search for moral coherence and honesty, society will ride roughshod over the individual. The elegance of a morally coherent universe might trample the diverse values individuals would seek. There are two aspects to this concern. One is that in collapsing the political/civil distinction such protections as are afforded by the political realm will be lost to the individual. This concern will be discussed below (cf. section V). The second problem is that Marx seeks, in the above manner, to impose a value monism on all individuals. Now, to begin with, I think it should be said that it is interesting and important to see freedom as Marx does not merely as a political concept, that of liberty, which characterizes but one aspect of life, but as a concept which characterizes our entire life, apart from any political/non-political dichotomy. Freedom — not liberty — is then taken to be the underlying motif of our (Western) lives. What justifies Marx's elevation of this value into the ultimate value of all values? Marx's reply would be that this is not *his* doing but simply his reading of the development of man and society. It is freedom, the struggle for freedom, which has dominated modern history. We no longer struggle for happiness so much as for freedom. Freedom is our chief desideratum, the dominant value in Western society. Evidence for this is readily at hand if one merely reflects on the central role that freedom plays in diverse philosophies and movements — from Marxism to existentialism, from religious movements to democratic, secular movements. Freedom is that to which revolutionary groups — as well as practically every government around the world — appeal to justify themselves — even before justice! It is not preposterous, then, to claim a privileged role and place for freedom (or liberation, emancipation) in the firmament of values. Accordingly, in reply to the charge that Marx's broad sense of freedom renders freedom meaningless and institutes a value monism, it might well be contended that it is just this broad, inclusive sense which opens up vistas and suggests new ideas. Freud, it should be recalled, was similarly charged with using the notion of sex in an overly broad sense. But in his case too, the broadening of the notion of sex was fruitful in stimulating new insights and ideas by which human behavior could be understood. The relevance of Marx today, then, is that he reminds us that freedom is at the center of Western, if not human, thought, as well as provides us with an analysis of that freedom — that freedom is bound up with self-development and that it is not to be found in escape from commitments to others, but in one's essential relations with others.

It is certainly clear, then, that for Marx freedom subsumes all other values. The collapse of the political/civil dichotomy crystallizes this fact. Freedom is not simply a political, but a human, value. Still, if freedom is taken as Marx's characterization of the free life, then two further conclusions might be drawn. Firstly, the charge against the breadth of his notion of freedom (at least as one political notion among many) is no longer plausible. One would expect an account of the free life to be broad and inclusive. Secondly, though Marx's view of freedom does bring all other values under it, it does not obliterate all other values. It does not result in a pernicious value monism, in which all variety, contrast, and spontaneity are abolished. Rather freedom is the basic value; it is the cardinal virtue. All other values or virtues are either contributory to freedom, or are part of freedom in the sense that they may be derived from it. Under communism, one would expect that courage, honesty, efficiency, love, helpfulness, creativity, etc. would remain values. Creativity could be said to be part of one's concrete self-objectification; helpfulness and love are part of the communal relation of individuals; efficiency and courage may contribute to the necessary bases for freedom, while courage may also, as well as honesty, be part of one's self-determination. Nevertheless, other traditional values such as justice – at least in the distributive sense – seem to be excluded under communism and hence play no role at all.

We see then that if Marx's view of freedom is identified in terms of rational self-mastery, as Berlin suggests, it is misleading to suggest that this 'one true purpose' implies a monism of values and ends.[25] Mac-Pherson is quite correct that Berlin's 'attributing to the doctrine of positive liberty the assumption that something as broad as [rational self-direction] is "the one and only true purpose of man" . . . can be dangerously misleading, for . . . it suggests a monism which in fact is not there.'[26]

Still, though Marx can be read, and is best read, in the preceding manner, it is appropriate to note that Marx is not wholly unambiguous on the present point. He does make various comments which legitimately give rise to concerns about a value monism and its imposition upon individuals. The following comment – attacking Max Stirner (Sancho) on racial differences – is a case in point:[27]

> Even naturally evolved differences within the species, such as racial differences, etc., which Sancho does not mention at all, can and must be abolished in the course of historical development. Sancho – who in this connection casts a stealthy glance at zoology and so makes the discovery that 'innate limited intellects' form the most numerous class not only among sheep and oxen, but also among polyps and infusoria, which have no heads at all – has perhaps heard that it is possible to improve races of animals and by cross-breeding to create entirely new, more perfect varieties both for human enjoyment and for their own self-enjoyment. 'Why should not' Sancho be able to draw a conclusion from this in relation to people as well? (*MECW*, 5:425)

Such a passage could be read to support the imposition of eugenic policies in order to create a 'single' human race. After all, why 'must' racial differences be eliminated unless Marx envisioned an extreme value uniformity? On the other hand, Marx might have been pointing out that if racial differences are not morally significant, and world history continues to develop as he saw it developing, then the elimination of racial differences would be an 'inevitable' consequence of historical development. In this sense, racial differences will necessarily (i.e. must) be eliminated simply by the future course of human actions. The point to be made is that Marx's views – or his statement of his views — lend themselves, at times, to interpretations which would be perniciously monistic. There is, in this sense, ever a tension in Marx between the individual and the universal. An acceptable contemporary Marxist ethics would have to make this tension in Marx clear and indicate its opposition to those baneful monistic interpretations which may be made of Marx's views.

The second troublesome feature of Marx's views concerns his claims that the transcendence of certain structural features of capitalism would result in the elimination of religion, alienated labor, egoism, etc., which he took to constitute restrictions on or corruptions of freedom. These claims can only be briefly referred to here. For all that one might agree with Marx's atheism, he surely neither deeply nor extensively considered this issue. His views were essentially a patchwork of views adopted from Feuerbach, Bauer, and others. He generally held that religion would be eliminated by communism, but it would seem more compatible with his views if it were said to be transcended, i.e. *aufgehoben*. What form it would then take, whether it might play a role in communal relations, is unclear. Indeed, given the conditions Marx sets for the end of religion, one wonders whether religion could ever end. In *Capital*, he says: 'The religious reflex of the real world can, in any case, only then finally vanish, when the practical relations of everyday life offer to man none but perfectly intelligible and reasonable relations with regard to his fellowmen and to Nature' (*Capital*, I:79). Now if 'perfectly intelligible' means that some people must both be able to understand the relations of man to nature and man to man, and be in a position to certify their intelligibility and reasonableness to others, we might agree that this situation could come about. But for the elimination of religion it would seem that such understanding must be true for all people. And yet it is doubtful whether the ability of all people to comprehend such relations is really comparable to what is needed. If it is not, might those who cannot comprehend such relations still retreat to religion? Accordingly, it would seem, either the conditions for the elimination of religion must be weakened by Marx, or if he saw correctly regarding these conditions, then, he should be more sceptical about the disappearance of religion.

Similarly, one might ask whether Marx was not too optimistic that the effect of eliminating alienated labor would be the elimination of other forms of alienation too? One of the problems here is that if one takes alienated labor to refer to the labor people engage in in industrial production, then surely Marx was too optimistic. But if alienated labor may refer to all (productive) activity, then perhaps he was not so optimistic depending on what is meant by or included under 'productive activity.' Marx sometimes simply includes all activities in which one objectifies oneself. At other times he includes only those in which surplus value is created. If Marx holds that the elimination of alienated labor in the broadest sense will bring about the elimination of all forms of alienation, that is plausible — but then his thesis seems to be but a matter of definition. On the other hand, if he meant alienated labor in some narrower sense, then its elimination certainly need not necessarily have the desired result. Further, inasmuch as Marx urged the transcendence of private property and the division of labor as central to communism in this task, it would seem that he had the narrower sense of alienated labor in mind. The question then becomes whether it is likely that such means as Marx advocates would achieve the ends Marx had in mind. Whether it would or not is an empirical question. However, surely Marxists must go further than simply advocating the transcendence of private property in those forms which we see today are compatible with state ownership and the alienated labor which may exist under it. They must more carefully define the sense in whch the division of labor is or can be transcended. We have seen that Marx is not out literally to abolish private property and the division of labor in all their forms. His principal objection to both was that their previous forms forced people into narrow and restricted lives. Thus, it is not simply implausible that, given some other incarnation of private property and the division of labor, the high material standard of living necessary for realizing human freedom might be possible under communism. But this issue cannot be resolved until Marxists develop Marx's ideas on the forms of private property and the division of labor which might exist under communism. In short, what is required is greater thought about and attempts to characterize forms of property and modes of production which are non-exploitative, conducive to freedom, and addressed to the late twentieth century.

V

The relation of the individual to others raises a third set of issues crucial to Marxist freedom. Without the harmony or identity of interests amongst individuals which Marx anticipates, communism and the realm of freedom would be a delusion. There are at least three consequences which would follow from such a lack of community. Firstly, the possibility that characteristics of pre-communist society such as the state, classes, the courts, and the police might be transcended would seem remote. Secondly, without close individual identification, the protections

227

afforded the individual by political rights, the state, etc. would seem not only necessary but also desirable. Finally, because Marx's ethics of freedom urges the creation of persons with co-operative dispositions and character traits, who define their very selves in a different manner than bourgeois individuals, he can more or less plausibly jettison rights, duties, and principles of justice from his ethics. Should, however, this inner transformation not be successful or plausible, the need for principles of justice and rules to guide and direct people would seem overwhelming. How plausible, then, is this crucial aspect of Marx's thought?

To begin with, Marx is unclear, as we have seen, on the nature and extent of this identification. It is unlikely that he could say that all people must identify with others to the same degree. Surely under communism there must be allowed to be lovers, friends, as well as strangers. If not, communism is wholly implausible. Even if, under communism, one person would treat all other persons with equal respect, share with them intimate details of his life, and enjoy mutually gratifying experiences, there would (due to our limitations) be some people with whom we would have done this more often. They would be closer to us. We would not have to explain everything to them. They would be our friends. Others would be strangers. This is true, even assuming one was not selective in the persons with whom one behaved in this way. If we were selective — some people were appreciated more than others — the difference of friends and strangers would be even greater.

But if we allow for various degrees of identification amongst people, still it is uncertain how much identification is needed amongst people in order to carry through Marx's plans. Certainly, there must be enough to eliminate the state, to eliminate coercion, to allow for the functioning of self-punishment, etc. This means, for example, that if the community decides to institute some plan, few if any of its members will seek to take personal advantage of the fact that most everyone else is following the plan. Those few would supposedly impose self-punishment on themselves. Community members will not only act in concert with others but also see their own advantage in co-operation with others. This clearly requires an extraordinary amount of identification with others. Perhaps Marx meant it to apply only on a certain level or to a particular area of human interaction. He was neither clear nor explicit on the matter. Suppose the identification occurs only on the level of general interests. This would not seem strong enough to eliminate the state, courts, etc. There must be a more thoroughgoing identification. The same might be said if it were suggested that the identification were only to hold for interests related to material production. Too many conflicts, quarrels, and differences which require the state are not attached directly to material production. Once again it seems that Marx's views require a strong and thoroughgoing identification among individuals. Three problems might be noted.

Firstly, the identification required for the state, coercion, etc. to be transcended is exactly on that level of general social interaction — i.e. where not simply friends but strangers meet — which is most problematic and difficult for close identification. Particularly this is so when one recalls Marx's view that communism cannot occur simply in individual countries, but must come about on a world level: 'Communism is only possible as the act of the dominant peoples "all at once" and simultaneously' (*MECW*, 5:49). Nevertheless, it is on this world level that people are supposed to co-operate voluntarily with others in pursuing ends rationally and jointly determined.

Secondly, Marx frequently voiced his concern for human individuality (cf. *MECW*, 5:440-1). However, in light of the close identification amongst people and the extended conception of the self, both of which Marx's concept of freedom seems to require, it is often claimed that such freedom threatens the submersion of individuality. However, this conclusion is too quickly drawn. Only if the concept of individuality necessarily implied that one swim against the stream, or act in ways opposed to others, would this have to follow. Certainly, friends and lovers can remain individuals within their relationships even though they experience an identity of interests and a merging of their selves. In such cases, or under communism, a person might develop his individuality by going the extra mile, making super achievements, or extraordinary sacrifices. Marx correctly responds that it is the transcendence of bourgeois individuality which the above objection fears (*MECW*, 6:500). Marxist freedom is misunderstood, that is, if it is taken to threaten, as such, the submersion of individuality. Perhaps, then, Marxist freedom should be said to threaten the *range* of individualities which may be developed. Certainly, it excludes the egoist, the capitalist, etc. But then surely capitalism too excludes other kinds of individuality. How one would measure which system might allow for the greatest range of individualities is far from clear. The objection, I think, might better be dropped.

Rather, the threat Marxist freedom actually carries concerns the possible authoritarian consequence if conflicts of interests are to be eliminated. Suppose a community formulates a plan, but one which is in fact misconceived, irrational. If this is not possible, then Marx is simply playing with words. Granted it is possible, what is a person (or a group of people) to do who (which) believes that the plan is irrational? Is he to go along? May they challenge the plan? May they work against it? If they do, is there then not a conflict of interests instead of a harmony of interests? This would seem to follow if the identification required for a community is a thoroughgoing one.

It might be said that, in such a case, there may still be an underlying harmony of interests; the disagreement is merely a factual disagreement. Of course, emotions and passions may run high in such matters, but there is no conflict of interests. This reply is not wholly implausible. Nevertheless, it is − and Marx was − overly optimistic that in a community it will be possible to find one rational plan which will harmoniously meet the interests of the community. Even granting that communism could solve the problem of production, it will not be able to solve the problem to which limited and uncertain knowledge, as well as different expectations and risk assessments, may give rise. Suppose that a community jointly has interests A, B, and C, which by their nature cannot be realized at the same time. In a certain instance, some in the community believe their situation to be characterized by facts w, x, y; others believe that their situation is actually characterized by facts x, y, and z. Accordingly, the former opt for plan M which will realize interest A; the latter opt for plan N which will realize interest B. Both groups believe that if the other plan is accepted neither interests A nor B will be realized. That neither group can finally and conclusively prove the 'true' nature of the situation is simply a consequence of human finite knowledge. A judgment is called for. This judgment, based on different beliefs, experiences, expectations, risk-assessments, etc., defines the situation above and beyond the facts either as one leading to interest A, or to interest B. When one group defends plan M and the realization of interest A, while the other group defends plan N and the realization of interest B, do we then have simply a conflict of facts, or also a conflict of interests? It is not implausible to say we have both. A situation not wholly dissimilar occurs in contemporary society in the debate over 'guns or butter.' it is a situation, I assume, in which most people would agree there is a conflict of interests. The upshot of this argument is that it is one thing for there to be a harmony of interests in a community. It is another for the actions and plans of a community to harmonize with those interests. Marx emphasizes the former. But unless both are true, a state, etc. may still be needed. The above argument suggests that Marx was too optimistic to think that both will be true.

Accordingly, either the community in Marx's strong sense seems highly unlikely, or the identity of interests it requires will be enforced through social pressures, and the like. But in such a case, there is potentially the suppression of truth and knowledge as well as the repression of individual beliefs and thought which may be of value to the community.

One can see, consequently, how authoritarian implications might be drawn from Marx's views of freedom, and specifically that aspect of it related to the community. Thus, the threat of Marxist freedom does not relate to central planning so much as the modification of individuals which must take place in order that such central planning does not take the form of the state, or require police, the courts, coercion, etc. Marx is surely correct that the extreme emphasis on the individual defined in opposition to others which characterizes bourgeois society is mistaken; he is correct that greater emphasis needs to be placed on some kind of social and rational planning of the economy for human needs. He is correct that we must replace the egoistic individual of bourgeois society with a person who is more socially conscious and constituted. Still, to demand the social individual which Marx's vision of the community requires is to demand too much.

Finally, one other consequence which stems from the strong individual identification required for the elimination of the state, the police, and the courts might be noted. These institutions can be eliminated only if people generally behave in appropriate ways and punish themselves when they do not. Now it might well be that a society in which such self-punishment was possible as the means whereby divergencies from the required behavior were controlled would be a society in which guilt feelings or feelings of shame would have to be rather strong. One would have to be sharply concerned about the nature and effects of one's actions and be sufficiently concerned such that if they went wrong one would punish oneself. Accordingly, another issue which Marx should have broached, but did not, was whether the identification communism requires would demand an unacceptable amount of feelings of guilt or shame in order to function. It is not implausible, that is, that a person might be freer if he did not have to internalize significant amounts of such forces of self-control. If this is plausible, then it might be more desirable to allow that anti-social behavior, if severe enough, would be punished by certain authorities determined by other aspects of Marx's views. This, however, would reintroduce into Marx's view of communism characteristics of society which he believed communism would transcend.

VI

There is a final set of questions which needs to be asked about Marx's views on individuals and the community. Suppose that whatever doubts might be raised concerning the extensiveness of the harmony of interests could be allayed. We must also ask about the bases for such identification. If Marxism is not to transform itself into an idealism, there must be some 'materialistic basis' for this identification. Marx held that the antagonism of interests was due primarily to private property and the division of labor. Consequently, one basis for the close identification required is the elimination of these obstacles. Attendant upon this would supposedly come the elimination of class conflicts, the elimination of the town and country division, etc. Marx seems to assume that once these institutions and conflicts are eliminated, a close identification of people will develop which will allow them to construct a communist society. Two questions seem paramount here.

Firstly, is it plausible that private property and the traditional division of labor are institutions such that their removal would bring about an end to the antagonism of interests in society? Surely Marx is correct that private property and the traditional division of labor have great, even ultimate, significance for social relations. But that is not at issue here. The question is whether their elimination, together with a sufficient production of goods, could be expected to eliminate all socially significant conflict such that the state, coercion, etc. could be transcended. And on this score, the prospect is much less clear. It would not seem inconceivable that, even in these circumstances, there might develop groupings of people (I will allow that they could not be called classes) with hostile interests they sought to impose. Unless all differences are eliminated by communism — something Marx does not advocate — it is not impossible to imagine that some of these differences could be seized on by some people as the basis for antagonistic distinctions between themselves and others. But in this case, Marx's suggested resolution to the problem of conflicting interests would not be sufficient. A community would not exist in such circumstances.

Secondly, suppose that the preceding argument is mistaken or not convincing. Perhaps the elimination of private property and the traditional division of labor would eliminate all significant conflicts of interests. Still, it should be clear that something more is needed for a community — and hence communism — to exist. Simply to eliminate the conflicts and institutions Marx proposes does not guarantee that identification with others which would characterize the community. Even if we all have similar interests, even if our interests do not conflict, it does not follow that these interests positively cohere, that we do not remain isolated (alienated) rather than unified and mutually identified in our interests. Something more is needed to forge a positive identification with others. One possibility is that this basis is found in the opposition to, and revolution against, the bourgeoisie. Certainly this factor played a role in the Paris Commune to which Marx on occasion pointed as exemplifying characteristics of a socialist or communist society. But this basis would hardly survive the successful establishment of communism.

Another possibility is that Marx simply assumed that humans have a natural, spontaneous affection for others, a tendency to identify with others, if obstacles and barriers between them are removed. This kind of assumption seems present in his view that mankind is not characterized by a tension between good and evil desires, but may be characterized as basically good — evil desires apparently arise from frustrated desires. Kamenka seems to adopt some such view in his claim that Marx conceived goods 'as being able to work and co-operate coherently, while evils conflict not only with goods, but with each other.'[28] Thus, if evils such as private property, etc. are eliminated, then the goods which remain will 'co-operate and form a harmonious system.'[29] A person whose life is constituted by good motives and desires is a person with a productive spirit who will voluntarily co-operate with others.[30] 'Goods require no censorship, no punishments, no protection as part of their ways of working.'[31]

Now even if this view is plausible, which I do not think it is, it could be only part of an answer to the present problem. Such underlying goodness and potential for identification with others could not be realized simply by the elimination of obstacles. Good motives and desires do not always assist others of the same kind.[32] My desire to help another person may conflict with my desire to keep a promise to help a third person. Spontaneous affections for others may harm them. Close identification with others may result in submerging one's own personality. On the other hand, bad motives and intentions may harmonize. Wanton murder is bad for the capitalist class and the proletariat class. The demand for security does not necessarily conflict with the security demands and needs for others.[33] Accordingly, the view that goods harmonize, that man is basically good, and that if evils are eliminated, a harmony of goods will arise is implausible. The good and the positive identification of individuals Marx seeks also require for their realization certain social structures which would give them a form compatible with communism. However, about such structures Marx was persistently silent. Yet some answer to this problem is essential.

Sometimes Marx says that communist man simply sees, in each situation, the answer to such questions (e.g. *MECW*, 5:41). But something less specific is needed. We have to be able to look ahead and not simply handle problems from day to day. How otherwise could there be rational planning? We must learn upon what structural bases communist

233

man may exist. We must be able to establish those positive bases upon which human identification could be founded. The effort to enlarge the self, to expand that with which the self identifies, is a noble effort. We see a progressive enlargement of these bounds in history — from the family or tribe to the region, country, and to mankind. It is not preposterous, then, to hold that in general people identify more broadly these days than in previous centuries, and that there are things we can and should do to extend this process of identification. As it stands, however, the basis as well as the social forms required for such a positive relation amongst individuals is not obvious in Marx's ethics. It is and remains a crucial problem in this thought.

The importance of this problem can be indicated in one final way. If such identifications were not attainable, questions concerning justice and rights, as well as mechanisms to ensure the social order, would have to be raised once again. The latter need not be oppressive or despotic, but they would have to exist — contrary to Marx's vision. Such rights of individuals and means to protect the social order become important in defense of those who can and do identify with others against those who do not or cannot. The danger with Marx's view (as we have seen in this century) is the temptation to try to impose on people the relations constituting the identification characteristic of communism. However, to do this without the necessary social and personal bases is, *ex hypothesis*, to violate the rights of individuals. Rights and justice are transcended only when there is such identification amongst people. If there is not such identification, and the bases for it do not yet exist, then rights and justice have not been transcended. To seek to impose relations of close identification on people would thus violate their rights. Accordingly, in contrast to the usual charge that Marxists, in attempting to achieve equality or justice, trample on freedom, it would seem more likely, if morality is transgressed, that the opposite is true — to achieve freedom, Marxists are tempted to trample on justice and rights!

It might be objected that I have tried too hard to make communist society plausible — or at least intelligible — to us today. According to the more radical proponents of Marxism, as well as such commentators as Heilbroner,[34] communism will be constituted by a society of humans utterly different from, and unimaginable to, us. Consequently, they might say, some of the features which I have maintained would constitute communism but which have, in some cases, suggested problems in Marx's views are simply remnants of a dying bourgeois period in history. Further, they might contend that to the extent that any socialist or Marxist group accepts an account such as given in the first two parts of this book, they would remain attached to social features which are bourgeois. They could not, therefore, constitute a radical force. The most they could do, within the confines of the above account, is to promote a bourgeois socialism or a socialist capitalism.[35]

These objections have, at least, the following merit. Obviously anyone's ability to imagine the future is limited by and tied to the past. Yet this must be said against them. Firstly, Marx apparently did not think that the difference between communism and capitalist times was so radical that he could not cite examples such as communist artisans of his time, the Paris Commune, etc. to illustrate various aspects of communism. Secondly, the account given of communism above includes the elimination of private property in the means of production, the transcendence of classes, of the town and country distinction, as well as formal punishment. It is hard to imagine such an account as simply an account of bourgeois socialism or socialistic capitalism simply because it retains some forms of private property, the division of labor, and individual punishment.[36] Thirdly, contemporary society differs significantly from medieval society. Concepts such as chivalry and piety which were significant previously are not significant in similar ways today. However, one cannot extrapolate from such examples to suggest, on the one hand, that contemporary society is wholly different from medieval society or, on the other hand, that communist society will be even more radically different from bourgeois society.[37] True, chivalry is dead. But the values of courage, honesty, loyalty, and generosity which were essential to chivalry have taken other forms. Similarly, one might expect their forms to be different, but recognizable, under communism. But that is a long shot from claiming that a wholly different moral form of life will appear with communism. Finally, if individuals and the life they lead under communism are virtually unimaginable, some other basis upon which to act in the present — than a conception of the moral life as exemplified by communism, which the objection says is impossible — is needed so as to change and remedy present society. It seems to make little sense to try to change this society towards something that I am told I cannot imagine or comprehend. To act to promote such a society is but a poke in the dark. If action now is to be rational and moral, it must have some end, ground, or reason that is intelligible and justifiable now. Thus, the above objection is to be viewed with suspicion. Much better to stretch our imagination in our conception of a more rational, more moral future society than to rest content in the *status quo*. However, it is also important not to stretch that imagination so far that it snaps and all action is simply a blind faith in some future-we-know-not-what!

In conclusion, Marx's ethics offers to contemporary ethics important and stimulating insights into the nature of morality and its role in society. However, his ethics also has significant problems and difficulties. But then this might be said of the work of any great thinker. Still, in contrast to previous moral philosophers, Marx's ethics requires a greater degree of explicit elaboration and extension. It also requires important revision. Indeed, Marx's ethics is most plausibly understood as an approach to problems of ethics rather than a set of final answers. However, there is no reason to think that Marx's views are not open to such further development as well as rethinking and revision. Marx's favorite motto was 'You must have doubts about everything.'[38] Only after such additional work could Marx's ethics take its place as a theory amongst the other significant theories of past and present. The present study is one step in this direction. Still, for an age ever more set in its ways but which increasingly experiences problems resulting from those ways, Marx's views are an open door to a renewal of critical thought. For a subject matter ever threatened by abstract thought and/or moralistic injunctions, Marx's ethics remains a healthy and potent reminder. And for those who believe that radical change is needed, but distrust appeals to transcendent sources, to intuitions, or to authority, Marx's ethics was a radical ethics in the best sense — an ethics which attempted to grasp the root of things and in so doing grasp man himself.

Notes

1 Marxism, moralism, and ethics

1 I distinguish between ethics and morality. 'Morality' refers to an actual or an ideal (i.e. reflective) set of moral principles, virtues, standards, etc. according to which people should live and/or act. 'Ethics' or 'moral philosophy' refers either to the process in which one engages while reflecting on morality, its nature and bases, or to the result of that reflection. In the latter instance, ethics and (ideal) morality overlap – at least in part. They might be said to be not identical because one's ethics may include various logical and methodological views which would not, as such, be part of one's (ideal) morality.

2 Werner Sombart, *Barun's Archiv für Sociale Gesetzgebung und Statistik*, vol. 5, 1892, p. 489, cited in Robert C. Tucker, *Philosophy and Myth in Karl Marx*, Cambridge University Press, 1971, p. 12. Other commentators who have held, in one place or another, that Marxism is essentially a science would include B. Croce, R. Hilferding, and K. Kautsky.

3 Lewis S. Feuer, 'Ethical Theories and Historical Materialism,' *Science and Society*, vol. 6, 1942, p. 269.

4 Donald Clark Hodges, 'Historical Materialism in Ethics,' *Philosophy and Phenomenological Research*, vol. 23, 1962, p. 6.

5 Michael Evans, *Karl Marx*, Bloomington, Indiana, Indiana University Press, 1975, p. 188.

6 Jacques Barzun, *Darwin, Marx, Wagner*, Garden City, New York, Doubleday, 1958, p. 163.

7 A list of the many persons who have contributed to this discussion would require several pages. I refer the reader to the bibliography and to the notes of this and the following chapters.

8 On the conditions for ethical inquiry, see Bertell Ollman, 'Is There a Marxian Ethic?' *Science and Society*, vol. 35, 1971, pp. 156-60.

9 Jeremy Bentham defended the view that those acts are morally obligatory which produce the greatest amount of pleasure; cf. Jeremy Bentham, *The Principles of Morals and Legislation*, Darien, Conn., Hafner Publishing Co., 1970.

10　Thus, I reject the contentions of Tucker, Ollman, and Popper that Marx could not have a moral theory because he did not suspend his commitments. Note that Tucker's discussion prejudices his answer by the additional fact that Tucker asks not whether Marx had a moral philosophy or a moral theory, but whether Marx was a moral philosopher; cf. Robert C. Tucker, *Philosophy and Myth in Karl Marx*, p. 15. One need not hold that Marx was a moral philosopher in order to hold that he had an implicit moral theory.

11　This is not to deny that they might have a moral theory. Allen Wood's comment represents the kind of view referred to in the text: 'At any rate, Marx seems to me no more a subscriber to any particular moral philosophy than is the "common man" with whose moral views nearly every moral philosopher claims to be in agreement' cf. Allen Wood, 'The Marxian Critique of Justice', *Philosophy and Public Affairs*, vol. 1, 1971-2, p. 281.

12　The sense of 'moralist' used in the text is that of one who applies various moral principles to concrete situations. This is distinct from the sense of 'moralist' in which a person's thought is primarily concerned with right and wrong. Yet another sense of 'moralist' is noted below at note 18.

13　The formulation used in this paragraph to capture the conditions of having a moral theory was suggested to me by an anonymous reviewer of this book.

14　Some have even maintained that Marx must be attempting *not* to use moral language; cf. William Leon McBride, 'The Concept of Justice in Marx, Engels, and Others,' *Ethics*, vol. 85, no. 3, April, 1975, p. 204.

15　Karl Marx and Friedrich Engels, *Selected Correspondence*, ed. S.W. Ryazanskaya, Moscow, Progress Publishers, 1975, p. 139.

16　In other circumstances or on other occasions, Marx's views indicate that his language must be clear and easy to understand:

> We are in full agreement with your view that the German Communists must emerge from the isolation in which they have hitherto existed and establish durable mutual contacts with one another; similarly, associations for the purpose of reading and discussion are necessary. For Communists must first of all clear things up among themselves, and this cannot be done satisfactorily without regular meetings to discuss questions concerning communism. We therefore also agree . . . that cheap, easily understandable books and pamphlets with a communist content must be widely circulated. (*MECW*, 6:54)

For a similar reason, Marx claimed to have popularized, 'as much as it was possible,' the analysis of the substance of value and the magnitude of value in *Capital* (*Capital*, I:7).

17 G.W.F. Hegel, *Philosophy of Right*, trans. T.M. Knox, New York, Oxford University Press, 1967, pp. 12-13. Hegel himself, however, did criticize various aspects of the society in which he lived.

18 The word 'moralist' is used in a rather ordinary sense here, but one distinct from either of the two senses noted above in note 12. In the present sense it suggests an officious person, one who seeks to impose his views of duty on other people against their wishes and in inappropriate ways or at inappropriate times.

19 The distinction between concept and word might be simply indicated as follows: The word 'alienation' stands for a certain concept, i.e. a certain set of ideas, meanings, etc., which might also be expressed by other words and languages. For example, the same concept might be signified in German by the word *'Entfremdung.'* Thus, two different words would stand for the same concept.

20 Cf. George Burgher, 'Marxism and Normative Judgments,' *Science and Society*, vol. 23, 1959, p. 253.

21 Cf. Donald Van de Veer, 'Marx's View of Justice,' *Philosophy and Phenomenological Research*, vol. 33, 1972-3, p. 369.

22 Karl Marx, 'Inaugural Address of the Working Men's International Association,' in *The Marx-Engels Reader*, ed. Robert C. Tucker, New York: W.W. Norton, 1972, p. 376. The German is *'befleckter Moral.'*

23 Other examples would include Marx's references to the 'evils oppressing us' (*Capital*, I:265); also 'The moral degradation caused by the capitalist exploitation of women and children' (*Capital*, I:399).

24 Karl Marx, 'Critique of the Gotha Program,' in *The Marx-Engels Reader*, 1972, p. 388.

25 Recall Marx's statements cited above on pp. 9-10.

26 Cf. William K. Frankena, 'Prichard and the Ethics of Virtue,' in *Perspectives on Morality*, ed. K.E. Goodpaster, Notre Dame, Indiana, University of Notre Dame Press, 1976; Lon L. Fuller, *The Morality of Law*, New Haven, Connecticut, Yale University Press, 1973; revised edition. Some of the formulations in the following paragraph stem from Fuller.

27 Cf. Allen W. Wood, 'Marx on Right and Justice: A Reply to Husami,' *Philosophy and Public Affairs*, vol. 8, no. 3, 1979, pp. 280-7.

28 Leslie Stephen, *The Science of Ethics*, New York, G.P. Putnam's Sons, 1882, pp. 155, 158, as cited in William K. Frankena, *Ethics*, Englewood Cliffs, New Jersey, Prentice-Hall, 1973, p. 63.

29 William K. Frankena, 'Prichard and the Ethics of Virtue,' p. 150.

30 The relevant German refers to *'moralische Schranken.'* Cf. also, Karl Marx, *Capital*, I:265. The point of this quotation is to offer textual evidence that Marx used (at least on occasion) the word 'moral' in a broad sense. The point is *not* to claim that Marx is here referring to the limitations of some 'true' or 'real' morality.

31 The view defended here also implies that some who have claimed that Marx did have an ethics but tried to find an ethics of duty in Marx are also mistaken. They did not recognize the radically different nature of his ethical views.

32 Allen Wood denies that Marx's views on freedom are moral views. His contention is that freedom (as well as security, self-actualization, community, etc.) is a non-moral good. He offers but one argument: 'We all know the difference between valuing or doing something because conscience or the "moral law" tells us that we "ought" to, and valuing or doing something because it satisfies our needs, our wants or our conceptions of what is good for us (or for someone else whose welfare we want to promote – desires for nonmoral goods are not necessarily selfish desires). This difference roughly marks off "moral" from "nonmoral" goods and evils.' Cf. *Karl Marx*, London, Routledge & Kegan Paul, 1981, p. 126. The argument is unacceptable. On the one hand, it is mistaken to suggest that Marx values freedom and community simply because they satisfy 'our needs, our wants or our conception of what is good for us.' Marx held that it is rational to value freedom, that people would value and demand freedom if they were not deluded, that there is (historical) justification for valuing freedom, and that we ought (to the extent possible) to strive to realize a free society (for a defense of these claims see Chapters 3 and 4). Surely this is to speak of a value that has many, if not most, of the makings of a moral value – and not simply a non-moral good. On the other hand, Wood's argument embodies a misleading ambiguity. If the phrase 'our needs, our wants' refers to the needs, wants, etc. of a single person, then surely there is a difference between this and morality. Even Marx would agree. His valuing freedom cannot simply be reduced to the fact that freedom would satisfy his (Marx's) needs, wants, etc. On the other hand, if 'our needs, our wants' refers to everyone's needs and wants, then even utilitarians would claim that a moral question is at stake. Marx is not a utilitarian. Still the point is that we have here to do with a moral question and not simply a non-moral question.

33 Cf. Arthur W.H. Adkins, *Merit and Responsibility*, Oxford University Press, 1960. Among those who have more recently denied that the Greeks had a morality is William K. Frankena, *Thinking About Morality* Ann Arbor, University of Michigan Press, 1980, p. 11.

34 Cf. G.E.M. Anscombe, 'Modern Moral Philosophy,' *Philosophy*, vol. 33, 1958, pp. 1-19. It has also been argued that an ethics of duty is conceptually linked with capitalism. If this is correct, then it would be nonsense (logically) to speak of Marx's ethics (cf. Lon L. Fuller, *The Morality of Law*, p. 24). But to characterize morality in such a narrow fashion is surely mistaken. It is an attempt to pro-

tect the term 'morality' which beggars our understanding. It is better to allow the scope of morality to range widely and then within that broad range show why certain particular moralities are themselves unacceptable, than by conceptual decree exclude them from consideration. It is this, I contend, we must do in order to understand and appraise Marx's discussion of morality, capitalism, and bourgeois society.

35 H.L.A. Hart, 'Are There Any Natural Rights?,' in *Political Philosophy*, ed. Anthony Quinton, Oxford University Press, 1967, p. 54.

36 Cf. p. 19.

37 Cf. Lon L. Fuller, *The Morality of Law*, pp. 6-11.

38 *Ibid.*, p. 24.

39 Karl Marx, *Grundrisse*, New York, Vintage Books, 1973, trans. Martin Nicolaus, p. 90. Also, Karl Marx, 'Letters from Deutsch-Französische Jahrbücher', in Karl Marx and Frederick Engels, *Collected Works*, vol. III, New York, International Publishers, 1975, pp. 142-4.

2 Ethics and historical materialism

1 Eugene Kamenka, *The Ethical Foundations of Marxism*, 2nd edn, London, Routledge & Kegan Paul, 1972, p. 96. Cf. Gordon Leff, *The Tyranny of Concepts*, Birmingham, Alabama, University of Alabama Press, 1969 p. 205.

2 Karl Marx, *A Contribution to the Critique of Political Economy*, New York: International Publishers, 1970, pp. 20-1.

3 The interpretation of historical materialism which is given in the following pages goes generally by the name of 'technological determinism.' It can be found in William H. Shaw, *Marx's Theory of History*, Stanford, California, Stanford University Press, 1978; and G.A. Cohen, *Karl Marx's Theory of History: A Defense*, Princeton, New Jersey, Princeton University Press, 1978.

4 Shaw, *Marx's Theory of History*, p. 13; cf. Cohen, *Karl Marx's Theory of History*, pp. 32-4.

5 There is some dispute amongst those who give accounts such as are being considered here as to whether the relations of production which constitute the economic structure of a society include simply social, ownership kinds of relations – such as those mentioned in the text – or whether they also include work or material relations of production (e.g. the relation of a foreman to his crew). For the former view, see G. Cohen, *Karl Marx's Theory of History*, pp. 35, 92-3, 111-14. For the latter view, see W. Shaw, *Marx's Theory of History*, pp. 28-30. The argument which follows does not depend on resolving this dispute one way or the other.

6 Shaw, p. 58; cf. Cohen, p. 46.
7 Shaw, p. 71.
8 *Ibid.*, p. 72.
9 Marx also claims that the following are productive forces: a communal economy (*MECW*, 5:76), social knowledge (*Grund.*, 706), capital (*Grund.*, 86). Cf. also *Grund.*, 308, 540, 543, 765; *Capital*, I:344, 386.
10 Shaw, p. 139.
11 *Ibid.*, p. 13; cf. Cohen, pp. 32-4.
12 Shaw, p. 13; cf. Cohen, pp. 32-4.
13 Ted Honderich also argues that such technological determinist accounts as Cohen and Shaw offer are defective in that they do not allow a role for human judgment, will, and desires; cf. 'Against Teleological Historical Materialism,' *Inquiry*, vol. 25, 1982. Honderich does not, however, push this point, as I do, to include values, both moral and non-moral.
14 Cf. Kamenka, *The Ethical Foundations of Marxism*, p. 142. Honderich maintains that 'once desires and judgments are on the scene in the given essential way, we have left behind Marx's fundamental line about the irrelevance of consciousness'; cf. 'Against Teleological Historical Materialism.' My argument, however, has been that Marx does *not* contend that desires, values, and judgments (i.e. consciousness) are irrelevant in the development of society. That this view is plausibly Marxist is what I now proceed to argue.
15 Brand Blanshard, 'Reflections on Economic Determinism,' *Journal of Philosophy*, vol. LXIII, March 1966, p. 165.
16 Frederick Engels, *Selected Correspondence*, ed. S.W. Ryazanskaya, Moscow, Progress Publishers, 1975, p. 394.
17 This list is not meant to be exhaustive.
18 Cf. Martin Needleman and Carolyn Needleman, 'Marx and the Problem of Causation,' *Science and Society*, vol. XXXIII, 1969.
19 Michael Harrington, *The Twilight of Capitalism*, Simon & Schuster, 1976, pp. 68-9. In this section, I am indebted to Harrington's own fine account of Marx's views on ideology and historical materialism.
20 Ollman maintains that the relations among the forces of production, the relations of production, and the superstructure can all be explicated as logical or conceptual relations; cf. Bertell Ollman, *Alienation*, Cambridge University Press, 1971. Cohen, Shaw, and Allen Wood attempt to explicate these relations in teleological or functional terms; cf. Allen Wood, *Karl Marx*, London, Routledge & Kegan Paul, 1981. Honderich, H.B. Acton, and many others have offered a causal interpretation of production forces, relations of production, and the superstructure; cf. H.B. Acton, *The Illusion of the Epoch*, London, Routledge & Kegan Paul, 1972.
21 Karl Marx, *Critique of the Gotha Program*, in *The Marx-Engels*

Reader, ed. Robert C. Tucker (2nd edn rev.; New York, W.W. Norton, 1978), p. 534.

22 Immanuel Kant, *Critique of Practical Reason*, New York, The Library of Liberal Arts, 1956, p. 100.
23 Karl Marx, 'Circular Letter to Bebel, Liebknecht, Bracke, and Others,' in *The Marx-Engels Reader*, p. 552.
24 Recall Kamenka's claim noted at the beginning of this chapter, p. 24. Cf. Kamenka, *The Ethical Foundations of Marxism*, pp. 96-7.

3 Ideology and moral justification

1 Karl Marx, *A Contribution to the Critique of Political Economy*, New York, International Publishers, 1970, p. 21.
2 Marx makes the same point when he later notes (regarding the ancient world) that 'as soon as *untruth* penetrated their world (i.e., as soon as this world itself disintegrated in consequence of practical conflicts – and to demonstrate this materialistic development empirically would be the only thing of interest), the ancient philosophers sought to penetrate the world of truth or the truth of their world and then, of course, they found that it had become untrue' (*MECW*, 5:136).
3 Brand Blanshard, 'Reflections on Economic Determinism,' *Journal of Philosophy*, vol. LXIII, March 1966, p. 177.
4 Cf. Frederick Engels, 'The Origin of the Family, Private Property and the State,' in Karl Marx and Frederick Engels, *Selected Works*, New York, International Publishers, 1970, pp. 455-593.
5 This is the problem noted above on pages 63-7.
6 William K. Frankena, *Ethics*, 2nd edn rev.; Englewood Cliffs, New Jersey, Prentice-Hall, 1973, p. 109.
7 Cf. 'The essence of man . . . in its reality . . . is the ensemble of the social relations' (*MECW*, 5:4).
8 Cf. Maximilien Rubel and Margaret Manale, *Marx Without Myth*, New York, Harper & Row, 1975, pp. 307, 321.
9 Karl Marx, 'The Future Results of British Rule in India,' in *The Marx-Engels Reader*, ed. Robert C. Tucker, New York, W.W. Norton, 1972, p. 587.

4 The ethics of freedom

1 The distinction between meta-ethics and normative ethics is a fairly common one in this century; cf. William K. Frankena, *Ethics*, 2nd edn; Englewood Cliffs, New Jersey, Prentice-Hall, 1973, chs 1 and 6. Many people are inclined to view normative ethics as the whole of ethics. This is a mistake to be guarded against. That this should

be necessary is ironic since amongst philosophers the opposite mistake has been common.

2 These interpretations may be offered in monistic and pluralistic forms. That bourgeois society is egoistic, greedy, and the like is simply a negative formulation of these interpretations.
3 Cf. Chapter 5.
4 Bertell Ollman, *Alienation*, Cambridge University Press, 1971, p. 117.
5 Eugene Kamenka, *The Ethical Foundations of Marxism*, 2nd edn rev.; London, Routledge & Kegan Paul, 1972, p. 102.
6 Adam Schaff, *A Philosophy of Man*, New York: Dell Publishing Co., 1963, pp. 112, 115. Also, Adam Schaff, *Marxism and the Human Individual*, New York, McGraw-Hill, 1970, pp. 154, 156, 158.
7 Karl Popper, *The Open Society and its Enemies*, New York, Harper & Row, 1967, vol. II, pp. 103-4.
8 Cf. John Stuart Mill, *On Liberty*, New York, Bobbs-Merrill, 1966, p. 13.
9 Schaff, *A Philosophy of Man*, pp. 112, 115.
10 Kamenka makes this mistake. Cf. Kamenka, *The Ethical Foundations of Marxism*, chs 9, 10.
11 Frankena, *Ethics*, pp. 62-7. Cf. William K. Frankena, 'Prichard and the Ethics of Virtue,' in *Perspectives on Morality*, ed. K.E. Goodpaster, Notre Dame, Indiana, University of Notre Dame Press, 1976, pp. 148-60.
12 F.H. Bradley, *Ethical Studies*, London, Oxford University Press, 1962, p. 232.
13 *Ibid.*, pp. 57, 215, 219, 232, 276-308.
14 Ollman, *Alienation*, p. 117 (emphasis added). Cf. also, pp. 116, 118, 139.
15 *Ibid.*, p. 117.
16 Plato, *The Republic*, in *The Collected Dialogues*, ed. Edith Hamilton and Huntington Cairns, New York, Pantheon Books, 1961, p. 599.
17 H.B. Acton, *The Illusion of the Epoch*, London, Routledge & Kegan Paul, 1972, p. vi.
18 Popper, *The Open Society and its Enemies*, vol. 2, p. 103.
19 *Ibid.*, p. 105.
20 George W. Dawson, 'Man in the Marxian Kingdom of Freedom: A Critique,' *Archiv für Rechts und Sozialphilosophie*, vol. 59, 1975, p. 365.
21 Derek P.H. Allen, 'Reply to Brenkert's "Marx & Utilitarianism",' *Canadian Journal of Philosophy*, vol. 6, 1976, p. 520.
22 Ollman, *Alienation*, ch. 4. Kamenka, *The Ethical Foundations of Marxism*, Parts III and IV. The claim made here is with regard to Kamenka's interpretation of Marx's later views.

23 I have emphasized 'mere' and omitted emphases on 'utility' and 'human' in Marx's statement.
24 Allen, 'Reply to Brenkert's . . . ,' p. 523.
25 *Ibid.*
26 G.W.F. Hegel, *Philosophy of Right*, trans. T.M. Knox, London, Oxford University Press, 1967, p. 45.
27 *Ibid.*, p. 42.
28 Hereafter, I will speak simply of the 'community' and not the 'real community.'
29 Allen, 'Reply to Brenkert's . . . ,' p. 520.
30 *Ibid.*
31 Richard Schact, *Alienation*, Garden City, New York, Doubleday, 1971, p. 90.
32 Cf. Ollman, *Alienation*, p. 109.
33 Karl Marx, 'The Civil War in France,' in *The Marx-Engels Reader*, ed. Robert C. Tucker, New York, W.W. Norton, 1972, pp. 555, 557.
34 Schacht, *Alienation*, pp. 99-100.
35 The relation of justice and freedom is discussed in Chapter 5.
36 Charles Taylor, *Hegel*, Cambridge University Press, 1975, p. 374.
37 Frankena, *Ethics*, p. 63.
38 Bradley, *Ethical Studies*, p. 225.

5 Capitalism and justice

1 Donald Van de Veer, 'Marx's View of Justice,' *Philosophy and Phenomenological Research*, vol. 33, 1972-3; Ziyad I. Husami, 'Marx on Distributive Justice,' *Philosophy and Public Affairs*, vol. 8, 1978; Harold J. Laski, *Karl Marx*, New York, League for Industrial Democracy, 1933; A.D. Lindsay, *Karl Marx's Capital: An Introductory Essay*, London, Geoffrey Cumberlege, 1947.
2 This is not simply an early comment. Marx makes roughly the same comment also in *Capital* (cf. *Capital*, I:618).
3 This can easily be documented. Not recognizing this fact can give rise to many difficulties and misinterpretations. On not speaking strictly according to his theoretical commitments, cf. *Capital*, I:174, 216, 227, 586.
4 I do not exclude the possibility that even Marx was guilty of this on occasion!
5 I assume that capitalism, in its restless search for surplus value, would not go beyond this point. Capitalism's nature is rapacious, unsatisfiable, but it is not consciously self-destructive.
6 Derek P.H. Allen, 'Is Marxism a Philosophy?' *Journal of Philosophy*, vol. 71, 1974, p. 603.
7 *Ibid.*, p. 604.

8   They might also ask about the ends of the labor — but this need not be discussed here.

9   My assumption in the present discussion remains that this is how wages should be determined.

10 I assume here that there is a difference between justification and justice. An act or situation may be unjustified without being unjust. Cf. below, pp. 159, 161.

11 John Stuart Mill, *Principles of Political Economy*, ed. Donald Winch, Baltimore, Maryland, Penguin, 1970, p. 370.

12 Allen W. Wood, 'The Marxian Critique of Justice,' *Philosophy and Public Affairs*, vol. 1, 1971-2, p. 256.

13 Robert Tucker claims that this formula is only used once by Marx in all his writings. Cf. Robert C. Tucker, 'Marx and Distributive Justice,' in *The Marxian Revolutionary Idea*, New York: W.W. Norton, 1970, p. 48. Tucker may well be correct in his claim; still, Marx does come quite close to this phrase on other occasions. Cf. *MECW*, 5:537.

14 Husami, 'Marx on Distributive Justice,' p. 46.

15 *Ibid.*, p. 39.

16 I assume here, for purposes of argument, that it is proper to speak of a communist principle of justice.

17 Husami, 'Marx on Distributive Justice,' p. 57.

18 Karl Marx, *Critique of the Gotha Program*, in *The Marx-Engels Reader*, ed. Robert C. Tucker, New York: W.W. Norton, 1972, p. 487.

19 *Ibid.*

20 *Ibid.*, pp. 388-9.

21 *Ibid.*, p. 386.

22 As we have seen above, capitalism opts for the latter view of justice.

23 Karl Marx, *Critique of the Gotha Program*, p. 388.

24 Cf. Donald Van de Veer, 'Doing Justice to Marx,' unpublished paper, p. 13.

25 The following additional comments are relevant to the point argued in the text. A capitalist may have great wealth, exercise great power over the fate of others as well as in the determination of his own course, and still not be said to be free in the Marxist sense. He is not free because of the power of the market over him, because of the manner in which he objectifies himself, and because of his antagonistic relations with others. Needless to say, the proletarian who works for the capitalist is also not free. He must execute the commands of the capitalist; he has little control over the fate of others let alone his own fate. Does he therefore have less freedom, less Marxist freedom, than the capitalist? This is not at all clear. The proletarian's relations with his compatriots might be significantly less antagonistic, he may be less consumed by greed, more concerned about the quality of the conditions under which

he works. One might even plausibly argue, in a manner reminiscent of Hegel, that it is the proletarian who has greater freedom (in the Marxist sense) than the capitalist! The point which should be emphasized, however, is that none of the members of the productive relations constituting capitalism is free. It makes little sense to ask which class under capitalism is more free, when the relations in which they exist condemn them all to an illusory freedom. Thus it is pointless to claim that capitalism is unjust because it distributes unfairly Marxist freedom. What is clear is that this entire social system of relations does not instantiate Marxist freedom. It is on this level that Marx brings his critique of capitalism.

26 Immanuel Kant, *Metaphysics of Morals*, cited in Bruce Aune, *Kant's Theory of Morals*, Princeton, New Jersey, Princeton University Press, 1979, p. 141.

27 Bruce Aune, *Kant's Theory of Morals*, p. 144.

28 Aristotle, *Nicomachean Ethics*, in *Introduction to Aristotle*, ed. Richard McKeon, New York, The Modern Library, 1947, p. 400.

29 Cf. John Stuart Mill, *Utilitarianism*, ed. Oskar Priest, New York, Library of Liberal Arts, 1957, ch. 5. G.E.M. Anscombe, 'Modern Moral Philosophy,' *Philosophy*, vol. 33, 1958.

30 David Hume, *An Enquiry Concerning the Principles of Morals*, in *Hume's Ethical Writings*, ed. Alasdair MacIntyre, New York, Collier Books, 1965, pp. 35-9.

31 Ivan Babic, 'Blanshard's Reduction of Marxism,' *Journal of Philosophy*, vol. 63, 1968, p. 752.

6 Revolutionary morals, violence, and communism

1 Karl Marx, 'Speech at the Anniversary of the *People's Paper*,' in *The Marx-Engels Reader*, ed. Robert C. Tucker, 2nd edn; New York, W.W. Norton, 1978, p. 577.

2 Karl Marx, *Critique of the Gotha Program*, in *The Marx-Engels Reader*, p. 529.

3 *Ibid.*

4 Friedrich Engels, 'Speech at the Graveside of Karl Marx,' in *The Marx-Engels Reader*, p. 682.

5 Karl Marx and Friedrich Engels, 'Address to the Central Committee to the Communist League,' in *The Marx-Engels Reader*, pp. 506-7.

6 Karl Marx, 'Speech at Amsterdam,' cited in David McLellan, *The Thought of Karl Marx*, New York, Harper & Row, 1971, p. 209.

7 *Ibid.*

8 Karl Marx, cited in Shlomo Avineri, *The Social and Political Thought of Karl Marx*, Cambridge University Press, 1971, p. 201.

9 Cf. H.B. Acton, *The Illusion of the Epoch*, London: Routledge & Kegan Paul, 1972, pp. 73, 81. Maurice Cornforth, *Materialism and*

the Dialectical Method, New York, International Publishers, 1971, pp. 53, 71, 82-3, 101-5.
10 *Ibid.*, p. 53.
11 Cf. Adam Schaff, 'Marxist Theory on Revolution and Violence,' *The Journal of the History of Ideas*, vol. 34, 1973, p. 268. Schaff suggests yet another reason why the peaceful transition to socialism need not be said to be a brand of reformism: 'Now, if today it is said in Marxist theory that it is *possible* to pass peacefully to socialism provided that appropriate conditions exist, this disclaims neither a violent revolution . . . nor the importance of the ultimate goal, i.e., Communism. . . . Hence, by definition we do not have to do with a reformist policy.'
12 Karl Marx, 'Marx to Ferdinand Domela Nieuwenhuis in the Hague,' in *Selected Correspondence*, 3rd edn rev.; Moscow, Progress Publishers, 1975, pp. 317-18.
13 Karl Marx, 'Marx to Vera Ivanovna Zasulich in Geneva,' in *Selected Correspondence*, p. 319. Cf. also p. 293.
14 Karl Marx, 'Circular Letter to Bebel, Liebknecht, Bracke, and Others,' in *The Marx-Engels Reader*, p. 555.
15 Obviously there were other necessary conditions as well, e.g. the importation of precious metals, the discovery of America, etc. Cf. *MECW*, 6:185.
16 Karl Marx, 'Circular Letter to Bebel, Liebknecht, Bracke, and Others,' pp. 551-2.
17 Karl Marx, 'Marx to Engels in Manchester,' in *Selected Correspondence*, p. 120.
18 Cf. John Harris, 'The Marxist Conception of Violence,' *Philosophy and Public Affairs*, vol. 3, 1973, pp. 192-220. For other instances of this sense of violence, see *Capital*, I:293, 470, 471, 475-77.
19 Karl Marx, cited in Bertell Ollman, *Alienation*, Cambridge University Press, 1971, p. 213.
20 This involves recognizing not merely the different sense of 'violence' noted in the text, but also the implicit ethics of freedom which lies behind these senses. Given such a broad view of violence, what is the relation of violence to alienation? If alienation is the lack of freedom, and violence is also the denial of freedom, are not alienation and violence about the same thing? Certainly, there is something to be said for this view. In 'Estranged Labor,' Marx claims that the alienation of labor is characterized, at least in part, by the fact that it is 'not voluntary, but coerced; it is *forced labor*' (*MECW*, 3:274). Nevertheless, we cannot simply identify violence (as well as coercion and force) with alienation. There are other aspects of alienation (and freedom) which, though they may be brought about force, coercion, and violence, are not simply the same as these concepts. For example, one is alienated to the extent one does not concretely, but abstractly, objectify oneself.

One who has an eye only for the monetary value of nature, but not its aesthetic aspects, is alienated. Such a characteristic of life under capitalism is not captured by any of the above senses of violence.

21 Robert C. Tucker, 'The Marxian Revolutionary Idea,' in *The Marxian Revolutionary Idea*, New York, W.W. Norton, 1970, pp. 17-18.

22 Robert C. Tucker, 'The Political Theory of Classical Marxism,' in *The Marxian Revolutionary Idea*, p. 61.

23 Cf. Shlomo Avineri, *The Social and Political Thought of Karl Marx*, pp. 185-201.

24 Karl Marx, cited in Maximilien Rubel and Margaret Manale, *Marx Without Myth*, New York, Harper & Row, 1975, p. 81.

25 Avineri, p. 188.

26 *Ibid.*, p. 194.

27 *Ibid.*, p. 190.

28 For an interesting discussion of Marx's concept of the dictatorship of the proletariat, see Hal Draper, 'Marx and the Dictatorship of the Proletariat,' *New Politics*, vol. I, 1961/2, pp. 91-104.

29 It should be recalled that it is through need, egoism, and self-interest that communism also comes about. Cf. *MECW*, 3:217.

30 Karl Marx, cited in Svetozar Stojanović, *Between Ideals and Reality*, New York, Oxford University Press, 1973, p. 179.

31 Certainly, this also seems to be corroborated by Marx's claim, in *The Holy Family*, that '*punishment, coercion*, is contrary to *human* conduct' (*MECW*, 4:179).

32 Karl Marx, *A Contribution to the Critique of Political Economy*, New York, International Publishers, 1970, p. 21.

33 In at least one place in his article, 'Marx, Engels, and the Future Society,' Irving Fetscher would seem to agree. He claims that with the withering away of the political functions of the state 'there is no longer a privileged class which must defend its interest, if necessary by force, by the constant threat of force.' He continues, 'from this hypothesis it follows that *most* incentives to individual crime will fade away' (emphasis added). Cf. Irving Fetscher, 'Marx, Engels, and the Future Society,' *Survey*, no. 38, 1961, p. 103. Nevertheless, this comment seems contradicted by his later comments on p. 110; cf. note 34.

34 *Ibid.*, p. 110.

35 G.W.F. Hegel, *Hegel's Philosophy of Right*, trans. T.M. Knox, New York, Oxford University Press, 1967, p. 70.

36 For an interesting and helpful discussion of Hegel's views on punishment, see David E. Cooper, 'Hegel's Theory of Punishment,' in *Hegel's Political Philosophy: Problems and Perspectives*, ed. Z.A. Pelczynski, Cambridge University Press, 1971, pp. 151-67.

37 Karl Marx, *Critique of the Gotha Program*, p. 539.

38 Karl Marx, 'Inaugural Address of the Working Men's International Association,' in *The Marx-Engels Reader*, p. 518.

39 Karl Marx, 'The Civil War in France,' in *The Marx-Engels Reader*, p. 640.
40 The words are William James's. Cited in William K. Frankena, *Ethics*, 2nd edn; Englewood Cliffs, New Jersey, Prentice-Hall, 1973, p. 70.
41 John Plamenatz, *Karl Marx's Philosophy of Man* Oxford, Clarendon Press, 1975, p. 273.
42 *Ibid.*, pp. 440-2.
43 John Plamenatz, 'Responsibility, Blame and Punishment,' in *Philosophy, Politics and Society: Third Series*, ed. Peter Laslett and W.G. Runciman, Oxford, Basil Blackwell, 1969, p. 190.

7 Moral implications and ethical conclusions

1 The prominence of this question in contemporary ethics reflects the influence of Kant. A good example would be Kurt Baier, *The Moral Point of View*, Cornell University Press, 1958. That this question is not a prominent one for Marx reflects his distance from Kant.
2 William K. Frankena, *Ethics*, 2nd edn; Englewood Cliffs, New Jersey, Prentice-Hall, 1973, p. 112. By 'free' Franakena means 'not coerced' – but not in the broad sense Marx would use.
3 Alvin Goldman has recently advocated 'a reorientation of epistemology' which would bring traditional (analytical) epistemology into close contact with psychology, as well as 'situational and institutional forces that affect the social dissemination or inhibition of knowledge.' That a reorientation of ethics is also required is a conclusion which I think we must draw from a study of Marx. Cf. Alvin I. Goldman, 'Epistemics: The Regulative Theory of Cognition,' *Journal of Philosophy*, vol. 75, 1978, pp. 509-23.
4 Karl Marx, 'For a Ruthless Criticism of Everything Existing,' in *The Marx-Engels Reader*, ed. Robert C. Tucker, 2nd edn; New York: W.W. Norton, 1978, p. 14. I have used the translation in the Tucker volume as being more revealing. A slightly different translation can be found in the Marx-Engels *Collected Works*, New York: International Publishers, 1975, vol. 3, p. 143. The conceptions of philosophy noted in the text were suggested by Leszek Kolakowski, *Toward a Marxist Humanism*, New York, Grove Press, 1968, p. 186; and by William Leon McBride, *The Philosophy of Marx*, New York, St. Martin's Press, 1977, p. 8.
5 I refer to a communist society in Marx's (ideal) sense – not in the sense of those societies which today call themselves 'communist.'
6 Karl Marx, *Selected Correspondence*, ed. and trans. Dona Torr, London, 1941, p. 472. This reference is to be found in Bertell Ollman, *Social and Sexual Revolution*, Boston, South End Press, 1979, pp. 133, 156.

7 The phrase is John Stuart Mill's. Cf. William K. Frankena, *Ethics*, pp. 105-16.

8 The example is mentioned in M.M. Bober, *Karl Marx's Interpretation of History*, New York, W.W. Norton, 1965, p. 9.

9 I assume that the preceding chapters have made plausible the compatibility of critical thinking and Marx's views. It is only a later and degenerate Marxism which insists on strict intellectual adherence to the party line. Cf. Leszek Kolakowski, 'Permanent vs. Transitory Aspects of Marxism,' in *Toward a Marxist Humanism*, pp. 173-6.

10 Cf. J.S. Mill, *On Liberty*, New York, Bobbs-Merrill, 1956, p. 13. Isaiah Berlin, 'Two Concepts of Liberty,' in *Four Essays on Liberty*, London, Oxford University Press, 1969, pp. 122-3.

11 *Ibid.*, pp. 121-2.

12 *Ibid.*, p. 122.

13 These various ways of characterizing positive freedom can be found in *ibid.*, pp. 131-44.

14 *Ibid.*, p. 133. There is a second reason why positive freedom is said to be dangerous in Berlin's essay. This has to do with the harmony of ends which constitutes positive freedom and which is said to allow only a 'single true solution' to value questions. The danger is that individual variety and creativity are excluded by positive freedom. This concern will be discussed below.

15 Even if one develops Marx's account in terms of people's real needs, Marx is not claiming that people 'really' seek that which they really need. Thus, any talk of real needs does not suggest the bifurcation of selves Berlin has in mind.

16 Berlin, pp. 133-4.

17 *Ibid.*, pp. 130-1.

18 Gerald C. MacCallum, 'Negative and Positive Freedom,' *Philosophical Review*, vol. 76, 1967, p. 314.

19 William A. Parent, 'Some Recent Work on the Concept of Liberty,' *American Philosophical Quarterly*, vol. 11, 1974, p. 151.

20 *Ibid.*

21 *Ibid.*, p. 152.

22 *Ibid.*, p. 151.

23 Berlin, p. 125.

24 *Ibid.*, p. 124.

25 *Ibid.*, p. 154.

26 C.B. MacPherson, 'Berlin's Division of Liberty,' in *Democratic Theory*, Oxford, Clarendon Press, 1973, p. 111.

27 Similar instances might be discussed under Marx's claims that there will be one literature, no town/country division, as well as one language. On Marx's views on language, cf. Bertell Ollman, *Social and Sexual Revolution*, Boston, South End Press, 1979, p. 77.

28 Eugene Kamenka, *The Ethical Foundations of Marxism*, 2nd edn rev.; London, Routledge & Kegan Paul, 1972, p. 99.

29 *Ibid.*, p. 100.
30 *Ibid.*, pp. 113, 159.
31 *Ibid.*, pp. 103-4.
32 Kamenka maintains the opposite view; cf. *ibid.*, p. 101.
33 *Ibid.*, p. 108.
34 Robert L. Heilbroner, *Marxism: For and Against*, New York, W.W. Norton, 1980, pp. 166-74.
35 *Ibid.*, pp. 171-2.
36 *Ibid.*
37 *Ibid.*, pp. 166-70.
38 Cf. David McLellan, *Karl Marx: His Life and Thought*, New York, Harper & Row, 1973, p. 457.

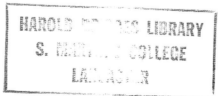